THE CIVILIZATION OF THE AMERICAN INDIAN

THE NAVAJO AND PUEBLO SILVERSMITHS

JOHN ADAIR

NORMAN
UNIVERSITY OF OKLAHOMA PRESS

INTERNATIONAL STANDARD BOOK NUMBER: 0–8061–0133–4

COPYRIGHT 1944 BY THE UNIVERSITY OF OKLAHOMA PRESS
PUBLISHING DIVISION OF THE UNIVERSITY
FIRST EDITION, AUGUST, 1944
SECOND PRINTING, FEBRUARY, 1945
THIRD PRINTING, NOVEMBER, 1946
FOURTH PRINTING, MAY, 1954
FIFTH PRINTING, FEBRUARY, 1958
SIXTH PRINTING, JUNE, 1962
SEVENTH PRINTING, NOVEMBER, 1966
EIGHTH PRINTING, NOVEMBER, 1970
MANUFACTURED IN. THE UNITED STATES OF AMERICA

For Ralph Linton
who taught me to look at art
as an integral part of
primitive culture

Preface

THIS BOOK is the result of investigations carried out over a period of several years. The principal field work was done during a six-months' period in the latter part of 1938. Work had been initiated the previous summer when, in early September, I undertook a preliminary study of Navajo silver technology. Before continuing research the next spring, I studied the collections of Navajo and Pueblo silver in New York, Philadelphia, and Chicago, and, on the way to the Navajo country, the collections of the Denver Art Museum, the Taylor Museum in Colorado Springs, and, finally, the most important and much the largest collection of all, that belonging to the Laboratory of Anthropology in Santa Fé. The text was finished in the spring of 1940; material collected subsequently will be found in Appendices II and IV.

The short study of technology and the museum research impressed upon me a fact which I had suspected before the inauguration of the whole project. The most interesting thing about Navajo and Pueblo silver is not the æsthetic object separated from its social setting and viewed abstractly in a museum case, nor yet the making of this object, but the sociological significance of the art form in Navajo and Pueblo culture. This whole aspect of the craft has hitherto been neglected, as it has been in the studies made of the arts of many other primitive peoples.

In the pages which follow I have attempted to depict the importance of silversmithing in Navajo and Pueblo culture. The book falls into two distinct parts. The first presents the study of Navajo silver. The second gives an examination of the art of silvermaking at the pueblo of Zuñi, which is the only pueblo where the craft is extensively practiced, concluding with a short survey, mainly of a historical nature, of the art in the other pueblos.

The Navajo and Zuñi sections are similar in outline, and each of them begins with a reconstruction of the history of the craft. I acquired my historical information in two ways: first, by questioning old residents, oftentimes men who in their younger days were silversmiths themselves, who have seen the growth of the art during their own lifetime; and second, by the use of written materials, both in historical studies and in random mentions in the reports of nineteenth-century ethnographers. I have placed in relief against this historical background a study of the craft as it exists at the present time. The process of making silver jewelry by various representative craftsmen is described. Following that, in both the Navajo and the Zuñi sections I have presented the social aspects of the art. How a silversmith learns the craft, to whom he sells his work, the æsthetic standards of the ethnic group, and other related matters are included. Finally, I have given an account of the economics of silversmithing, which is necessarily linked closely with the social functions of the craft.

Without the help of many individuals and institutions this study could not have been accomplished. For financial support in the study I am indebted to the Southwest Society, to Mr. J. J. Augustin, who realized the need for a book on this subject, to Dr. Clyde Kluckhohn, of Harvard University, who secured for me an anonymous grant, and finally to my father, Mr. Arthur B. Adair, who generously supplemented these funds. I am deeply grateful, also, to the American Council of Learned Societies, whose liberal grant-in-aid helped make publication possible.

Through the co-operation of Dr. Scudder Mekeel, Dr. H. P. Mera, and Mr. Kenneth Chapman, of the Laboratory of Anthropology, Mr. Frederick H. Douglas, of the Denver Art Museum, Mr. Mitchell Wilder, of the Taylor Museum, Dr. Paul Martin, of the Field Museum, and the late Mr. Charles Amsden, of the Southwest Museum, I found my museum work greatly facilitated and most enjoyable. They all made their collections easily accessible and rendered many other favors.

An essential part of the field study was pursued in trading posts on the Navajo and Zuñi reservations. I should like to express my gratitude for their aid to Mr. William Stewart of Pine Springs, Mr. Harry Boyd at Smith Lake, the late Mr. Burtin I. Staples of

Coolidge, and Mr. Charles Kelsey, Mr. George Rummage, and Mr. C. G. Wallace, all of Zuñi. Many of my photographs are of silver which they have at their posts. Many other traders also extended courtesies, and to these unnamed ones, I am equally grateful.

Members of the Burnsides family at Pine Springs acted as my principal interpreters and informants on Navajo silver. They showed me the kindness and patience typical of their people. Tom Burnsides, who worked at his anvil during the hot summer months, when he normally would have spent the time out-of-doors tending his sheep and cattle, deserves warm thanks. I consider him an excellent artisan and a good friend. I should like to thank other informants: Chee Dodge, Charlie Bitsui, Ambrose Roanhorse, and Dooley Shorty, all Navajo; Mrs. Lewis and her family, of Zuñi, Okweene Neese and Horace Aiuli, of that pueblo; and Pablo Abeita, of Isleta.

Richard Van Valkenburgh, of the Navajo Service, was most helpful in making suggestions relative to obtaining historical data. Mrs. Gerald Cassidy and Mrs. Cornelia Thompson, of Santa Fé, and Mr. M. L. Woodard, of Gallup, showed much interest in my research and kindly allowed me to photograph pieces from their beautiful collections. I owe thanks to my sister, Mrs. R. J. Cameron-Smith, and to Mr. Gordon Adamson for their generosity in lending me photographic equipment.

I am indebted to the late Dr. Elsie Clews Parsons and Dr. Leslie Spier for reading and criticizing that part of the manuscript dealing with the Pueblos, and to Mr. Frederick H. Douglas and Dr. Gladys Reichard for reading the whole of the manuscript. I would like to thank Dr. Clyde Kluckhohn, who also read the manuscript in its entirety, for making many valuable suggestions during the course of my research.

I am grateful to my wife, Carolyn, for her assistance in preparing the manuscript for publication.

JOHN ADAIR

Contents

Sources

Sources of the individual pieces of silver shown are: Field Museum of Natural History (Chicago), 11B, 20A (two pieces at right); Laboratory of Anthropology (Santa Fé), 2B, 5D, 8A, 8D, 9, 10D, 10E, 12G; Santa Fé Indian School, 15B, 15C; Hubbell Trading Post (Oraibi, Arizona) pawn rack, 4A; Pine Springs (Arizona) Trading Post pawn rack, 7D, 12B; Kayenta (Arizona) Trading Post pawn rack, 8G; Mrs. Pablo Abeita (Isleta), 10F; Mr. and Mrs. John Adair, 10C, 11C; Mrs. Gerald Cassidy (Santa Fé), 12D, 20D; Mr. and Mrs. Kenneth B. Disher (Albuquerque), 2E, 7A; Chee Dodge (Crystal, Arizona), 14A; Mrs. Harold Helmer (San Antonio), 12E, 12F; Mr. and Mrs. William Lippincott (Wide Ruins, Arizona), 8I; Okweene Neese (Zuñi), 20C; Burton I. Staples (Coolidge, New Mexico), 4C, 5A, 7B, 7C, 15F; Mrs. Cornelia Thompson (Santa Fé), 2A, 2D, 8E, 8F, 14B, 14D, 20A (left); C. G. Wallace (Zuñi), 14C, 20B, 20E, 22C, 22D; Robert L. Wallace (Zuñi), 10G, 10H; Mrs. John Wetherill (Kayenta, Arizona), 5B, 10A, 10B, 12H; M. L. Woodard (Gallup), 5C, 8B, 8C, 12I, 15A, 15D, 15E.

The rawhide tobacco canteen (11D) is in the Denver Art Museum; the iron Mexican cinch buckle (2C) belongs to Ralph Meyers (Taos); the Zuñi ceremonial head ornament (12A), to Frances Quarles (Taos); and the brass tobacco canteen (11A), to Mrs. Cornelia Thompson.

Photographs used in Plates 3A, 24A, and 24B are from the Southwest Museum, Los Angeles; in 3B and 5E from the Ben Wittick Collection, Laboratory of Anthropology, Santa Fé; the photograph in 5D is also from the Laboratory of Anthropology. All other photographs are by the author.

Plates

Tables

Map & Chart

Foreword

THIS is one of those rare books which will please, I think, both the specialist scholar and the layman of broad interests. The professional anthropologist will find here that wealth of beautifully documented detail which alone will serve as basis for scrupulous induction. Yet these necessary minutiæ bear a definite relationship to each other. They are sharply focused upon questions which are rich with meaning for every thoughtful human being. The magnificent photographs demonstrate that in this field, at least, American Indians have created their own imperishable achievements of beauty. But how does it happen that we find these particular forms fashioned by these specific technologies? In response to what total social pressures do styles change from decade to decade? What is the relative role of conservative persistence of artistic tradition and motor habit as opposed to availability of new techniques and the stimuli and demands (æsthetic and unæsthetic) of a wealthier, externally more powerful culture? Wherein and to what varying degrees has this craft altered the general social equilibrium of the various Pueblo cultures and of Navajo culture?

Because Mr. Adair treats each small fact not as an end in itself, not of importance as satisfying an idle and perhaps perverse curiosity, but as material bearing upon these and other fundamental problems, he never wearies the reader, who is quite properly impatient of the trivialities of "material culture" as such. Authors of anthropological treatises on "material culture" have all too commonly appeared to wallow in detail for its own sake. If I may borrow a phrase which Mr. H. G. Wells has applied to academic psychology, the description of the technology of nonliterate peoples has tended to become "a happy refuge for the lazy industry of pedants." With tremendous proliferation of particulars we have been informed how many twists to the right were made at a given point, what the native names for such and such raw materials were, and the like. But the relationship of such data to the charm or serviceability of the finished product, the dependence upon the historical experience of the given people, the satisfactions which the craftsmen derived from the performance of such acts—these and similar truly *anthropological* queries have too often been left unilluminated. Only occasionally—as in Dr. Reichard's *Navajo Shepherd and Weaver*—does the "anthropos" remain constantly on the scene in anthropological studies of material culture. Modally, at least up to the present, the published account of a technology has emerged as a revolting and shapeless colloidal mass of verbiage. By contrast, *The Navajo and Pueblo Silversmiths* seems to me to have a sharp, crystalline structure. The details are grouped into determinate form which pleases and satisfies. In no other study known to the writer is the relationship between art form and social framework so clearly depicted.

Anthropologists have devoted many pages to the meaningless question of whether history or function determines observed cultural forms. Both do, of course. And here, on this comparatively small canvas, one sees it sharply and clearly. The basic technology of silversmithing in the Southwest is determined not by inner configurations of Zuñi or Navajo society nor by temporary social equilibrium, but by knowledge diffused from cultures of European origin. But that all of the details of style, technique, and craftsman's place in the society are not so determined is unmistakably proved by the differences between Pueblo and Navajo silver and the role which the crafts and the craftsmen occupy in the respective social systems. In my opinion, this book is a product of true functional social anthropology, a social anthropology which scrupulously follows out the interrelationship of cultural forms and the interactions of living human beings and is nevertheless tempered by awareness of historic significance: the influence of pre-existing cultural content and pattern in both the aboriginal and the acculturating societies is carefully traced. Mr. Adair so skillfully devotes himself to that too often neglected question—How is a particular aspect of a culture transmitted?—that we see plainly how old patterns and configurations change more slowly than the content of the overt culture to which additions and changes are made readily enough. Some, at least, of the techniques of European culture are received. The products, however, have their own quality. Imitations of Navajo silver are always palpable imitations. "Es ist der Geist der sich den Körper baut." And the changes which the introduction, development, and spread of the art and craft have brought about in Navajo society are not those which the same events would have wrought in a small American community. The exposition of all this history, of all these social and cultural processes in their wealth of data, is a significant human document, an anthropological contribution in the best sense.

CLYDE KLUCKHOHN

PART I

The Navajo

CHAPTER I

History of Navajo Silver

From its Origin to 1880

SILVERSMITHING is not an ancient art among the Navajo. They did not learn the craft until after the middle of the nineteenth century, although they had been wearing silver for many years. They acquired knowledge of the art from the Mexican *plateros (silversmiths)* who lived in villages in the upper Rio Grande valley and at the southeastern edge of the present Navajo reservation. It is not surprising that they did not learn to make silver earlier, for they were continually at war with the Mexicans and made frequent raids into their villages. Hostility such as this was not conducive to the learning of an art which requires instruction over a period of time. Furthermore, the Navajo had no tools. Even if a man had wanted to learn the craft and had watched one of the *plateros* at work, he would not have been able to produce any work of his own without a hammer, an anvil, and files.

Today the older men of the tribe remember the Navajo who was apparently the very first member of their tribe to learn the art. His name was Atsidi Sani, which in English means Old Smith.[1] To the Mexicans he was known as Herrero, the Iron Worker. One of the Navajo who learned the craft directly from him lives today at Sunrise Springs, not far from Ganado, Arizona. This man, known as Grey Moustache, is close to eighty years of age and no longer works at the craft, for he is totally blind. Grey Moustache told the following story of how Atsidi Sani learned the art from the Mexicans.

---

[1] The statements of my informants to the effect that Atsidi Sani was the first Navajo silversmith, and that he learned from a Mexican, not only check, but also corroborate the data collected by the Franciscan Fathers and published in the *Ethnologic Dictionary of the Navaho Language* (Saint Michaels, Arizona, 1910), and the statement to that effect made by Arthur Woodward in *A Brief History of Navajo Silversmithing* (Bulletin No. 14, Museum of Northern Arizona [Flagstaff, 1938], page 14).

"Atsidi Sani was my father's uncle by marriage; he married my grandmother's sister. He was the first Navajo to learn how to make silver, and my grandmother told me that he had learned how to work with iron before that. He learned how to do this from a Mexican by the name of Nakai Tsosi [Thin Mexican] who lived down near Mt. Taylor. He thought that he could earn money by making bridles. In those days the Navajo bought all of their bridles from the Mexicans, and Atsidi Sani thought that if he learned how to make them the Navajo would buy them from him. So he went down to the region of Mt. Taylor, and there he watched this Mexican smith at work. Nakai Tsosi also knew how to work silver, but Atsidi Sani didn't learn to do that until some years later.

"Nakai Tsosi and Atsidi Sani became good friends. He used to go down and stay with the Mexican, and the Mexican used to come up and stay with him, at his hogan near Crystal. This smith didn't charge him anything for teaching him how to work iron. I remember watching Atsidi Sani make bridle bits out of pieces of scrap iron. He made them with jingles hanging from the bottom. Some of these he exchanged for buffalo hides with the Utes.

"Atsidi Sani had four sons. All of these boys learned how to work iron from their father, before they were taken to Fort Sumner in 1864. The names of these sons were: Big Black, who was the oldest and the first one to learn, Red Smith, Little Smith, and Burnt Whiskers. At this time Atsidi did not yet work with silver. It was not until the Navajo came back from Fort Sumner that he learned how to make silver jewelry. It is not true that the Navajo learned silversmithing from the Mexicans while they were there. They did wear some silver at that time, mostly rings and bracelets, which they bought from the Mexican smiths, but most of their jewelry was made of copper and brass.

"After Atsidi Sani learned to make silver, he taught his sons how to work it. He told them that silver was very easy to work. He never made very much silver, but spent most of his time making iron bits. His sons made lots of silver, especially Red Smith. They told the Navajo to wear jewelry of silver because it was much nicer looking than that made of brass.

"It was ten years after I returned from Fort Sumner [1878]

that I learned how to make silver from Atsidi Sani. At that time I was fourteen years old. We lived near his hogan and I used to watch him at work. I decided that I wanted to learn how to make jewelry. I first learned by making *conchas* [plaques of silver, worn on a belt].[2] Then I learned to make bridles and bracelets. Some other men who also learned the craft from Atsidi Sani were Smith Who Walks Around, Big Smith, Crying Smith, and Red Smith. All of these men were great craftsmen.

"Atsidi Sani was a great man. He was a leader and spokesman of his people. He was also a medicine man, and he knew the Mountain Chant and the Shooting Chant."

Chee Dodge, a well-known Navajo, who for many years has been a leader of his people, lives near Crystal, Arizona, close to the place where Atsidi Sani used to live. Of him Chee said: "I knew Atsidi Sani well. He used to live over near Washington Pass, just a short way from my house. When he was an old man he used to come over here and talk with me. He was blind at that time, and I used to lead him around by a cane. He died some twenty years ago [*c.* 1918], and at that time he must have been over ninety years old. He told me that he learned how to work iron when he was a young man, I guess he must have been about twenty-five then. He didn't learn that up in this country. He used to go down to the south where there were Mexicans living, and it was there that he learned it from a Mexican blacksmith.

"The Navajo didn't make any silver of their own while they were at Fort Sumner [1864–68]. How could they? The Navajo were locked up there just like sheep in a corral. They had only a very little silver in those days, which they bought from the Mexicans. But they had lots of copper and brass which was pounded up into bracelets. They used to gamble for those bracelets."[3]

[2] In oral usage and as a trade term, *concha* is frequently pronounced and spelled *concho*. This corruption of the Spanish may, in time, supplant *concha*, but at present *concho* and its plural, *conchos*, are not recognized in authoritative dictionaries.

[3] Chee's statement that the Navajo at Fort Sumner wore very little silver is further substantiated by a survey of photographs which were taken of Navajo during the Fort Sumner period. The absence of silver is evident. No conchas, wrist-guards, or najahe show up in these pictures. Only two rings are to be seen

From these statements of Grey Moustache and Chee Dodge, we learn that the Navajo knew the art of blacksmithing before they were taken as captives by the United States government to Fort Sumner. According to Chee, Atsidi Sani, who may well have been the first Navajo to work iron, learned the trade from a Mexican about eighty-five years ago. That would have been about 1853. According to Grey Moustache, Atsidi Sani learned this art twenty years before he first worked silver, which was not until after his return from Fort Sumner. That could not have been before 1868, and was possibly several years after that date. Therefore, he must have learned blacksmithing about 1850. This information checks with Chee's statement.

The year in which Atsidi first made silver is not so clearly established. These informants say that he did not learn the art until after the return from Fort Sumner.[4] However, Arthur Woodward has evidence that Atsidi Sani learned the art prior to Fort Sumner, and that the Navajo had some knowledge of the art when they were at the fort.[5] Because of the conflicting evidence, the origin of silversmithing can not be accurately dated, nor is it likely that it will be in the future. At this time the facts are vague in the memory of the oldest members of the tribe, and the written accounts which mention the subject are meager. All that we can say is that the art may have been taken over from the Mexicans as early as 1850 or as late as 1870.

A subject of greater interest, and about which more information is available, is the early development of the art following 1870. Grey Moustache continued his story, telling of the early history of the craft.

"Some of the silver that the Navajo made they traded to the Utes. Before that we used to trade iron bits and blankets to them

---

and only a few simple bracelets, buttons, and hoop earrings. One pair of tweezers, which may have been of silver, appears. These pictures are deposited in the Labortory of Anthropology, in an album entitled, *Souvenir of New Mexico*, and are the property of John Meem. For contrast, see Plate 3B, which shows Navajo about 1890.

[4] Statements made by three other informants: Old Lady Gordy, Wide-Earrings, and Long Moustache corroborate the fact that the Navajo did not know the art of silversmithing until after their return from Fort Sumner.

[5] Woodward, *op cit.*, pages 14–17.

for buckskin or mountain lion and buffalo hides. Sometimes we got beaded buckskin shirts and trousers. Those Utes wore bracelets and rings of a yellowish color. They also had ornaments on their bridles of that same metal. It wasn't like our silver; I know because I got some of it from a Ute one time, and I tried to melt it up, but no matter how hot I got my charcoal, I couldn't do it.

"When I was a young man [1880–90] the silversmiths made some things that they don't make today. We used to make silver bells out of quarters. [Plate 2A]. We took these quarters and hammered them down into a cup-shaped hollow made in the log which held the anvil. The quarter was hammered into the hollow with a piece of scrap iron that had a rounded end which just fitted the hole in the wood. These pieces of silver were thinned around the edges, a small loop was soldered inside at the top, and a small bit of silver or copper was tied to this loop. It made a fine bell. The Navajo learned to make these from the Mexicans many years ago, when they first learned to work silver. We sold these to both the men and the women. The older women wore them attached to their sashes, so their sons-in-law would know when they were coming. The men wore them tied to their garters when they danced in the Yeibichai, and both men and women wore them at the war dances.

"The smiths also made small silver tobacco cases shaped like canteens. Before the Navajo knew how to make silver, the Mexicans made these and sold them to the Navajo. They were very expensive, and there were only a few Navajo who had enough money to buy them. But after we learned how to use the metal, we made them for ourselves. We never carried anything but tobacco in these canteens; we had other things to carry corn pollen and medicine in. The tobacco cases were carried in the leather pouches every man wore by his side. The medicine men wore these on their right side, other men wore them to the left. I made several of those tobacco canteens and was paid a horse or a calf for each one that I made. Some people think that we used to carry gunpowder in these canteens, but they were too small to hold much, and it would take too long to open the leather pouch, take out the canteen, and pour out the powder. No, the powder was carried in regular powder horns which were made out of cow's horn. These were carried by the right side, held by a strap which passed over the left shoulder. The powder was poured out of these into silver measures [Plate 2B], which were worn on the strap of the leather pouches. There they could get at them quickly and measure out the powder and pour it into the gun.

"In those days I used to make many silver-mounted bridles. You don't see many of those today except on the pawn racks in the trading posts. At that time every Navajo who could afford a silver headstall had one on his horse. They cost lots of money. A good bridle was worth at least sixty dollars, and one with lots of silver would cost a hundred dollars. That is about what they were worth in cash, but it was seldom that cash was paid for one, because the Navajo didn't have as much cash in those days as they do now. I used to pawn my bridle for eighty dollars in the trading post. I remember selling one bridle for a good horse, with a saddle-blanket and saddle. In the early days we made these headstalls, and all the other silver, out of American dollars and other American coins. I used to make silver for old man Hubbell at Ganado.[6] He used to get the American pesos for us, and he supplied us with them for twenty years. Then the government sent out an order telling us that we were not to melt up any more silver money [*c.* 1890]. From that time on Mr. Hubbell got Mexican silver for us to work. It was softer than the American money, and easier to melt up and pound out.

"Many years ago the Navajo used to make lots of cast silver. We learned how to do this from the Mexicans. They used clay molds for casting the metal. The first Navajo smiths used rock for casting. The rock wasn't soft and powdery like that we use now but was hard, and darker in color. In fact I had never seen the soft, powdery kind until forty years ago [1898] when I made a trip up to Sunrise Springs. I saw some white rock on the side of a hill and I thought that it might make good molds for my silver, so

[6] Roman Hubbell informed me that his father, John Lawrence Hubbell, brought a Mexican silversmith from St. Johns, Arizona, to Ganado to teach the Navajo in that region how to make silver more than forty years ago. Chee Dodge said that a Mexican smith who worked for Hubbell at Ganado was known to the Navajo by the name of Thick Lips.

I got some of it and made a cast for a *ketoh* [bow-guard, frequently spelled *gato*]. But that stone was too soft and cracked all to pieces. Then I went back a second time and got some more, and this time the stone was just hard enough, and I made a good ketoh in that mold.

"My brother-in-law, Atsidi Chon, saw this stone, and he asked me where I got it. I told him and he went over to that same place and got some for himself. After that time we always used that stone for our molds.

"Atsidi Chon was a very good silversmith. He used to live over near Klagetoh. He was the first silversmith to set turquoise in silver. The first piece that he set was in a ring. That was at the time when I was learning how to make silver from Atsidi Sani [*c.* 1878]. This ring had just one stone in it. At that time the only rings that the Navajo had were of silver with some designs filed into the metal. I remember when this ring was finished, many Navajo gathered around to see it, and all of them thought that it was very pretty. After he finished making that first piece, he made some more jewelry with turquoise in it. He made a *najahe* [crescent-shaped pendant, frequent spelled *naja*] and several bracelets. Young fellows used to come up to him and say, 'I want to learn how to make silver; I want to learn how to make jewelry like that.' He used to say to them, 'You have two eyes, you can see; watch me and you will learn how for yourselves.'

"The Hopi and the Zuñi used to trade the Navajo turquoise and shell beads for silver work. I used to make ketohs for the Zuñi, and I would trade one of those for a necklace of shell beads. I went down to Zuñi several times each year to sell my silver. I had several friends there in the village with whom I used to stay at Shalako time. I think that those Zuñi Indians got their turquoise out of old ruins. They had dark blue stones that were finer than the stones you see nowadays.

"It was twenty years ago [*c.* 1918] when the Navajo women first began to make silver. In those days money was falling down just like rain, and everyone went crazy. The women began to make silver for money and put sacred things on blankets. When I first heard about some women over near Gallup making silver, I felt sort of silly. I thought that I was better than a woman because I could make silver jewelry and they couldn't. But when I heard this, I had to admit that women were just as good as I was. I think that it is all right if women make silver. They can earn good money that way.

"I taught many men how to make silver. Most of them were either friends or relatives. I didn't ask them for anything in payment, but every once in a while one of these fellows would give me fifty cents or so.

"I used to dream about silver. I didn't dream about the designs that I was going to put on. But one time I dreamed that my tools were all around me. My anvil, my bellows, and my hammer were all right there. I dreamed that I was going to start work on another bracelet. In my dream someone told me that I was going to go blind because I was using bellows like that.

"The next day I thought that it was strange to dream that. So I had someone perform motion-in-the-hand over me.[7] I wanted to find out why I had that dream. This man told me that I must have a sing. He said that I must have Navajo Wind Way Chant, and that if I didn't I would get sore hands, and then I would go blind. I didn't believe what this man said, so I made some more silver. I felt perfectly all right, so I didn't have that sing, but later on my hand began to itch. Then it got sore on both sides and blistered all over. I wasn't able to sleep. When I put my hand under the blanket it was hot, and it pained. My eyes began to go bad, and I couldn't see things clearly. They got worse and worse, until I couldn't see anything. So I called the same man in again to do motion-in-the-hand, and he told me the same thing he had before. So I had the sing and medicine was put on my hand. After the sing was over, I felt better. I was able to see once more. When the sing began, I wasn't able to see a thing.

"After that time my eyes were better. I could see a little bit. I could see the sky, the trees, the road, and where there is sand. But I couldn't see as well as I could before I had that dream. I used to be

[7] Motion-in-the-hand is a Navajo method of diagnosing disease and prescribing the ritual for the cure of the particular illness. See Leland Wyman, "Navajo Diagnosticians," *American Anthropologist*, Vol. XXXVIII (1936), pages 236–46.

able to track horses, but I couldn't do that any more. I felt pretty good for about fifteen years, then I became sick again, so I had another sing. It was the same one I had before, Navajo Wind Way. I felt better after that, but my eyes were just the same. I think that I burned my eyesight looking at the red hot charcoals. I think that those coals baked my eyes.

"The second sing didn't help my sight, so I went to see a white doctor. That doctor told me that I could have my eyes fixed if I would go to a hospital in Albuquerque. But I didn't want to do this. I told him that I didn't want to have them fixed if I had to leave the reservation to have it done.

"From that time on, I couldn't see well enough to make silver, so I had to give it up. But I knew how to do some medicine singing and praying. I had learned how to do that first when I was learning to work silver. I knew the prayers that are said while someone is doing motion-in-the-hand, and I knew many different prayers and short songs, but I didn't know all of any one chant. I just helped at different sings, for which I was paid, but I never worked as a regular chanter. For the last twenty years I have been earning money that way. Making silver is hard on the eyes. I know many men who used to be silversmiths, who are blind now. They took up medicine work, just as I did. That is about the only thing that a blind man can do."

In his story, Grey Moustache mentioned the Ute's wearing "bracelets and rings of a yellowish color." These were made of brass, copper, and German silver. The Ute as well as the Comanche, Cheyenne, Kiowa, and other tribes of the Southern Plains area wore rings, bracelets, brooches, conchas, and hair plates. These tribes obtained the metals from the Indian traders to whom they sold hides.[8] Evidently the metal that fell into the hands of Grey Moustache was either copper or German silver, both of which have a much higher melting point than silver.

The tobacco cases which he mentions were never very common. In fact there were so few of them made that most of the Navajo have never seen one. While the older men of the tribe re-

[8] Woodward, *op. cit.*, page 7.

member seeing a few of them in the past, they are distinctly a novelty to the younger men, who, when shown one of these old pieces, inquire what it is. One reason that there are so few of these is that they are extremely difficult to make and require more technical ability than any other silver object.

The tobacco canteens have an interesting history. Their origin, like that of many other types of Navajo pieces, was Mexican [Plate 11]. The Mexicans of the Rio Grande valley carried tobacco cases made of rawhide. These were small, flat, oval or circular cases, which had stoppers made of wood cut to fit in the opening at the top. The *plateros* made these cases out of metal also. Copper seems to have been used most frequently for this purpose. The cases had a metal spout at the top through which the tobacco was poured in and out. This spout was attached to the body of the container by small, triangular, metal flanges extending down on each side, holding the spout in place. The body of the flask was decorated, as much of the Mexican silver was, with simple, engraved designs cut into the metal with a sharply pointed tool.

It is not definitely known whether or not the Mexican smiths made these canteens out of silver. They did make silver tobacco cases of a different shape—oval in cross-section, with a flat bottom and a lid that fitted down over the top. One can not be certain whether the Navajo smiths copied the shape of the copper canteens made by the Mexicans and substituted silver for copper, or whether they had seen the Mexican tobacco cases made of silver. In any case the Navajo knew how to make them by 1880. In that year Washington Matthews, an army medical officer who was posted at Fort Wingate, published an account of Navajo silversmithing in which one of these silver canteens is described and illustrated.[9] The piece which he described was very much like a canteen which I photographed in the Field Museum of Natural History in Chicago [Plate 11B]. A naturalistic deer is depicted on one side of the canteen, and a rabbit on the other side. There is a silver braid of twisted wire around the outside, covering the seam where the two sides of the case are soldered together. This braid,

[9] Washington Matthews, "Navajo Silversmiths," *Second Annual Report, 1880–81*, Bureau of American Ethnology (Washington, 1883).

which is on all Navajo tobacco cases, is not present on the Mexican ones made of copper. It seems likely that the braid was put on in imitation of the roping found on the army water canteens. There is little doubt that these tobacco canteens were made on occasion at the request of the soldiers, who took them back East as souvenirs. Matthews mentions one smith, known to the soldiers as Jake and to the Navajo as Letter Carrier, who lived at Fort Wingate and made silver pieces for the soldiers.[10]

Washington Matthews also describes and illustrates a powder measure, such as the one that Grey Moustache mentions. These pieces are scarce today, being even more rare than the silver canteens. They passed out of use when modern guns and shell ammunition were introduced. In all probability nearly all of these powder measures, which at one time seem to have been fairly common, were melted down and made into other objects when there was no longer a use for them.

Grey Moustache says that the rock that the Navajo used for casting silver in the old days was hard and dark in color. This is quite true. Almost any fine-grained sandstone that could be found in the region was used. A mold for a buckle was made of such rock by Largo, a famous smith who used to live near Thoreau, east of Gallup. The pumiceous rock that Grey Moustache found near Sunrise Springs is quite rare, occurring in fine grain in only a few places on the reservation. Today, if a smith can not obtain a piece of it, he will use a hard rock. While it takes a much longer time to carve the design out of hard rock, the mold can stand much greater temperatures and lasts indefinitely.

Atsidi Chon (Ugly Smith) was one of the most important early craftsmen. It was from him that the Zuñi first learned the art, when he set up a shop in their pueblo during the 1870's. Roman Hubbell says that he was the first Navajo to make silver in the vicinity of Ganado. Although Grey Moustache said that Atsidi Chon was the first smith to set turquoise in silver, his testimony can not be taken as conclusive evidence. It would be more accurate to say that he was the first one to set turquoise in silver as far as

[10] Washington Matthews, *Navajo Legends, Memoirs* of the American Folklore Society, V (Boston and New York, 1897), page 9.

13

Grey Moustache knew. Many Navajo informants say that this or that silversmith was the first one to make a concha belt, or the first one to make a string of beads or some other piece. In interpreting such historical data, it is best to qualify such statements with the phrase, "as far as his knowledge goes." The Navajo reservation covers a huge territory, and the tribe has many thousands of members. An informant is able to give accurate information of this nature only with reference to that particular part of the reservation where he lives. While Atsidi Chon may have been the first Navajo in the region of Sunrise Springs to set turquoise, one can not be sure that he was the first of all the Navajo to set the stone; that honor may be claimed for some other silversmith who lived a hundred miles away.

It is fairly certain that Atsidi Chon was the first smith in this region to set the stone in silver. This same information was given by Long Moustache, who lives at Klagetoh, which is just to the south and slightly east of Sunrise Springs, near the place where Atsidi Chon's hogan was located. The date for the setting of turquoise by a Navajo is accurate as far as our information goes. A Navajo smith presented Matilda Coxe Stevenson, a government ethnologist who lived at Zuñi for many years, with a ring which he had set with turquoise. According to Mrs. Stevenson, this was the first setting of turquoise in silver by the Navajo, and it occurred about 1880.[11] J. W. Bennett, a trader who has been active longer than any other man in the business, says that when he opened his post at Houck, Arizona, in 1882, the Navajo were wearing turquoise set in silver. Another trader, Robert B. Prewitt, says in a letter: "I went to Farmington in 1883. At that time there was considerable silver being made and they were putting some turquoise in the rings and possibly the bracelets."[12]

While turquoise was first set in silver by the Navajo about 1880, it was not until after 1890 that the stones were used in the jewelry in considerable quantities. In 1880 turquoise was scarce, for this was before the modern mines in Colorado and Nevada

[11] Matilda Coxe Stevenson, *Pueblo Clothing and Ornament,* unpublished manuscript in the Bureau of American Ethnology, Washington, D. C.

[12] This letter was written to Mr. H. H. Garnett, of Colorado Springs, on January 8, 1936, and I am indebted to him for showing it to me.

PLATE I

MABLE BURNSIDES, NAVAJO

PLATE 2

A. Old Navajo Bell

B. Old Navajo powder measure

D. Old Navajo cast buckle

C. Mexican cinch buckle (iron)

E. Navajo wrought buckle

began to export the stones to New Mexico and Arizona. The stones that were used earlier were, for the most part, native to New Mexico. Many of the stones were obtained at the mine known as Los Cerrillos, located a few miles south of Santa Fé. The Pueblo Indians of Santo Domingo obtained stones from this mine and other sources, and traded them to the Navajo for weaving, silver jewelry, and livestock. This barter continues today; the Santo Domingans polish turquoise and work it into beads which they trade to the Navajo. John Lawrence Hubbell, who founded the famous trading post at Ganado, imported Persian turquoise in the 1890's. Some pieces of this fine blue turquoise may still be seen in the jewelry of Navajo living in that region.[13]

Once the Navajo had learned the art of setting turquoise in silver, they turned to ornamenting jewelry with other stones less scarce than the valuable turquoise. Native garnets, jet, and malachite were used; and occasionally bits of abalone shell and even pieces of colored glass were set. As turquoise became more and more plentiful, the other stones fell into disuse, and many of them were pried out of the bezels and turquoise set in their places. Rings with these other stones are seldom seen today. They, like the powder measures and the mother-in-law bells, have become museum pieces.

[13] I owe this information to Mr. Herman Schweizer, of the Fred Harvey Company.

CHAPTER II

History of Navajo Silver

From 1880 to the Present

THE report of Dr. Washington Matthews is the only old historical account of silversmithing which we have. His notes, published by the Bureau of American Ethnology in its annual report for 1880–81, were made after he had persuaded a Navajo smith to set up his forge at Fort Wingate, and pursue his art where he might be observed.

The bellows which this smith used were much like those in the picture, from the Southwest Museum, of a smith in his hogan [Plate 3A]. This picture was taken about 1885 and will serve to illustrate Matthews' description of the tools which were used by the craftsmen of that era: "A bellows, of the kind most commonly used, consists of a tube or bag of goatskin, about twelve inches in length and about ten inches in diameter, tied at one end to its nozzle and nailed at the other to a circular disk of wood, in which is the valve. This disk has two arms: one above for a handle and the other below for a support. Two or more rings or hoops of wood are placed in the skin-tube to keep it distended, while the tube is constricted between the hoops with buckskin thongs, and thus divided into a number of compartments."[1]

The forge which may be seen in this photograph is also much like the one that Matthews discusses and illustrates in his report. He describes its manufacture: "In the first place, he [the smith] obtained a few straight sticks—four would have sufficed—and laid them on the ground to form a frame or curb; then he prepared some mud, with which he filled the frame, and which he piled up two inches above the latter, leaving the depression for the fireplace. Before the structure of mud was completed he laid in it the wooden nozzle of the bellows. . . . then he stuck into the nozzle a round piece of wood, which reached from the nozzle to the fire-

[1] Chee Dodge said that Atsidi Sani used to fan his fire with turkey feathers.

16

place, and when the mud work was finished the stick was withdrawn, leaving an uninflammable tweer. When the structure of mud was completed a flat rock about four inches thick was laid on at the head of the forge—the end next to the bellows—to form a back to the fire, and lastly the bellows was tied to the nozzle, which was built into the forge, with a portion projecting to receive the bellows."

The photograph illustrates the description given by Matthews in all but one or two minor details. The bellows that this smith uses have twice as many compartments as the bellows described, and the front part of the forge is constructed of blocks of stone cemented together with adobe.

This type of forge and bellows was widely used by the smiths of that period, but today not a single forge of this sort is to be found. The old, handmade, goatskin bellows disappeared when the traders introduced the manufactured heart-shaped bellows, and the adobe and stone furnace was supplanted by the tin bucket. An ordinary bucket with a hole cut in the front, into which the nozzle of the bellows is fitted, and the interior of which is filled with charcoal, makes a more efficient forge than the old kind. It is more portable; it may be taken apart and stored until needed; and the bellows furnishes a better draft.

Matthews mentions the other tools which the smiths used in 1880. He speaks of crucibles: "The Navajos are not good potters. . . . their crucibles are not durable. After being put in the fire two or three times they swell and become very porous, and when used for a longer time they crack and fall to pieces. Some smiths instead of making crucibles, melt their metal in suitable fragments of Pueblo pottery, which may be picked up around ruins in many localities throughout the Navajo country, or purchased from the Pueblo Indians." It is interesting that the Navajo smiths continue today to use fragments of Pueblo pottery for crucibles, to supplement those which they buy from the trading posts. It is also interesting to know that the Navajo men sometimes make crucibles. Pottery-making is a woman's art among the Navajo, and restricted to them, with rare exceptions. Its manufacture is surrounded by many taboos observed by the women while they are working with the clay. Mary Burnsides informed me that her husband's brother, Wide-Earrings, used to make his own crucibles, and that there were no restrictions which governed behavior when men worked the clay. She said that the temper for the pottery consisted of ground-up pot-sherds. The pottery was baked until it was red hot, surrounded by charcoal covered with sheep manure. No slip was put on this pottery. The vessels were triangular at the rim and looked much like the crucibles bought in the stores. Mary said that she had made crucibles of this type for her husband.

Other tools which Matthews mentions are: sandstone ingot molds, which the smiths fashioned out of rock native to the country; an anvil, made of any large suitable piece of iron—such as a bolt or a wedge—which is sunk into a log; tongs made of scrap iron; scissors of the ordinary variety, with which the smiths attempted to cut the metal; pliers, hammers, and files. Of the files he said: ". . . they usually employ only small sizes, and the varieties they prefer are the flat, triangular, and rat-tail. Files are used not only for their legitimate purposes, as with us, but the shanks serve as punches and the points as gravers, with which figures are engraved on the silver." Matthews mentions also the use, in the making of beads, of homemade cold chisels, awls, dies, and matrices made out of scrap iron. The smith made his own blowpipe, usually by beating a piece of thick brass wire into a flat strip, and then bending it into a tube. The pipe was about a foot long, slightly tapering, and curved at one end. "The flame used in soldering with the blowpipe is derived from a thick braid of cotton rags soaked in mutton suet or other grease."

A number of these tools may be seen in the photograph [Plate 3A]. Several hammers are in evidence. An ingot mold of sandstone rests against the anvil. A pair of tongs is held in the hand of the smith; several files and what appears to be a cold chisel rest on the blanket in the lower left-hand corner of the picture. The anvil in this photograph is not made of scrap iron, but is a small blacksmith's anvil.

By 1880 the Navajo had given up mining their own flux and had begun to use borax, which they obtained from the traders, for this purpose. The report states that, for polishing, the smiths used sandpaper and emery paper, which they also obtained from the trading posts. Matthews commented: "... but these are expensive, they are required only for the finishing touches, the first part of the work being done with powdered sandstone, sand, or ashes, all of which are used with or without water." The smiths of that day whitened their silver, after the metal had been heated for the last time, with a substance which some of them continue to use today. Of it Matthews reported, "... they use a mineral substance found in various parts of their country, which, I am informed by Mr. Taylor, of the Smithsonian Institution, is a 'hydrous sulphate of alumina, called almogen.'"

In a survey of the history of Navajo silver, it might be said that the technical refinement of the silver was in direct proportion to the type of tools employed. Fairly crude jewelry was produced with a limited number of tools which were primitive in character. Technical facilities were increased with the introduction of better tools, and jewelry more exact in workmanship and greater in variety was made. This does not mean that beautiful silver was not made by smiths who worked in the early days with crude tools, for many of the finest pieces of Navajo silver were made during those years. But it is true that the tools a smith uses limit, to a certain degree, the possibilities and the scope of the craft in both design and variety of form, as well as in perfection of finish of any given piece.

Thus we find that the tools mentioned in the report of Washington Matthews are indicative of the state of the silversmith's art as it existed in 1880. The art had made tremendous progress since it was first practiced by the Navajo. Matthews said: "Old white residents of the Navajo country tell me that the art has improved greatly within their recollection; that the ornaments made fifteen years ago do not compare favorably with those made at the present time; and they attribute this change largely to the recent introduction of fine files and emery-paper."

While it is true that the smiths had made great progress in their art by 1880, an advance that seemed very significant to contemporary white men who witnessed the development, nonetheless the art was very crude when compared with its later development. In his report Matthews described the technology of several different pieces, and the finished pieces are illustrated in the text. There are a tobacco canteen, a string of beads, several buttons, two powder chargers, and two bracelets. While it is hazardous to say just how fine the finish of these pieces was, one may venture to guess that it was quite rough, because of the very limited supply of emery paper and fine files which were at the disposal of the craftsmen. At that time the smiths did not have metal saws or shears, two tools which are essential to the production of fine handmade silver.

The most significant fact to note with regard to the technical state of the craft in 1880 is the limited means of decoration. There is not a single piece of silver described or illustrated in this report which is marked with stamps. All of the pieces listed above were decorated with an awl, with the exception of one button and the beads, which bore no decoration whatsoever. In addition, one of the bracelets is decorated with simple diagonal marks, probably put on with a cold chisel; and one of the powder chargers is marked with straight lines of a similar sort. The only other tool used in decorating the silver was a simple punch, with which a small, round indentation was made in the metal of the powder chargers.

From this evidence we may conclude that the Navajo smiths were not using the designed stamps at that time in their art, or if they were, we know that the use of them was restricted to a few smiths. Evidently these stamps were not employed at all by the silversmiths until a later date, for, if they had been used at this time, Matthews, who was a keen and accurate observer, would certainly have been aware of their existence. Nor is it probable that the smiths who made the powder chargers, whom Matthews describes as being "two of the best workmen in the tribe," would have been unaware of the designed stamps if they were in general use then.

The Navajo smiths did not learn the art of die-making from the Mexican *plateros*, for they did not use dies. The designs applied to Mexican silver made in this region were applied with an awl, like that the early Navajo smiths used, and other chasing tools. The silversmiths copied the designs which the Mexican leatherworkers employed in stamping figures on saddles, bridles, and other leather goods. From these leatherworkers they borrowed the technique of filing such designs on the ends of old pieces of scrap iron. When these dies were pounded down into the silver while the metal was cold, an impression was obtained exactly like that the Mexicans made in leather. A photograph taken at Oraibi, Arizona, shows an old concha belt with a border of crescent-shaped designs stamped on the leather to which the plaques are attached [Plate 4A]. These designs had been applied with a silver stamp, yet the design is the same as that applied by leather stamps. The tools are identical, except for the fact that the leather dies are slightly larger than some of the silver dies.

At first the stamped silver was quite simple in its decoration, being marked with only one or two dies. This was because fine files, which are essential to the making of these stamps, were rare. It was not until along in the nineties that these tools became accessible, and the smiths made an ever-increasing number of dies for stamping their silver.

In a Mexican leather shop in Los Angeles, I saw many punches identical with those used by the silversmiths. Crescents, rosettes, triangular figures with a radiating pattern, wavy and zig-zag lines, all of which are common dies among any Navajo smith's tools, were being used by these modern leatherworkers.[2] The Mexican designs continue to be stamped on saddles, and a saddle made by a large mail-order house in Denver has the same type of designs as that used by the smiths [Plate 4B].

With the introduction of designed stamps, the awl went out of use as a tool for decorating silver. This change in technology was accompanied by a change in the design of the jewelry. It became more elaborate; frequently the whole surface of a bracelet or a button was marked with stamped patterns. By 1895 the stamps had become very common, and the vogue for elaborately stamped pieces had reached its peak. Often such naturalistic design as that

[2] F. H. Douglas, of the Denver Art Museum, informed me that he has seen these same designs on Spanish leather several centuries old (in photographs in the Hispanic Museum, New York).

of the arrow, which was introduced about 1895 by the white man as a design motif, was seen on the silver, stamped on the metal by an iron die.

But in the period of which Matthews writes the art was still fairly crude both in technology and in design. "A large majority of these savage smiths make only such simple articles as buttons, rosettes, and bracelets; those who make the more elaborate articles, such as powder-chargers, round beads, tobacco cases, belts, and bridle ornaments are few," reported Matthews.

One of these "few," a silversmith who was well versed in the craft, was a man by the name of Beshthlagai-ithline-athlsosigi (Slender Maker of Silver), who was the younger brother of Atsidi Sani and lived near Crystal, New Mexico. Chee Dodge says that he was one of the best of all the Navajo silversmiths. The fine quality of his work is also mentioned by the Franciscan Fathers, who say: "An old silversmith, Beshthlagai ithlini athltososigi, or the slender silversmith, who is still living [1909], and who at one time was considered one of the best, if not the best silversmith in the tribe, is said to have originally learned his craft from Mexicans."[3]

That he learned the craft directly from Mexicans is subject to doubt. Chee Dodge, who was a friend of his, says that he learned the art from his brother, Slender Old Silversmith. According to the notes of Richard Van Valkenburgh, Slender Maker of Silver was "the innovator of new forms and refinement of silversmithing, particularly active in the 1880–1890's."[4] These notes state that he died in 1916.

There is a photograph extant of this craftsman [Plate 5E].[5] The picture was taken about 1885 by Ben Wittick, a photographer

[3] Franciscan Fathers, *op. cit.*, page 271.

[4] Richard Van Valkenburg, field notes to Woodward's *A Brief History of Navajo Silversmithing*, page 61.

[5] I was prompted to write to the National Museum after I had read the statement of Peshlagai Atsidi, Appendix 4, in Woodward's *A Brief History of Navajo Silversmithing:* "When shown a picture from the National Museum, of a Navajo silversmith whose name was given as Boi-ie-schulch-a-ichin, the old man looked at this picture a long time, he thought he could remember him, and that he had died a long time ago and he remembered his name as Peshlagai-ilim altsosigi (Slender Silversmith)." I was informed by the National Museum that the spelling of this smith's name apparently varies. The spelling on the Wittick photograph is the one given as such in the text.

who was active in the Southwest during the last two decades of the nineteenth century. Wittick gave the name of his subject as "Beich-schluck-ich-inel-tzuz-zigi," but there is no doubt that this is a crude spelling of the same Navajo name recorded by the Franciscan Fathers.

Slender Maker of Silver made several pieces of jewelry for Chee Dodge. Among them are a tobacco canteen, a bridle, and a string of what are usually called squash-blossom beads. This string of beads is the only one that I have seen that has a row of blossoms facing inward as well as outward [Plate 14A]. It is also unique in that it has two small najahe in addition to the large one at the bottom of the strand. These unique features testify to the originality of this smith.

I have met the son of Slender Maker of Silver; he lives at the present time in Los Angeles, where he makes Navajo silver for the tourists who visit Olvera Street. His name is Fred Peshlakai, and he said that he learned the craft from his father over twenty-five years ago. He also said that his father had a regular silver shop and paid more than ten men to help him with his work.[6]

Slender Maker of Silver is shown in the picture wearing silver which presumably was made by himself, but one can not be certain of this, since Wittick photographed many of his subjects with properties that he carried with him. However, the silver shown is typical of the period. He wears a string of plain hollow beads with a large najahe at the bottom. The other, shorter strands of beads appear to be made of turquoise. Looped through these is what looks like a pair of the old-fashioned silver earrings. In his ears are turquoise pendants. He is wearing a concha belt and is holding another one spread out across his lap. The belt which he is wearing has a diamond-shaped slot in the middle of the concha, through which the leather has been laced, and is the older of the two in type, for the solid type of concha was developed later.

Slender Maker of Silver wears dyed buckskin leggings with

[6] It is quite possible that this man is the nephew and not the son of Slender Maker of Silver. According to the Navajo method of reckoning kinship, the father and the father's brother are called by the same term. In this case he would be the son of Slender Old Silversmith, the brother of Slender Maker of Silver, who was also the brother of Atsidi Sani.

large silver buttons running up the outer side. When the traders introduced American-made clothes, leggings of this type went out of style, but buttons similar to those shown in the picture are still worn on moccasins. A headstall and several bracelets complete a list of the silver which may be seen in the picture. On none of it is there any evidence of die-work; all of the designs have been applied with simple punches, files, and cold chisels.

In 1897 Washington Matthews wrote: "The [silver] work has improved since I wrote of it in 1881, with the introduction of better tools. Then the smith built his forge on the ground and squatted to do his work. Now he builds it on an elevated frame and sits on a stool or chair to work."[7]

During the eighties and the nineties more trading posts were established on the Navajo reservation. The traders imported an ever-increasing supply of tools for the Navajo silversmiths. Metal-workers' saws, dividers, crucibles, and fine files were introduced to the Indian craftsmen. The introduction of the fine file enabled the smiths to develop the stamps with which they impressed designs on their silver. In making these stamps, pieces of scrap iron, such as old rivets, bolts, nail-sets, and worn-down cold chisels were used. Upon one end of such a piece of metal a design was filed. Very fine files were required to cut the designs, which, as mentioned above, were derived from the stamps of the Mexican leather-workers. The Navajo smiths may possibly have made stamps of this sort as early as the late 1870's, but it is certain from the evidence of Washington Matthews' report that the stamps were not common in 1881.[8] With the introduction of the fine file the stamps became a more common tool.

It is certain that by 1890 stamps were being made. Among some pieces of silver in the Laboratory of Anthropology in Santa Fé, which were collected by a resident of Durango, Colorado, before 1890, there are several bracelets marked with stamped designs. In fact the die-work on some of these pieces is elaborate and shows evidence of accurately made stamps. One is led to the conclusion that if elaborate and well-made stamps were in use then,

[7] Matthews, *Navajo Legends*, page 19.
[8] See page 101 for my conclusions regarding the use of designed stamps.

the art of stamp-making must have originated sometime during the latter part of the 1880's.

Up to that time practically all of the silver work produced by the Navajo smiths was for Indian use. The greatest part of the jewelry was made for fellow Navajo tribesmen. A small part of it was made for the Pueblo Indians by Navajo smiths who set up their forges in the pueblo villages, but for the most part the Pueblo Indians obtained silver from the Navajo in trading.

The only silver made for the white man before 1890 was a small amount which the soldiers at Fort Wingate ordered from the smiths. In his shop near Fort Wingate, the smith Jake, or Letter Carrier, made tobacco canteens, powder chargers, buttons, and other objects which the soldiers wanted as souvenirs. A small quantity of silver jewelry was obtained from the Indians by white settlers who traded them various objects for their handiwork. But this silver, and that which the soldiers obtained, was just like the silver that the Navajo made for their own use or for the Pueblo Indians. The fact that a white man was the purchaser made no difference to the smith.

The commercialization of the craft began in 1899 when the Fred Harvey Company first started to order silver made up expressly for white consumption. Before that time, the Fred Harvey Company had bought pawned Navajo silver from the traders. It had proved to be too heavy for sale to the tourists, who wanted lighter jewelry which they could wear in the East. In 1899 Mr. Herman Schweizer, who for many years has been in charge of the Harvey Company's curio department, asked a turquoise-mine owner in Nevada to cut stones into flat, square, and oblong shapes for Indian use. Schweizer took these stones and some silver to a trading post at Thoreau, New Mexico. He asked the trader there to have Navajo smiths make jewelry lighter in weight than that which they made for their own use. This method of "farming out" to the trading posts silver and turquoise, which had been polished and cut to the right size and shape, proved to be a very satisfactory method of obtaining jewelry for the tourist trade. Therefore, the Harvey Company sent the raw materials to other posts to be made into rings, bracelets, beads, and other jewelry. The traders at

Sheep Springs, Smith Lake, and Mariano Lake gave this silver to the Navajo silversmiths and paid them by the ounce for the finished products. The Harvey Company sold these bracelets, rings, and beads on the trains which traveled over the Santa Fé line and in stands in the stations along the route.

Other companies were soon to follow this system of "farming out" silver and turquoise. The big mercantile companies in Gallup, which supplied the trading posts with merchandise, adopted this method of buying silver for the tourist trade and for the rapidly growing markets in other parts of the country. This commercialization, begun in a small way by the Harvey Company, grew to tremendous proportions in the middle of the 1920's; and the sale of silver to white people had a great effect on both the design and the economics of the craft.

The silver which was made during the late years of the last century and the early years of this century has a characteristic appearance. It tends to be heavily stamped with designs. Frequently there are arrows and swastikas on the bracelets. These designs were introduced to the Navajo by the traders, who knew that the white man preferred to have designs on silver jewelry which were, to his mind, typical of Indian art. The swastika and the arrow appealed to the Navajo silversmiths, and they began to stamp the silver which they made for themselves with these designs. During those years turquoise was more scarce than it is today. Many bracelets, ketohs, and other pieces were made without any sets. The smiths frequently covered whole surfaces of the jewelry with designs which they applied with the recently invented metal stamps. This stamping gave the silver a very different appearance from the earlier silver, which was marked only with punches, files, cold chisels, and awls. With the cold chisel and the file, only straight lines could be produced, which gave the designs a geometric appearance. The punch was used to make a small circle on the silver, or if knocked more firmly with the hammer, it made a circular hole in the silver, like the holes seen around the edge of a concha. The awl produced a small featherstitch so thin and shallow that it does not stand out from the silver as the stamped designs do. The stamps afforded a method of applying curvilinear designs to the jewelry, and the small stamps which bore curved designs were combined with each other, so that the component parts made up a larger curvilinear design.

As the tourist trade grew in size during the first two decades of the century, the demand for Indian-made silver increased. At that time tourists traveled almost entirely by train. Many who came to New Mexico and Arizona were passing through these states either on their way to California or on their way back to the East. The Harvey Company sold great quantities of silver on the Santa Fé trains and in its hotels at the Grand Canyon and at Albuquerque. It was not long before the Navajo smiths were making cheap bracelets, light in weight and decorated with a few small pieces of turquoise, and inexpensive rings and beads, to fill the orders of the traders who sold the jewelry to the wholesale traders and the mercantile companies. Small pieces of Pueblo-made pottery and this silver became the popular souvenirs of a visit to the West. They became stereotypes of the art of the southwestern Indians, just as the miniature totem pole, the toy tomahawk, and the birch-bark canoe had become associated in the minds of tourists with the art of Indians in the Northwest and the eastern woodlands.

As tourist trade grew throughout the western states, the fame of Navajo silver spread to the surrounding regions. The demand for "Indian-style" silver was so great that manufacturers began to imitate the handmade Navajo silver. In 1910 a firm in Denver began to manufacture this imitation jewelry, using white labor. By mass production techniques the manufacturer was able to undersell the traders. Dealers in curios in the southwestern cities followed the example of the Denver firm and opened small shops, but unlike the Colorado company, these firms in Santa Fé and Albuquerque employed Indians to make the silver. Most of this Indian labor was not Navajo, but Pueblo, from the Rio Grande villages, which had their own traditions in silversmithing.

Beginning about 1870, in fifty years the craft of silversmithing had grown with tremendous rapidity from a very crude art, known to only a few craftsmen, who learned the art of working metal from the Mexican blacksmiths and silversmiths, to a craft that was known to hundreds of Navajo Indians, who made jewelry not only for themselves and the neighboring Indian tribes, but for the white man as well. During those fifty years the design of the silver had evolved from a crude state, in which the decoration was not only simple but also rough in execution, into a highly developed art, in which the decoration was much more complex and, in fact, baroque in character.

CHAPTER III

The Development of Design

U NTIL approximately 1890, American silver dollars, fifty-
cent pieces, and quarters were melted by the silversmiths
for making jewelry. During those years some Mexican
pesos were melted for the same purpose, but they were a minor
source of silver. About 1890, when the government authorities
began to enforce the laws which prohibit the defacing of cur-
rency, the traders began to import Mexican pesos for the use of the
Navajo smiths. The silversmiths preferred this silver to that of the
American coins, as it had less alloy; being purer in silver content,
the metal was softer and more easily worked. The jewelry made
from the old American coins, because of the great percentage of
copper, tends to have a slightly more yellowish cast than that made
from the Mexican silver. Some authorities have attempted to date
Navajo silver by its color, claiming that those pieces which have
the yellow cast are older than the others. While it is true that the
American coins were used before the Mexican, it is certain that
during the early period some Mexican coins were used, and it is
equally certain that silversmiths in remote parts of the reservation
continued to use American coins after 1890. Other factors com-
plicate the picture. The annealing of the silver, the amount of heat
used while pounding, and the amount of solder used will affect the
color of silver as much as the alloy of the metal. Therefore, individual pieces can never be dated accurately on the basis of color.
One can say only that jewelry made with the American coins is
probably older than that made with the Mexican, and this gen-
eralization may be used only in connection with a large number of
pieces, and never when speaking of an individual piece.

The Concha

Arthur Woodward has conclusively demonstrated that the
Navajo derived the concha[1] from the Plains Indians. The Ute,

[1] See page 5 n.

Kiowa, and Comanche, all traditional enemies of the Navajo, wore round and oval plaques of German silver as hair decorations, and as ornaments strung on leather belts around their waists. The Navajo obtained such silver ornaments as loot in their battles with the Southern Plains tribes. Woodward says that the art of making conchas, as well as wide, flat bracelets, rings, and earrings, diffused to the Plains Indians from the Delaware and the Shawnee, two eastern tribes skilled in the art of silversmithing, who moved from the East to the Plains area. The designs of their silver had been derived from those of the colonial white silversmiths who made silver for the Indian trade. The forms and designs were passed on to the Plains tribes, and from them to the Navajo, who copied them in coin silver.

The earliest Navajo conchas were round in form, thin, and light in weight. The oldest concha in the collection of the Laboratory of Anthropology, one which formerly belonged to the collector in Durango, Colorado, mentioned on page 24, has this form. It was held on the belt by a diamond-shaped slot transversed by a bar over which the leather was laced. The edges of the concha are scalloped; there is a row of perforations just inside the scalloped edge, and between these holes there is a light tracing, applied to the silver with an awl. More tracing surrounds the slot and forms a border inside the row of perforations.

Although there can be little doubt that the Navajo derived the concha from the Southern Plains tribes, nevertheless, it seems to me that the decoration of it was derived from the Mexicans, who ornamented the headstalls of their horses with silver conchas. Woodward contends that the Navajo copied the designs from the Plains Indians, whose conchas, like the early ones of the Navajo, were simple in form. It is true, as he points out, that the Mexican headstall conchas were much more complicated in design than the early Navajo conchas; but, on the other hand, many of the oldest Navajo conchas, like the Spanish bridle ones, have scalloped borders, a decorative feature extremely rare on those made by the Plains Indians, whose conchas usually have a smooth edge. An old Mexican cinch buckle [Plate 2c], found in the pueblo of Taos, has this same scalloping on the edges, and the feeling of its design is

PLATE 3

A. Navajo silversmith (c. 1885)

B. Navajo (probably c. 1890)

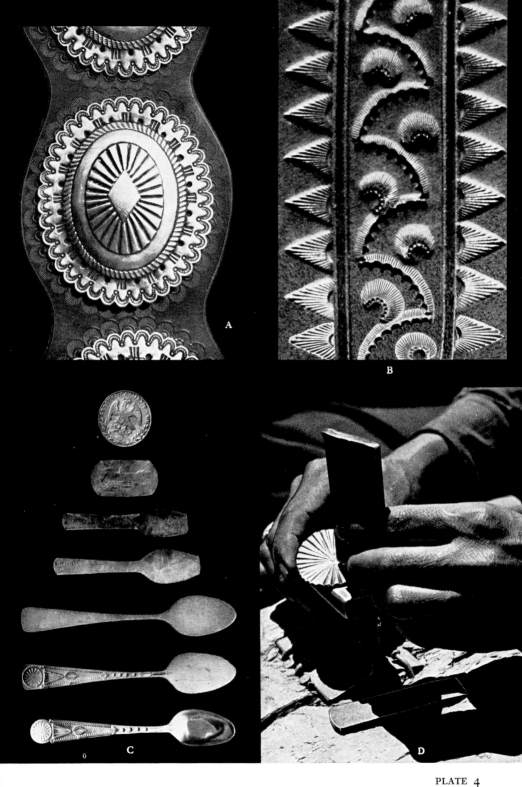

PLATE 4

A. Concha mounted on stamped leather (belt)

B. Stamping on leather stirrup strap

C. Steps in the making of a spoon

D. Marking concha with cold chisel

very similar to that of the Navajo conchas. Because of this, it appears to me highly probable that the Navajo copied the basic form of the conchas worn by the Plains tribes and applied to it Spanish designs, which at first were of a simple character, but which became more complicated as the smiths became more skilled in their craft and had better tools with which to work.

At a slightly later date the Navajo began to make oval conchas [Plate 7]. These were identical in design with the round ones. As silver became more plentiful, the conchas became heavier and larger.

The next important change in form occurred when the smiths made the plaques with a solid face. Up to that time the conchas were held in place on the belt by the slot with the transverse bar, through which the leather was laced. When the craftsmen became more expert in their art, they learned to use solder, and by means of it they were able to attach a loop of silver or copper to the back of each concha, so that the faces of the plaques could be left solid. The smiths were accustomed to seeing a diamond or oval opening in the center of the conchas, and as they liked the design effect of the slot, they felt a need for a similar design on the conchas of the new type; therefore, they stamped a diamond or a circular design on them with cold chisels.

During the 1880's, when the metal stamps came into use, the conchas became more complicated in design. The ones with the slot in the center had been severely plain, having little decoration, while those with the solid face had designs in the middle, and frequently there was a sunburst effect achieved by the use of straight lines impressed with a cold chisel [Plate 4D]. These lines radiated from the central diamond, or circle, to the designs around the edge. Sometimes this radiating design was raised in relief from the rest of the concha. This was done by using two dies, the common male die and a female die. The silver was placed between the two, with the latter on the upper side of the concha, and when the die was struck with a hammer, the silver was impressed into the female die by the male die. Stamped designs were then added to the patterns made by the cold chisels and punches. These were usually applied to the center of the concha and around the edge. One rare

31

belt shows a pattern stamped into the leather around the edge of the concha [Plate 4A]. Here the identity of the Mexican leather stamps and the Navajo silver stamps is strikingly illustrated, as was pointed out on page 21. The smiths also continued to make some conchas with a slot in the center, but they now surrounded it with stamped designs.

Lieutenant J. G. Bourke described thus the concha belts which he saw when he was at Fort Defiance in May, 1881: "The grand prize of the dandy Navajo buck is his belt; this is of leather completely covered by immense elliptical silver plaques, 4" x 3" in the transverse diameter horizontal; each of these contains from 5 to 6 silver dollars and the workmanship is very striking. Of these Chi's belt had seven, besides a little one. He told me he had given the silversmith $15 for making it, besides the silver."[2] On the same day Bourke noted: "When made into a baldric, as many as fifteen of these silver plaques will be strung on a leather belt and worn from shoulder to hip."[3]

The setting of turquoise in the silver plaques is a comparatively recent development in the design of the concha. Beginning about 1900, when turquoise became more plentiful, some conchas with sets were seen, but they did not become common until after 1920. Usually there is but one set—a round or oval stone placed in the center of the concha; but even more recently conchas have been made with a ring of small sets around the edge.

Another element adding to the complexity of the design of the concha belts, and developed about the same time as the curvilinear stamps, was the placing of separate pieces of silver between the conchas. Such a piece was usually wrought and stamped and was held in position by a loop of metal on the under side. Its usual shape is roughly like that of an hourglass, with an indentation at the top and the bottom, so that the edges follow the lines of the

---

[2] Lansing Bloom (ed.), "Bourke on the Southwest," *New Mexico Historical Review*, Vol. XI, No. 3 (July, 1936), page 226. The Navajo mentioned here is Chee Dodge, who as a young man was employed by the government as an interpreter.

[3] *Ibid.* Bourke is referring to the shoulder strap of the leather pouches. I have never seen one with conchas. These straps are usually decorated with coins or buttons.

conchas on each side. Belts with this decoration are popular with the white buyers of Navajo silver, who like the pleasing effect of the alternating rhythm formed by the vertical line of these pieces offsetting the horizontal line of the conchas. This separate piece of silver is sometimes an elongated oval in shape, set upright [Plate 7C], a position which affords an even more striking contrast to the horizontal line of the conchas.

During the past twenty years the traders have encouraged the silversmiths to make small conchas which are light in weight and especially suited to the tastes of the white women. Frequently they are less than two inches in diameter and weigh only a fraction of an ounce, a dozen or more being needed to fill out a belt.

The Buckle

The first buckles were very simple in form, small circular loops of silver with a crossbar holding the tongue in place. They were like any ordinary buckles on leather belts or straps, purely functional in character. These buckles were the most inconspicuous part of concha belts, as they were much smaller than the conchas and served only to hold the two ends of the leather belt together. As the art of the Navajo silversmith developed, the decorative possibilities of the buckles were realized, and they were increased in size, until they became as large or larger than the conchas. A variety of forms developed. Sometimes the buckle was made in the form of a concha, with a tongue held by the bar transversing the central slot. Another common type bore the same marginal designs as the conchas, but was rectangular in shape, with two winglike pieces on each side [Plate 6]. Others were rectangular in outline with elaborate stamping across the face. A common design for the rectangular buckles was composed of four shallow s-shaped figures, two of which were stamped at the top of the buckle and two at the bottom [Plate 2E]. It will be noticed that when viewed in a vertical position, the design, as well as the feeling, of the total form of such buckles is very similar to that of the ketohs. The four curves converge in a central rectangular slot where the end of the belt is held by the tongue.

Large and elaborate buckles may be wrought, or they may be

33

made by casting the silver in a mold. In the former case, the designs will be stamped on the flat silver. If the piece is cast, the curvilinear designs will be in the form of solid bars of silver, which will stand out in an open pattern against the wearer's clothes [Plate 2D].

The Ketoh

Navajo men used to wear a leather strap or ketoh around their wrists to protect them from the snap of the bowstring. In the days before silver-working, ketohs were simple, undecorated pieces of leather, about four inches wide, held together by lacing. Wrist guards of this old type[4] may be seen even now on the northwestern edge of the reservation, where the bow is still used to a considerable extent. When the Navajo learned the art of silverworking, they began to decorate these straps with the metal. The first ornamentation consisted of a solid plaque of silver, bent to fit the curve of the wrist and fastened to the leather by copper or silver shanks [Plate 8A–C]. The metal was decorated with marks impressed with files and cold chisels, or with designs applied with a stamp; and the decoration on the early silver-mounted ketohs was always simple in character.

As the smiths acquired more technical skill, other types of silver ornaments were fastened to the leather of the ketoh. Openwork designs were developed, and, as in the case of the concha and other pieces, when the smiths became more proficient and as more tools were introduced, the designs became more elaborate. These openwork designs were made in one of two ways, either by pounding out separate pieces, which were soldered together, or, more frequently, by casting [Plate 8D–I].

Ketohs decorated with openwork produced by casting have a characteristic design, which is built up of the elements which lead from the center to the edges of the ketoh. Frequently there are the four shallow *s*-shaped bars, like those found on the buckles. Each of these four bars leads out to a corner. The *x* thus formed is quartered, four bars of silver leading out to the edges, midway

---

[4] Occasionally the leather of these unmounted wrist-guards is stamped with the dies used on silver. A ketoh in the Denver Art Museum is decorated with a simple design composed of crescents and chevrons.

between the corners. Very often the bars, in a vertical position and radiating from the center of the ketoh to the midpoints of the top and bottom edges, have smaller curvilinear bars branching from them in a leaflike pattern. The horizontal bars, extending to midpoints on the vertical edges of the ketoh are shorter and simple in design. This style of composition makes the center of the ketoh the focus of interest. A turquoise is usually set in this area, giving just the accent needed to complete the design. From old ketohs it seems that this design existed before turquoise was set in silver; however, once the art of setting was learned, stones were used.

Silversmiths continue to make bow-guards by fashioning the metal into thin rectangular sheets. The designs which are stamped on these sheets are very often similar in form and composition to the designs of the cast ketohs. Many times there will be not only the single set in the center, but one at each corner as well.

The Navajo men wear their ketohs today more for decoration than for protection when using the bow. Bow-guards may be seen on dress occasions: at squaw-dances, at sings, and when the men come to town. The silversmiths make ketohs for the Pueblo Indians as well as for the men of their own tribe. During the summer rain-dances in the Hopi villages and at Zuñi, the dancers wear bow-guards, which are an essential part of the dress of many of the Kachina dancers.

The ketoh is one of the few pieces of Navajo silver which has not been commercialized by white men. It alone, of all Navajo silver, remains the exclusive property of the Indian. From the point of view of design, many of the finest pieces of Navajo silver have been ketohs. Many of them are still being worn, and fine ones are still being made by the smiths.

The Bracelet

Of all Navajo silver the bracelet is perhaps the best known. It is the piece most frequently bought by tourists as a souvenir. The wholesalers of Navajo-made silver, whose stores are mainly in Gallup and Flagstaff, sell more bracelets than all other types of silver combined, and the Navajo themselves wear more bracelets than any other article of jewelry. Men as well as women wear them. Poor indeed is the Navajo who does not have two or three bracelets, although many Navajo do not have any silver buttons or beads. Frequently a well-to-do Navajo will have a dozen or more bracelets, while he will have only one or two strands of beads or a single set of moccasin buttons.

The bracelets have been also the favorite pieces of white people who have built up collections of Navajo silver, mainly because this kind of jewelry has the greatest variety of forms and designs, whereas the finger rings, the bridle mountings, and the beads have only a few distinctive styles. The often repeated statement that no two pieces of Navajo silver are exactly alike is especially true of the bracelet.

The first bracelets that the Navajo made were of copper and brass, lengths of round, heavy metal wire bent to fit the wrist. What little decoration they had was either a thin chasing engraved with a pointed awl-like instrument or simple diagonal marks, sometimes arranged into chevrons, cut into the metal with cold chisels.

J. W. Bennett, who now has a post at Lupton, says that the Navajo continued to wear bracelets of brass and copper well after 1900: "At that time silver was not plentiful as it is today, and the Mexican silver didn't begin to come into this country until after 1885. I used to buy long bolts of heavy copper wire in hundred-pound lots. The Navajo men and women came into my post and bought lengths of it right off the spool. In those days the Navajo men didn't dress as they do now. They wore cotton pants and calico shirts. I remember many a time when they came into the store, bought themselves some cotton and sat right down here by the counter and made themselves a pair of pants, put them on over their old ones, and walked out of the store."

It is quite probable that the first silver bracelets had the same form as the old brass and copper ones: simple bars of metal, round or oval in cross section, bent to fit the curve of the wrist [Plate 10A–B]. These had very little ornamentation, and what there was, was applied with the same type of tools used on the brass and the copper.

At an early date a form of bracelet was made which has always been popular with the Navajo and is still worn today. This bracelet is triangular in cross section and one-quarter to one-half inch in width. In the early days of silversmithing, it, too, was stamped with a cold chisel. Another basic type of bracelet which was developed many years ago was the flat, broad band. This type also has a copper and a brass prototype made from metal wire pounded flat. All of these broad, flat bracelets were made of silver melted and wrought into a single piece. The simplest of the compound bracelets was the type which was composed of two pieces of heavy, round silver wire twisted together. Sometimes three wires were twined together, making a bracelet similar in appearance, but with a tighter twist.

From these elementary forms the more elaborate types of bracelets were developed. From the single, flat broad band came the ridged band, which was made by filing, or by forming with a cold chisel rounded or pointed ridges which ran parallel to the edges of the bracelet. This motif broke the flat expanse of the band into different levels, and often there were also short lines and grooves which ran in a transverse direction.

After the Navajo smiths had attained knowledge and control of the soldering process, many compound forms were produced. The triangular bar, the twisted round wire, and the flat bar, of various widths, were combined with each other to form complex pieces. Two triangular bars were placed on each side of a heavy twist of wires, all three parts being held together at the back by short end-pieces. Or two separate twists of wire, each composed of two or more strands, were placed next to each other, giving a braided effect. Less often the triangular bars were placed on each side of a narrow, flat bar.

When the Navajo smiths began to stamp designs on their silver, the total design of the bracelets became much more complicated. Up to that time all of the decorative patterns were achieved by using files and cold chisels, and on the oldest pieces, chasing had been applied with an awl. These patterns were largely rectilinear because of the nature of the tools. Now, with the stamps which bore designs derived from Mexican leather stamps, curvilinear patterns were applied to the metal. Design units, made of straight as well as curved lines, could be combined with each other to form an infinite number of patterns. These patterns were most frequently used on broad, flat bracelets where there was an area large enough for patterns of a fairly good size.

These stamps were used not only to form larger curvilinear patterns, but also to form straight lines and borders. A short, crescent-shaped figure, composed of small radiating lines, is often seen on the triangular-shaped bars, when used both individually as complete bracelets in themselves and as parts of compound bracelets. Such a figure repeated many times in a straight line provides a scalloped line, pleasing as a border design.

The full potentialities of Navajo bracelet design were not realized until about 1880, when the smiths began to set turquoise in silver [Plate 10D–E]. The stones were set in all the types of bracelets mentioned above. Single large stones were put in the broad, flat bands, and sometimes two smaller stones were set on each side of a large one. The bracelets made of two separate bars of twisted strands were especially suitable foundations for turquoise sets. For the past fifty years, bracelets of this type, set with three or more massive pieces of turquoise, have been very popular. The stones vary in shape; sometimes they are cut and ground by the Indian turquoise-workers into round or oval shapes, other times, into square or oblong shapes. Oval-cut stones are preferred for bracelets and are set in either a crosswise or a lengthwise position.

Turquoise used to be mounted on the silver by a quite different method from that employed today. The bezel, or rim, into which the stones were set was deep and level with the top of the stone. This rim was often bent over the top of the turquoise, forming a small cup which held the stone securely in place. Sometimes there was notching on the edges of these crude bezels, giving a pleasing saw-tooth pattern which formed a decorative relief against the turquoise. Shallow bezels, extending but halfway up the sides of the stones, were not developed until a later time, when the smiths had acquired a greater dexterity in the craft.

All of the aforementioned types of bracelets were wrought; the silver was fashioned from an ingot which was pounded into the desired shape while hot. However, bracelets were also made by the casting process, by which molten metal was poured into a rock mold carved approximately into the shape of the finished bracelet. Pieces made in this way are different from the wrought pieces in both form and design. In the former, the bracelet is a solid band with straight parallel sides and an unbroken surface, whereas in the cast bracelet, the surface is broken up into curvilinear bars separated by spaces, and the sides of the bracelet are not straight. The decoration of the wrought pieces depended on file and die-work and marks of the cold chisel. The decorative effect of the cast bracelets, like that of the cast buckles and ketohs, was achieved by the curves of the silver seen in outline against the wrist of the wearer.

Cast bracelets date back to about 1875, which is the approximate date of the oldest cast bracelets in the collection of the Laboratory of Anthropology [Plate 9]. These first cast bracelets had no sets, but later a common type was made with one large stone set in the middle of the piece; less frequently there are smaller sets on the side.

In the past twenty years turquoise has become more accessible to the Navajo craftsmen. The stones are imported from mines in Colorado and Nevada by the traders, who are able to sell them to the smiths for much less than they could have forty years ago. As these stones became more common, the silversmiths used an increasingly great amount for ornamenting their bracelets, and by 1920 set most of them with stones, although they continue to this day to make many bracelets of the lighter, simpler sorts, with no sets, for the tourist trade and for themselves. In the eyes of the Indians a bracelet without a single set looks bare, unfinished, and curiously old-fashioned. If the smith can not afford to buy large stones to set in his jewelry, he buys small, broken-up pieces in a rough state, which he grinds and polishes himself. These small pieces are a by-product in mining the larger stones and are sold for much less. Recently they have been set in single and double rows the entire length of the bracelet and in clusters surrounding the larger stones. This use of turquoise was derived from Zuñi, where the Pueblo smith is less interested in the quality and design of his silver than in the turquoise.

Zuñi use of turquoise exerted an influence on the design of other Navajo silver. Rings, necklaces, brooches, and earrings were more elaborately set. During this same period, the Navajo smiths tended to stamp their bracelets and other silver with many dies. As better tools were introduced, finer and more delicate work was turned out. Such mechanical aids as gasoline torches and rollers enabled the smiths to produce more intricate silver, and in addition, the smiths developed a greater dexterity in handling the medium than the early ones had had.

This facility in handling the metal led the craftsmen to make their silver jewelry more and more elaborate. Design became baroque. We find in the history of silversmithing, as of other arts, that there is a period of development during which the artists perfect their technical skill. As the techniques are refined, the forms and designs increase in number and variety. Once the craftsmen have attained proficiency in handling their medium, they begin to play with these forms and designs, experimenting with them and combining them into new and more elaborate patterns. The inevitable outcome is a baroque phase in the history of any art, in which period the artist becomes more interested in exploiting his technical abilities to their fullest degree than in the aesthetic effect of the whole. In other arts of the American Indian, for instance, we find this same tendency towards overelaboration resulting from experimenting and playing with forms. Pomo basket weavers who wove shells and feathers into their baskets, Navajo women who wove blankets of Germantown wool during the nineteenth century, and the modern potters of Acoma and Zuñi have all used designs so elaborate that they are unæsthetic.

To counteract this development, the Indian Arts and Crafts Board of the Department of the Interior during the last few years has encouraged the Navajo smiths to make bracelets in more simple styles. Old types have been reintroduced in the silver shops of the Indian schools [Plate 10c]. The filed bracelet of the type worn fifty years ago has been copied by the young craftsmen in the schools, and pieces of this kind have found considerable favor among the white people, but the Navajo on the reservation still prefer their bracelets with many sets of turquoise.

The Bridle

That part of a bridle which is mounted with silver is the head-stall, which is frequently elaborately ornamented [Plate 5A–B]. The silver is held on the leather by copper loops, and the straps are encased by seven to thirteen closely fitting pieces of silver. In addition, there is a concha on each side of the headstall. The bits used during the nineteenth century were made either by the Mexicans, or, at a later date, by the Navajo in the same style. Some of them had a fringe of metal loops which hung down below the animal's mouth and jingled when he walked. One other piece of silver found on almost all of the old headstalls is crescent-shaped and just like the pendants which the Navajo wear on their silver necklaces [Plate 12G]. This ornament, called by the Navajo *najahe*, is suspended from the center silver piece on the headstrap, to which it is attached by a small metal loop. There is considerable variation in the shape of these najahes. Sometimes the crescent-shaped bar is not single, but double or even triple, all of the bars joining at the lower ends; and sometimes the piece is closed at the bottom. Usually there are buttons at the ends, and on many of the old najahes there are small hands with four or five fingers [Plate 12B]. These hands are fashioned in various ways; on some pendants they are highly stylized, on others, the depiction is naturalistic. Extending down on the inside of the najahe there is often a turquoise set in a rim of silver.

In ascribing the origin of the najahe to the Old World, Woodward says: "This emblem was old when Columbus crossed the ocean to the new world. It was wide spread from Africa to Serbia. In short, it was an Old World amulet fastened to horse trappings, preferably the bridle, to ward off the evil eye from the animal. These crescent shaped amulets were made of two boars tusks joined together or fashioned out of brass, iron, silver, gold, or bronze. The Romans had them, so did the Moors. The bridle trappings of the *conquistadores* no doubt carried these same traditional ornaments."⁵ A pin from North Africa, made by a Mohammedan silversmith of the Kabyle tribe, has this same crescent-shaped ornament [Plate 12D].

It is Woodward's belief that the Navajo obtained the najahe not directly from the Spaniards, but from the Indians of the Southern Plains. He points out that the Delaware, the Shawnee, and the Comanche all had similar bridle ornaments. He argues that the Navajo probably obtained the najahe from these Indians rather than from the Spaniards, for if they had obtained them from the Spaniards, "their presence would have been noted much earlier."⁶ This reasoning does not seem valid. If the conquistadores had ornaments of this type, there is no reason why the Navajo could not have obtained them directly from the Mexicans and the Spaniards who settled in the region now called New Mexico. It is unnecessary to attribute their origin to the round-about diffusion across the Southern Plains in order to satisfy the time element, for after all there were other types of Mexican silver which the Navajo obtained as late as the mid-nineteenth century. Buttons and squash-blossoms, the origin of which Woodward assigns to the Mexicans, were not reported to have been worn at a date earlier than that when the silver-mounted headstalls were first seen among these Indians. From what little is known, the Navajo probably did not wear much silver until the nineteenth century, after they had been in contact with the Mexicans in wars and raids for several centuries.

The early bridles, just like the other pieces mentioned, were marked with an awl. These first bridles were very plain. A bridle made by the famous silversmith, Atsidi Chon [Plate 5D], is in the Laboratory of Anthropology.⁷ The simplicity of this headstall suggests that it is very old, as Navajo bridle-mountings go, possibly dating back as far as 1875. The center piece on the head band is quite unusual in that it is round; it also has a loop from which a najahe probably once hung.

Later the headstalls were marked with dies, and still later an

⁵ Woodward, *op. cit.*, page 36.
⁶ *Ibid*, page 37.
⁷ I am indebted for this information to Dr. H. P. Mera, of the Laboratory of Anthropology in Santa Fé.

occasional one was set with turquoise. Except for these variations, there was very little change in their design. Those that are made today are much like the old type. Silver-mounted bridles, old or new, are not seen today in large numbers. At a squaw-dance, or at other ceremonies where there is a large gathering of Navajo, two or three such bridles may be seen. Many Navajo who can not afford to buy the amount of silver necessary for a bridle will ornament their headstalls only with conchas. Bridles are frequently made of braided buckskin, and most of the silver-mounted bridles are kept for the greater part of the year on the pawn racks of the trading posts, where the owners have pawned them for credit or cash. Their intrinsic value, because of the large amount of silver on them, makes good collateral.

The Necklace

Chee Dodge states that in the early part of the nineteenth century, before the Navajo were rounded up and taken to Fort Sumner, they wore bits of scrap tin and other metal strung on leather. These leather ornaments they wore around their necks or their wrists.[8] It is quite possible that such crude beads were the forerunners of necklaces composed of spherical beads, made of two halves soldered together. A craftsman would have to have some knowledge of soldering in order to fasten the shank to the inside of the bead, but such a process is simple compared to soldering two half-beads together.

Washington Matthews, in his account of Navajo silversmithing of the early 1880's, gave a description of bead-making which parallels the method used today, except for minor details.[9] Thus, it

[8] In the Laboratory of Anthropology there is one photograph which was taken in the 1860's, about the same time as this imprisonment, which shows a man with one of these ornaments around his wrist, and there is another one which shows a woman with a similar thong of leather strung with bits of metal, possibly silver, around her neck. Still another picture taken during the same period shows a woman wearing a necklace of hemispherical beads which have been strung with alternate beads facing in opposite directions. It looks as if each bead, which is actually but half of a complete bead, were fastened to the leather by a shank on the inside.

[9] Matthews, "Navajo Silversmiths."

is very probable that the Navajo learned how to solder two hemispheres together to make one bead sometime during the 1870's.

The first beads of this type were large, unornamented, and round. From the simple round beads, others more complicated in form, such as the fluted beads and the oval ones, were developed. Dimes and quarters were sometimes fastened by a shank to the necklaces and interspersed with beads.

The best-known type of necklace [Plate 12B], which is called the squash-blossom necklace, probably did not come into existence until sometime after 1880. Washington Matthews did not mention beads of this type in his report.[10] Arthur Woodward has pointed out a very interesting fact in his discussion of the beads of this shape. He says that they were "originally Spanish-Mexican trouser and jacket ornaments . . . which were fashioned to resemble the pomegranate."[11] He says that the pomegranate was a common Spanish decorative motif, painted and carved on missions in Mexico and used as silver trim on men's clothing. Woodward shows the similarity in the forms of the Navajo squash-blossom bead, the Mexican ornament, and the pomegranate, by a drawing and by photographs of the Navajo bead and the Mexican clothing ornament. One may also compare the Navajo squash-blossom to a photograph of the young fruit [Plate 12C], and see that the two are practically identical in form.

It would seem that the Navajo smiths used the Mexican buttons as models for their beads. Their word for beads of this shape, literally translated, is "bead which spreads out." There is nothing in the word which denotes the squash-blossom. It is highly probable that this term was coined by a white man, who, upon asking a Navajo what the bead represented, was told a squash-blossom. The Navajo did not mean that the bead was symbolic of the flower, but merely that the bead looked like the flower.[12]

[10] *Ibid.*

[11] Woodward, *op. cit.*, page 31.

[12] I received the following information from Mr. F. H. Douglas: "In 1916 I was in Kayenta. Mrs. John Weatherill was talking about Navajo silver. She told me that the Navajos in her region thought of the naja as the bow of Nayenezgani; and said that what we call a squash-blossom did not represent that flower, but instead one of the little units that go to make up the central part of a sunflower."

The squash-blossom necklace has a pendant, usually the najahe, shaped like the pendant on the headstrap of the bridle. The early ones were cast in the form of one crescent-shaped bar, while more elaborate types with turquoise sets, composed of two or three bars held together by a cross piece, were developed later, after the smiths had become more expert at casting their silver. Crosses were also worn as pendants. These were of two types, the common cross with the single crossbar and the one having the double crossbars. Smaller crosses were sometimes strung on the necklace, taking the place of the squash-blossom as a decorative motif. Pendants of this type were also copied from the Mexicans, who wore metal crosses as Catholic emblems. To the Navajo the cross was simply a decorative form, void of any religious value. Many old necklaces, having large pendant crosses with smaller ones interspersed with the beads [Plate 14D], have been attributed to the Navajo, but were not made by them. This type of necklace was always more popular with the Pueblo Indians than with their Navajo neighbors. The silversmiths of Isleta and Laguna made such pieces in great numbers.

In recent years the Navajo squash-blossom necklace, like the concha belt, has become a popular item with the white residents of the Southwest and, to a lesser extent, with the tourists. The traders have encouraged the smiths to make strands of small beads which are much lighter in weight than those they formerly made. A type of necklace commonly made today is a double or triple strand of small beads held together at the lower end by squash-blossoms which have large bases set with stones. This use of stones on the beads is again Zuñi influence, and beads like this have, in recent years, become popular with the Navajo (as well as with white people), so that today they make beads of this style for themselves.

Buttons and Pins

With the exception of the bracelet, the Navajo buttons have a greater variety of form and design than any other sort of their silver. These forms range from very simple buttons, which are merely undecorated hemispheres, to intricate ones with elaborate die-work and settings. A collection of buttons in Gallup contains several hundred items, and each one of the buttons is different from the others.[13] Buttons are worn for the most part by the women, who decorate the fronts of their velvet blouses with trims of silver, and put buttons on the collars, and along the sleeves [Plate 16]. Today the men wear comparatively few buttons, usually on the moccasins. In former days they wore them on their leggings and leather pants.

The first type of button was round, about the size of a fifty-cent piece and slightly convex. There were two holes in the center through which a thong or twist of woolen yarn was passed to fasten it to the clothing. Buttons of this type were made very early in the history of the craft, when the Navajo women were still wearing dresses of their own weaving. These buttons, worn at the shoulder, held together the front and the back pieces of the dress.[14] Today they are extremely scarce. Three of them were obtained a few years ago by Ralph Meyers, of Taos, to whom they were sold by a Cheyenne Indian who said that they were obtained in a raid on the Navajo over sixty-eight years ago.

About this same time the Navajo began to use Mexican and American coins as buttons. Dimes, quarters, and fifty-cent pieces were made into buttons simply by fastening a copper loop to the back of the coin. Such buttons were used not only for decoration of their clothing, but also for ornamentation on the sides of the ketoh straps and on the leather pouches worn by the men. I saw a Navajo near Kayenta wearing one of these pouches which had fifty-two quarters sewn to the shoulder strap and thirty rounded buttons made of quarters on the pouch itself, with a single fifty-cent piece in the center.

13 This collection belongs to Mr. M. L. Woodard, who very kindly allowed me to photograph it.

14 Again I am indebted to Dr. Mera. Possibly it was a button of this type to which Lieutenant J. G. Bourke referred in his journal on May 25, 1881: "The dress of [Navajo] women consists of moccasins, leggings, (held up by garters); a blanket robe, made of two blankets sewed together at top of both shoulders and from waist to bottom hem. This robe reaches to the knees. When the woman is wealthy, she fastens large, beautiful silver clasps at the shoulder seams." (Bloom [ed.], *op. cit.*, Vol. XI, No. 3 [July, 1936] page 224.)

It is interesting to note the quantity of silver that was worn by the Navajo less than fifteen years after they had returned from Fort Sumner, where the only silver that they owned was made for them by the Mexicans.

PLATE 5

B. Navajo headstall concha
C. Navajo belt ornament (cast)
D. Early Navajo headstall

A. Navajo bridle
E. Slender Maker of Silver (c. 1885)

PLATE 6

WHITEHAIR, NAVAJO

Coins were pounded down into spherical and conical molds, made either in the wooden stump which served as a stand for the anvil or in a piece of scrap iron. When the coin was removed from the mold, it presented a concave side, to which a loop of copper was soldered, and an outer convex side, smooth in surface, the edge of the button retaining the notching on the coin. Such silver bosses were also used for decorating the leather of leggings and pouches.

These conical and hemispherical pieces of silver were ornamented with designs and used as dress buttons. Some of the oldest buttons may be seen with simple patterns scratched into the silver by a pointed tool. Many were decorated with file marks radiating from the center, and others were deeply grooved with a cold chisel, making the button corrugated on both surfaces [Plate 15A]. Large buttons made from melted pesos were treated in the same way. At a later date the smiths stamped designs on their buttons, and later still they set them with turquoise.

Buttons were also fashioned out of several pieces of silver, pounded as separate pieces and fastened together with solder. Wire, made by pulling silver bars through a drawplate, was used in this way. Delicate tendril-like wires were fastened to a bit of silver on which a stone was mounted [Plate 15D].

Buttons were also cast. One form was a round, flat button with radiating points, at the end of which were small knobs. The number of points varied; some buttons had but six, others had eight, twelve, or more of them. Silver was cast in a wheel-like pattern with bars spreading out like spokes from a hub. Oval buttons were made in the same way [Plate 15E].

These cast buttons are remarkably like certain pieces of Islamic silver. A modern ring from Fiume, made by a Mohammedan silversmith, is almost identical in form with one of the Navajo buttons [Plate 12F & I]. It is very probable that certain forms of Islamic silver were diffused to the New World by the Spanish silversmiths, the roots of whose craft may be traced back to the metal work of the Moors. Such forms as the najahe and cast buttons spread northward from Mexico to that region which is now New Mexico and Arizona. In turn the Navajo silversmiths copied the designs wrought in silver by the Mexican *plateros*.

All of these types of buttons are still worn by the Navajo today. Even buttons of the simplest type, coins to which a loop of metal has been attached, continue to be worn in great numbers. Anyone who has visited the Navajo reservation has received, as change in the trading posts, dimes which have these loops, or a bit of solder which formerly held loops, attached to one side. Navajo women also wear buttons which have more recently developed forms. A favorite type is a long button, which consists of a row of small oval units that form a scalloped edge. Another modern button is roughly like a butterfly in outline.

The Navajo button has not been commercialized by the dealers in southwestern silver who sell jewelry to the white people. Only in the past few years the government Indian schools have encouraged the young silversmiths studying the craft in the school shops to make pins that may be worn by white women in the style of some of the old Navajo buttons [Plate 15B–C]. These pieces have met with enthusiastic approval on the part of the buyers, and such a program should insure the production of buttons of the highest quality of design and workmanship.

Earrings

Navajo men wear turquoise pendants as earrings. These nuggets of turquoise are fastened to a pierced ear by a bit of string which is threaded through a hole drilled in the stone. There are many who wear earrings of this type, especially the older men of the tribe and those Navajo who live on the least accessible parts of the northern reservation. If one had visited the reservation fifty years ago, very few of these turquoise pendant earrings would have been seen. At that time two types of silver earrings were still being worn by the men of the tribe. One of these was a large, hoop-shaped ring with a small hollow silver ball at the bottom, just like the ones that the Pueblo Indians used to wear [Plate 21C]. Sometimes these hoops of silver had a squash-blossom bead in place of the ball. The other type was truly a pendant earring, consisting of one long, cone-shaped piece, which hung with the large end down, with a small squash-blossom having short "petals" hanging from it. These earrings were sometimes as much as three or four inches long. Neither type was decorated; the surface of the silver was left perfectly plain. Less often a hoop, flattened and stamped with dies, was worn [Plate 20A].

In 1881 Lieutenant Bourke described the silver worn by a "well-dressed" Navajo: "Frequently, a dandy will enter the agency wearing large silver hoops in his ears, a necklace of silver balls the size of small cherries, a baldric and belt as above described, silver buttons down the outside seam of his leggings from knee to ankle and a corresponding amount of barbaric decoration upon his pony's bridle and saddle."

When turquoise came into the reservation in quantities about the turn of the century, earrings of these types were discarded or melted down and made into other jewelry. I did not see a single pair of the old style being worn by a Navajo on any part of the reservation, not even in the most remote parts. All of the men who wear earrings now wear turquoise ones.

The history of the women's earrings is quite the opposite. The Navajo women wore, for the most part, loops of small turquoise beads in their ears, at the bottom of which were fastened several bits of red shell. These loops were as much as four or even five inches long. They are rarely seen at the present time, having been outmoded by silver earrings, often elaborate in design, set with many stones, and surrounded by bits of bent wire. This style, of course, reflects again the Zuñi influence that has recently affected Navajo silver work. Today the loops of turquoise beads are worn at the bottom of the longer necklaces of shell beads, interspersed with larger pieces of turquoise.

Rings

As one would expect, the first rings were merely bands of plain metal with no design work whatsoever. Then these bands were marked with designs, first by the awl, and later by dies. About 1880 the first turquoise was set in rings, and such sets were held to the ring by a very high, rudely-made bezel. On these first set rings we find what are known as raindrops, small balls of silver which are set in clusters and rows on each side of the stone. The back and the side of the ring was made either in a single band or in the form of three or more prongs which converged at the back to form one band. A raindrop was set on each of the prongs next to the stone. This type of ring, which was developed at an early date, has always been the most popular form [Plate 15F]. Rings were also made by the cast method, but they have never been as popular as those which were wrought. Before turquoise had become plentiful, the Navajo set other stones in their rings and bracelets. Malachite, cannel coal, garnets, all of which are found on the reservation, and even bits of glass were set in these old silver rings. Garnets were fairly abundant on the northern reservation near Round Rock and also above Kayenta at Garnet Ridge.

After turquoise became more plentiful, three and four stones were set in a vertical row, or perhaps one large stone was surrounded by a circle of smaller ones. On occasion, a smith made a ring with three or four rows of stones, each row containing three or more stones. The larger stones set as solitaires often have small holes drilled in them. Such stones were formerly used as earrings or as part of a necklace.

The setting of polished petrified wood is a modern development. This stone is never polished by the Indians because it is too hard for their tools. It is mechanically polished by professional white stonecutters. Pieces of petrified wood are often set in a ring in a form different from the traditional Navajo type. The band is broad in the front and comes up almost flush with the top of the stone. It has the appearance of being made of solid silver; actually it is hollow on each side of the stone, and is composed of two separate pieces of silver with a space between.

With the exception of the bracelet, the ring has more of a tourist sale than any other piece of Navajo silver. Because the tourists want cheap souvenirs, and care little for quality of design and workmanship, the traders and dealers in silver have encouraged the Navajo to make rings light and flimsy, with sets of a poor grade of stone. Often the stone is not genuine turquoise at all, but malachite, or synthetic turquoise, or a very cheap grade of turquoise, dyed darker.

The Tobacco Canteen

One of the most interesting objects made by the Navajo silversmiths is the tobacco canteen, a piece of silver known today to few Navajo and white men, because of its exceeding rarity. Most of the canteens in existence are in museums or private collections, and the few left on the reservation remain on the pawn rack for most of the year.

In Chapter 1, the origin and early development of the canteen was traced, and it was shown how it developed from the Mexican tobacco cases, which were first made of rawhide and of copper or brass [Plate 11A & D]. The early canteens were made for the soldiers in the army posts, but there were also a few made by the silversmiths for their own people. Chee Dodge has such a piece, made by Slender Maker of Silver.

These canteens varied in size and thickness. The one Chee has is about two and one-half inches in diameter and about an inch and one-half in thickness. Others were an inch larger than this in diameter, but thinner. The smiths also made some very small canteens not more than an inch in diameter. These were constructed in just the same manner as the larger canteens. There are a number of them in the collection of the Laboratory of Anthropology. Dr. H. P. Mera tells of a silversmith who lived near Mariano Lake who used to make miniature canteens. He says that the Navajo women would buy perfume at the trading post and put it in these and then carry them tied to the bottom of their strands of beads.

The stopper which fitted into the spout of the canteen was attached to the rim of the flask by a silver chain. Sometimes there were two chains, one attached to each side of the spout. At a later period the canteens were decorated with stamped designs, which were applied in such a way as to form a large design, which was built up around the center of the canteen. A few canteens were made with a turquoise set in the center of this decoration.

In 1937 I borrowed an old canteen from the trading post at Ramah, New Mexico, and took it to Zuñi, where there is a large group of Navajo silversmiths who make jewelry for the trading posts there. I requisitioned the services of one of the silversmiths, a Navajo by the name of Charlie Bitsui, and asked him to make a canteen, using the old one as a working copy. Charlie had made but one canteen before, and he found the work quite difficult, although he is a very skilled smith.

The trader found the finished piece so pleasing that he had Charlie make several other canteens. During the next year the smiths made several more, set with oyster shell (an idea of the trader's), and these were exhibited in Gallup at the arts and crafts exhibit held at the time of the Indian Tribal Ceremonial. They attracted a good deal of attention there, so that the tobacco canteen is now enjoying a revival. But those that are being made are all sold to the white people, and, as far as I know, the Navajo smiths have not made any more of them for their own people.

Miscellaneous Pieces

In the nineteenth century the Navajo craftsmen made certain pieces which are no longer fashioned. One of these was the mother-in-law bell, and another, the gunpowder measure. The design and nature of these pieces are described in chapter 1. The leather pouches which are ornamented with silver buttons continue to be worn by the older men of the tribe, but few if any are being made today. The buttons that are sewn to these pouches are no different in design from those made for use on clothing. A pouch from the pawn rack of a post in Kayenta has a piece of silver sewn to it which is unique in design, suggesting the form of a cornstalk [Plate 13D].

Some Navajo men wear silver hatbands on their wide-brimmed hats. The origin and the date of the first appearance of these among the Navajo is unknown. The silver band is an inch or so wide and very thin, since the band is made in one long, flat strip, which must be thin enough to be easily bent when cold. Simple designs are stamped on the metal, and a rosette shaped button is attached at the place where the two ends are fastened together. Some hatbands are made with a small prong at one end and holes at the other end, into one of which the prong is inserted, thus allowing the size of the band to be regulated to fit any size of hat. These hatbands are more frequently seen on the western and the northern edges of the reservation than they are in the central part. Many of them may be seen at the annual celebration which is held at Flagstaff, to which hundreds of western Navajo come. They are seen also at the Navajo fair, held every year at Shiprock, on the northern border of the reservation. But relatively few are to be seen worn by the Navajo who come to the Ceremonial at Gallup.

All Navajo men pluck their facial hair. This they do with a pair of native-made silver or brass tweezers, often worn on a chain about the neck. They are an inch or more in width, made of a single piece of metal which has been bent double like a hairpin. Most of the Navajo men prefer tweezers made of brass, since they retain a temper better than the silver ones, which lose their spring after a short while. Designs of the usual sort are stamped on the tweezers.

In the past forty years the traders and the curio dealers have encouraged the Navajo smiths to make souvenirs for tourists. The smiths have made not only the pieces of jewelry similar to those that they make for themselves, but they have made pieces foreign to their native craft. Boxes, ash trays, forks and spoons, and letter openers are a few of the objects that the white man has introduced to the silversmith.

In the making of these pieces, the smiths have used their old designs. The same patterns found on buckles we see on boxes. Concha designs have been put on ash trays and silver bowls; bracelet designs, on watch bands and letter openers. Some of them are beautiful works of craftsmanship. Other pieces are shoddy, poor in design, and even worse in craftsmanship. Some people bemoan this whole development in Navajo silversmithing, saying that the art died when it became commercialized. They refuse to see any beauty in the modern pieces, no matter how fine the design and the craftsmanship. They would have the smith return to the ways of his father.

This is hardly a realistic manner of viewing the present situation. The craft has been commercialized over a long period of years, and the demand for such objects as Navajo-made silver boxes gives employment to many smiths. To go back to the old ways would be to throw many smiths out of work, and employment is highly essential to the majority of the younger men who work at the craft. While it is true that much of the silver being made is poor in quality, some of it is very fine, and such craftsmanship is to be encouraged. In order to understand the present situation of Navajo silversmithing, we must know something of the modern technology and economics of the craft. Then we will be able to understand why the silversmiths can not revert to the methods of fifty years ago. Much of the silver made today, both that which is copied from the old pieces and that which consists of modern commercial objects such as the boxes, tableware, and ash trays, has a beauty in its own right which compares favorably with the silver made by modern white smiths.

CHAPTER IV

The Modern Craftsman: I

TOM BURNSIDES is a young Navajo silversmith twenty-seven years old. He lives a mile north of the trading post known as Pine Springs, which is in Arizona just forty miles west of Gallup, New Mexico, and ten miles north of U.S. highway 66. Tom's hogan, where he does all of his work, is a small, single-room log structure, not more than eighteen feet in diameter. Here he lives with his wife and their three young children, in pleasant surroundings of cedar, juniper, and scrub pine. South of the hogan is a cornfield, the joint property of his wife and his mother-in-law, who lives with her family on the other side of the field. Back of the hogan is a small corral where Tom and his wife drive their sheep in the evening, and several hundred yards in front of the house is a larger corral which Tom and his brothers use for a small herd of cattle.

Tom first learned the art of silversmithing, when he was twenty years old, from his half-brother, John, a man eight years older than he, who lives in a hogan several miles to the north. It took Tom just about a year to learn the craft; that is, it was that long before he was able to master the fundamental processes such as hammering, soldering, filing, and die-working. Within that time he had learned how to make fairly good bracelets and buttons of a simple type. The first pieces he made were some buttons which he gave to the children of his sister, Nazbah. Tom learned to do only wrought work from his brother, but he learned how to cast silver from Left-Handed Red, an old silversmith who lives at Houck, down on the highway. Tom watched this man do casting for one day; then he was able to cast for himself. He paid Left-Handed Red a bracelet for letting him watch him at work.

One day, during the month of June, I went to his hogan to watch Tom at work [Plate 17]. He had agreed to let me watch him make silver, and he had also promised to teach me how to work the metal. Because Tom did not speak a word of English, all these arrangements had been made and all communication had to be carried on through an interpreter, Isadore Burnsides, who is Tom's uncle (his mother's brother). When I entered his hogan early that morning, Tom was busy setting out his tools, which he kept in wooden boxes lining the north side of the hogan and on the shelves of a small rack. His anvil had been put out of the way, by the wall, as Tom had not made any silver in over a month, since he had been busy shearing sheep, herding his cattle, and planting corn. The anvil consisted of a wooden block about a foot square on which was fastened a piece of railroad track, approximately eight inches in length, which Tom said he got from the nearby station at Houck. The piece, which originally had been four feet long, he had carried home in his wagon. Other silversmiths in the region heard that Tom had the track and came over and sawed pieces off. Tom said that it took him one whole morning to saw through that track with a hack saw.

After Tom had laid out his tools, he placed the block of the anvil in a shallow depression, first wetting the earth of the hogan floor so that dust would not fly up when he hit the anvil with the hammer. Then he took three and one-half silver slugs out of a cigar box and put them in a small, triangular crucible. These slugs were bought at the Pine Springs trading post. Slugs which come from refineries in Los Angeles are used almost universally today in place of the Mexican pesos. Each slug weighs an ounce and is about an inch and one-half square and one-eighth of an inch thick. An alloy of copper or brass hardens the metal and makes it less brittle. The slugs handled by the traders are between .900 and .925 fine, which is the fineness of coin. Sterling silver, which has a fineness of .925 or more, is often considered too soft to be made into jewelry and does not have the wearing quality of the silver with more alloy, although it does have a more pleasing silvery color.

After he had put the silver into the crucible, Tom filled a tin bucket with charcoal, which he had previously prepared from piñon wood, and placed the crucible containing the silver down in the coals. The bucket, which is Tom's forge, has a hole cut in the front, several inches in diameter and a few inches from the bottom of the bucket. Tom lighted the charcoal and placed a pair of bellows to the hole. Within a few minutes the coals were red hot, and after about seven minutes he sprinkled a pinch of borax (which lowers the melting point) on the silver in the crucible. After heating the metal for approximately thirty minutes, he removed the crucible from the forge and poured the molten silver into an open ingot mold, which had been greased with mutton tallow to prevent the metal from sticking to the stone. The depression in the mold was about three inches long, one inch wide, and one-half inch deep. The silver blazed up when it hit the mold. Silver solidifies very rapidly, and after a moment Tom blew out the flame, and waited for the metal to cool a bit before he took it from the mold. In a minute or so, when the silver had turned from a glowing red to black, Tom turned the stone over, emptying out the silver ingot. He allowed it to cool for a few more moments, in the meanwhile lighting a gasoline torch. (Torches such as this are used by the majority of the smiths today in place of a natural flame and blow-pipe.[1]) Then he picked up the bar of silver with a pair of pliers and sat down tailor-fashion in front of his anvil. Holding the silver on the anvil, he began to pound it with a heavy hammer.

I had asked Tom to make one of the old-style filed bracelets, similar to one that I had bought at the Santa Fé Indian School. Tom is well known as an expert in making silver of this type. Ambrose Roanhorse, the Navajo silversmith who taught the craft at the Santa Fé school, had been out to Pine Springs during the previous summer (1937) under the auspices of the Indian Arts and Crafts Board, and had encouraged Tom and several other smiths to make silver in this old style. Tom held the silver on the anvil with the pliers and struck a blow on the diagonal with the corner of the hammer head. He explained that the silver spreads more rapidly if it is struck with the edge of the hammer rather than with the flat surface. Then he turned the bar around and pounded the end that he had been holding. After that he held the bar with the thin edge on the anvil, pounding first one edge and then the other, thus keeping the bar the same thickness along its entire width.

---

[1] In the region around Smith Lake the silversmiths make their own torches out of beer cans, a metal spout, and a length of rubber tube [Plate 13c].

After striking about three dozen blows, Tom placed the bar on an asbestos pad, which rested on a small iron grill beside the anvil, and heated it with the flame of his gasoline torch. Pounding hardens the metal, but if the silver is pounded when it is too cold, it will harden unevenly and will crack. If it is alternately heated and pounded, the hardening will be even, producing a finished piece that is fine in grain, with no flaws. If the silver is pounded when it is too hot, it will get brittle and flake off when cool. Therefore, Tom allowed the metal to cool for a few moments before he placed it on the anvil to pound it again. He continued to pound and heat alternately for about an hour, pounding on the four surfaces each time. During this annealing process, the metal bar was lengthening, and as it lengthened it became increasingly thinner and slightly wider. When it was about eight inches long, an inch and one-half wide, and one-sixteenth of an inch thick, he stopped hammering.

The bar was allowed to cool for a few minutes; then Tom took a ruler and marked a line about one-sixteenth of an inch from one edge, and with a cold chisel made a groove along the ruled line. Then with a large pair of tin-shears he cut along the groove, making one edge perfectly smooth; with the use of dividers he then drew a line parallel to this edge, and slightly in from the other side. He cut along this line in the same way. Both edges were then filed to make them absolutely smooth, and the ends of the bar were trimmed in a similar way and filed. With the dividers Tom marked eight lines, four on each side of the center, lengthwise on the bracelet, and along each line he made eight even grooves with the cold chisel. In doing this, he began with the center lines and progressed outward, alternating from one side to the other, so that the silver would spread evenly and the edges of the bracelet would be kept parallel. Then he heated the bracelet and bent it so that the surface on which he was working was slightly convex. Next he picked up a fine file and filed off the edges of each of the grooves. He caught all of the silver dust in a box top. He melts this with scraps and saves it to make other pieces.

Tom then picked up a die made out of an old file, with a small and simple pattern on it. This he marked along first one edge of the bracelet and then the other. He held the die firmly and struck a gentle blow with the hammer. He moved the die about an eighth of an inch and then struck it again. He had not marked the places, but was simply judging the correct distance with his eye, and it was amazing to see that each mark looked exactly equidistant from the next. When the border of die-work was finished, Tom once more took up the filing, this time using even finer, triangular files, and rounding off the sides of the grooves so that the spaces between were given curved surfaces. He filed on the bracelet for two hours, smoothing both the outer and the inner surfaces. Then he smoothed the inside surface of the bracelet with a piece of emery paper, and filed for another hour, making the grooves absolutely even, and the surfaces between evenly curved. At five o'clock Tom stopped work for the day. He had worked steadily on that bracelet since eight-thirty in the morning, with only a few minutes rest at noon for a cup of coffee and some *tortillas*.

The next morning Tom began work once more. He heated the bracelet and at the same time put some of the scraps of silver, which he had trimmed from the edges of the silver bar, into a small cup-shaped crucible. It was not the same crucible that he had used the day before; it was made from a bit of prehistoric black-on-white pottery, which he said that he had found on a ridge near his hogan. He told me that old pottery of this kind is a better crucible than many of the modern ones bought at the trading posts. He heated the silver with his torch, and when it was molten, poured it into a small ingot mold, holding the flame of the torch next to the crucible as he poured. If he had taken the torch away, the silver would have cooled in just a fraction of a second, and a thin crust would have formed on the surface before the metal was poured into the mold. This would have prevented the silver from flowing correctly, and it would have had to be reheated.

When the silver was cool, Tom made two narrow pieces, just as long as the bracelet was wide, which were to be attached to each end of it. When the pieces were the correct size, he placed one of them against one of the ends and with tin-snips and files made it exactly the same thickness as the bracelet. Then he soldered the two pieces together with a solder made of borax and water and small bits of silver. With a pair of tweezers, he put some of this mixture on the surface which he was soldering and sprinkled some dry borax over it. Next he heated the bracelet, beginning at the farther end of the piece, and gradually bringing the flame up to the place where he was going to solder. When the flame was pointed at the point where he had put the solder, he touched the small bits of silver with a piece of pointed steel wire. They melted and flowed evenly, joining the two pieces of silver together. The other end of the bracelet was treated in the same way. Then he did some more filing, rounding the end pieces so that they were perfectly smooth and even. Finally, he bent the bracelet to fit the wrist, by holding the silver band over the edge of a hammer head and tamping with a piece of wood, first with one end down and then the other, until the band was curved to a symmetrical oval. The ends of the bracelet were not joined; an opening an inch wide was left in the back so that the band could be easily slipped on and off the wrist. When Tom tried the bracelet on, he felt a rough spot on the inside; therefore, once more he used his files and emery paper to polish the rough spot.

From the heat of the fire the silver had become coated with a thin black film, or fire-coat, which Tom removed by heating the silver again and dipping the bracelet into a bowl of diluted nitric acid.[2] He allowed it to remain there for just a moment, and when he took it out, it was a dull grey-white color. He then put it in a bowl of water and brushed it vigorously with a wire brush in order to restore the luster of the metal. He felt the inside of the bracelet again, and, finding that it was still not quite smooth enough to suit him, rubbed a handful of dirt from the hogan floor on it. The particles of sand in the dirt acted as an abrasive and smoothed the metal so that it had a shiny surface, which looked more like tin than silver. Then Tom got a grindstone off a shelf, clamped it to a chair, removed the carborundum wheel, and attached a buffing pad on which jeweler's rouge had been rubbed. He held the silver against the buffer for a few moments, giving the metal a high pol-

---

2 Various materials are used for blanching the silver. Rock salt, which is native to the region, alum, sulphuric acid, and muriatic acid, are all used for this purpose.

ish. For the first time in the manufacture of the bracelet, the silver had the luster and shine that we associate with it.

If Tom had been making the bracelet for a Navajo, it would then have been finished. The Navajo likes to have his jewelry as bright and as shiny as it is possible to get it; he wants his silver to look new, whereas, when the white man buys silver, he wants it to look old. Since Tom was making this piece for me, he artificially oxydized the silver, giving it a tarnished and old appearance. This was done by heating the silver and rubbing a dauber, which had been dipped in liver of sulphur, over the surface. This blackened the silver, and then once more the bracelet was buffed so that the artificially produced tarnish would remain only in the grooves made by the files and the die, thus making the pattern show up against the highly polished surface. If silver were not artificially oxydized, it would be some while before the action of the air on the metal would tarnish it enough so that the bracelet would appear to its best advantage.

This one bracelet was finished after Tom had spent twelve and one-half hours making it. It is a beautiful piece of craftsmanship, perfect in design and form. Tom, like many Navajo craftsmen, is a perfectionist, and his work never has the slightest blemish. In fact, the trader in the near-by post often pays Tom to finish any sloppily made jewelry that the other less careful smiths turn out. Ordinarily, however, the average Navajo smith working for a trading post would not spend twelve hours making a single bracelet. I showed this particular bracelet to one of the curio dealers in Gallup who buys the work of a good many Navajo smiths. He admired it, and then asked me how long it took the smith to make it. I told him, and he said: "Well it ought to be good; if a smith that worked for me spent that much time on one piece, it would be just as good as that one, but I give them too much work to do. I have to fill the orders which I get from the wholesalers, and I must have a half a dozen bracelets produced in one day, so they can't be as good as that one." This is one of the reasons why much of the silver that is sold to the tourists is poor in quality. Because the smiths are paid by the number of ounces that they work up into silver, the more ounces per hour the better for them, as long as the finished piece is good enough for the traders to sell. Tom remarked that the bracelets which he made for the traders would be as good as this one if he could spend as much time on them.

A filed bracelet, like this one, is a difficult piece to make. Much more time is required to make it than one with a good deal of die-work and one or two sets of turquoise, and even more patience is needed to spend hour after hour on one piece in order to get the filing perfectly even.

Tom has a well-equipped silver shop, but it is primitive compared with the shops of some of the silversmiths who spend the whole of their time at the craft. He sits on the floor of his hogan to work, just as the silversmiths did fifty years ago, although most of the smiths today work at benches set up in their hogans. Many of the smiths who work at the craft month in and month out, year after year, those who depend entirely upon the craft for their livelihood, have many more tools than Tom has. A mechanical roller is frequently part of their equipment. With this they can roll out silver slugs in a fraction of the time it takes to hammer them out by hand. Some have mechanical devices which facilitate drawing silver through the drawplate, and many have a complete set of saws, dividers, pliers, and a vise. Like most of the Navajo, Tom makes many of his tools out of odds and ends: the grill that he rests the asbestos pad upon, the forge made of a tin pail, and the cold chisels made of old files. His set of tools is typical of the silversmith who earns two or three hundred dollars a year from the craft, working but part of the time and doing most of his silver work during the winter. Tom does not work through the summer months, for then he must care for his sheep and cattle and work in his cornfield. Nonetheless, a set of tools only as large as his costs several hundred dollars, at the current prices charged by the trading posts. A list of these tools follows; an asterisk denotes the ones Tom made himself.

*	2 anvils		1 keyhole saw
	2 gasoline torches	*	1 oval crucible
	1 bellows	*	1 crucible holder (wire)
	3 hammers	*	4 ingot molds
	2 pliers		3 snub-nose pliers

PLATE 7

NAVAJO BELT CONCHAS

A　　　　　　　　　B　　　　　　　　　C

D　　　　　　　　　E　　　　　　　　　F

G　　　　　　　　　H　　　　　　　　　I

PLATE 8

NAVAJO KETOHS (BOW-GUARDS)

1	hack saw	4	heavy files
1	tweezers	12	fine files
* 1	iron grate	1	screw driver
1	asbestos pad	* 1	scales
1	ring-bar	1	wire brush
2	drawplates	* 30	dies
1	grindstone	* 10	cold chisels
2	buffing pads	1	monkey wrench
1	triangular crucible	1	metal-shears
* 1	forge	1	nail set
1	tin-snips		emery paper
* 3	steel pointers		emery cloth
1	dividers		borax
1	ruler		nitric acid
* 1	tongs		jeweler's rouge
			liver sulphur

Although Tom spends much of his time making filed silver, he is also an expert at making silver by the casting method [Plate 18]. I asked him to make a cast ketoh. At the time he had no stone with which to make the mold; therefore, he went fourteen miles south of Houck, where there was an outcropping of the rock which the smiths use for casting. This rock, which is erroneously called sandstone, is tuff, a volcanic ash similar to pumice.[3] There are a number of places on the reservation where this tuff may be obtained, but the finest of it comes from this region and from around Ganado. Tom removed the tuff, which comes out in chunks and is very light in weight, from the ground with the aid of a crowbar.

On the next day I found Tom sitting under a juniper tree in front of his hogan, starting to make the mold for the ketoh. First of all, he took one of the large pieces of tuff and trimmed it roughly with a hand axe to the shape he wanted, and then with a breadknife he trimmed it to a rectangular form about seven and one-half inches by six inches, and approximately two and one-half inches thick. Another piece, which was to serve as the top of the

[3] Dr. J. T. Stark of the geology department of Northwestern University kindly identified this rock for me.

mold, was trimmed to the same size. One surface of each of the stones was made perfectly smooth first by carving with the knife and then by rubbing with a file. Finally Tom rubbed the two smooth surfaces together until they were so even that the one fitted perfectly against the other. It took him half an hour to prepare the tuff in this way. Then with a pair of dividers he marked construction lines on the surface of the piece which was to be the mold for the silver; the other piece was to be used as a lid for the mold. Following the construction lines, Tom began to carve in the design with a small scalpel-like knife, which he had made for this purpose out of an old file. The tuff is very soft and carves easily, and the dust is almost as fine as chalk. As Tom carved, he blew away the powdery white dust from the incised lines. First he carved the rectangular border which was to form the outside edges of the ketoh. Then he began to fill in a design within this area. Four featherlike lines were drawn from the corners to the sides of a square depression in the center, which was where the turquoise would later be set. Two shorter lines leading out from the sides of this square joined the vertical borders. Then Tom made two leaf-shaped uprights which led from the square to the horizontal borders. This is the conventionalized design which is to be seen on many of the old ketohs.

It took Tom two hours to carve the mold. After it was carved, he rubbed a pointed piece of charcoal through the grooves which had been incised in the tuff. This charcoal was to prevent the silver from adhering to the stone. He also cut a channel from the outside edge of the tuff down to one side of the rectangular border. This channel was trifurcated at the lower end, and was to be used in pouring the silver into the mold. Then he incised four very shallow grooves leading from the corners of the border to the corners of the tuff, which acted as channels to allow air to escape from the mold when the silver was poured in.

Next, Tom prepared the forge. Four slugs were put in the crucible, which he buried in the charcoal.[4] The silver was heated

---

[4] Tom makes his charcoal as follows: several logs of piñon are allowed to burn for about forty minutes. Then the burning wood is covered with dirt, smothering the fire. Two hours later he uncovers the charred wood, and it is

for about twelve minutes, during which time Tom greased with a cooking compound the groove through which the silver was to be poured. The lid was tightly tied on to the mold with heavy rubber bands, made from an old inner tube. Tom set the mold near the forge so the rocks would heat, for, as he explained to me, if they are cold when the silver is poured in, it will cool too rapidly and crack. Tom used the bellows on the fire, and then took the mold and rested it upright near the base of the forge, bracing it with a large piece of tuff and an iron grate. Once more Tom used the bellows. Then he quickly took the charcoal out of the top of the pail, deftly lifted out the crucible with a pair of tongs, and poured the silver in the hole of the mold [Plate 19A]. It took him but a moment to do this. He said that if he didn't move rapidly the silver would solidify before it had flowed down into the mold.

After about five minutes Tom undid the bands, took off the lid, and opened the mold. There was a perfect cast! The silver had flowed evenly to every corner of the mold. Tom was pleased and smiled. He said that he didn't always have such good luck as this. He told me that the last time he had cast silver, the metal had leaked out of the bottom of the mold. Another time he had been working too close to the door of the hogan, and the silver didn't flow correctly; and when he opened the mold, the silver was all cracked because it had cooled too rapidly.

With a cold chisel Tom cut away from the one border the silver which remained in the channel that led to the ketoh. Silver had flowed over the edges of the grooves. This he removed with tin-shears, finishing the job first with a jig saw and then with a file. He continued filing all around the edges of the silver bars, first using large files, and then progressively smaller ones [Plate 19B].

All of this work was done in a day, and Tom put up his tools at six o'clock that evening. Early the next morning he was at work again, once more filing the curved bars of the ketoh. Then he stamped the upright, leaflike portions with a simple crescent-shaped die, which he placed carefully on the silver and then pounded with the hammer. A slip of the die would have ruined

ready for use. This charcoal holds up for only one or two heatings before it turns to ash.

the whole ketoh, as once the metal has been stamped, a mistake can not be corrected, and the ketoh has to be melted and a new one made. Tom, however, made no mistake. He placed the die so that it extended but halfway across the portion of the silver he was stamping. Seven times he marked the metal, each time gauging the distance with his eye. Then he stamped seven more crescent-shaped marks on the silver, touching the others halfway across the silver. The other leaflike part was stamped in the same way. Then Tom spent three more hours filing and papering the ketoh.

Next Tom took a piece of turquoise out of a paper bag which was on the shelf. The day before he had taken the unfinished ketoh to the trading post, and luckily enough he had found a stone that was just the right size and shape for the bow-guard. The turquoise was a stone cut by a professional lapidary, but if the trader had not had a stone the right size, Tom would have bought a lump of raw turquoise and cut the stone from the matrix himself, using the carborundum wheel to do the job. Tom placed the turquoise on the square section of the silver, which was in the center of the ketoh. A housing had to be made which would hold the stone tightly against the silver. He had some thin strips of silver which he had previously made for this purpose, pounded out from scraps of silver left over from the bracelet. He measured a piece by bending the silver around the circumference of the turquoise and wired it to the silver of the ketoh with some steel wire, which he got by unraveling some window screening. Then the housing was soldered to the base, the wire removed, and the turquoise fitted. The housing was just a fraction of an inch too large on all sides, but that was just the way Tom wanted it. He removed the stone, as it would not be set permanently until the ketoh was completely finished.

The under side of all cast pieces is pitted with minute holes. This is the surface which lies next to the lid of the mold, for as the silver solidifies, oxygen is released, leaving these holes in the silver. To make the back smoother, Tom filed for over an hour. He then made four small loopholes of silver and soldered one to each corner, on the back of the bow-guard. Leather thongs would be laced through these to hold the silver to the leather wriststrap on which it was to be mounted. As the silver was perfectly flat, Tom bent it to fit the curve of the leather strap. This he did by gently tamping the silver with a section of a wooden ax-handle, a tool that he always used for this purpose, while he held the ketoh on the wooden base of his anvil. The piece was then ready for blanching in the acid, brushing, oxidizing, and polishing, all of which he did in the same way that he had treated the bracelet.

Last of all the turquoise was set. A small piece of cardboard was cut from the side of a match box, and made to fit inside the housing. The stone was then put in, and the sides of the housing were pushed up to the stone with a small wooden block. The cardboard acts as a cushion, allowing just the right amount of give when the housing is pressed against the turquoise. If it is not used, there is danger of breaking the stone when the rim is pushed in.

It took Tom two full working days to finish this ketoh. He did not have any leather for mounting it. This I had done by Dooley Shorty, the Navajo teacher of silversmithing at the government Indian school at Fort Wingate. This bow-guard [Plate 19c&D] won a first prize at the Navajo tribal fair when it was shown at Window Rock in September, 1938.

The finished ketoh was praised by the Navajo to whom I showed it. They admired the perfection of the craftsmanship. The perfect symmetry and the clean sweep of the curved bars appealed to the Navajo's sense of beauty.[5]

The tobacco canteen is the most complicated of all the pieces made by the Navajo smiths. It is intricate in construction in that it is composed of several separate pieces soldered together. It takes an expert craftsman to make a canteen which is neatly put together and well designed. I asked Tom to make one and showed him the canteen that had been made by Charlie Bitsui, one of the Navajo smiths who work at Zuñi. Tom had never made one of these before; in fact, he had never even seen one. I wanted to see how he would solve the technical problems with which he would be confronted in making a piece such as this.

[5] This ketoh is now in The Taylor Museum for Southwestern Studies, in Colorado Springs.

Tom weighed the canteen with a pair of scales which he had made out of two tin lids from baking powder boxes, some string, and a crossbar of heavy wire. The canteen weighed three and one-half ounces. Allowing for waste, which amounts to more than sixteen per cent of the silver used, Tom first melted two ounces of silver and poured it into an open ingot mold which was round in shape. Then he followed the same procedure with two more ounces. These two round pieces of silver, which were to be the sides of the canteen, were pounded out on the anvil. It took Tom just forty-five minutes to hammer out each piece. When he had finished, each one was three and one-half inches in diameter and one-sixteenth of an inch thick. Before they were pounded, each had been one and one-half inches in diameter and one-half inch thick. With the dividers, Tom found the center of one of the pieces and inscribed a circle on the metal. He cut around the circumference of the circle with the shears, and then he marked and cut the other piece. Construction lines were marked on the metal, the first being a circle one-half inch in from the edge of the piece. Then with a crescent-shaped stamp Tom followed around the perimeter of the piece, making a continuous scalloped design around the edge of the silver. With a nail set, which he used for a stamp, he punched a small circle where each of the crescents joined the next one. Following the other construction lines a smaller circle of crescents was made nearer the center of the piece. He next used a very small, circular die which he stamped in the exact center, encircling the stamped design with small crescents, to which were directed a pattern of lines radiating from the center. These were made with a small cold chisel. Tom then marked the other piece of silver with a design varying only slightly from the one he had just applied.

Next he bent the pieces so that each would have a convex surface. He did this by pounding a circular depression in the wooden block to which his anvil was attached, and, holding the edge of the silver over this depression, he hammered, turning the silver slightly after each stroke, and curving the metal the most at the outside. He placed the two shaped pieces on a flat surface (a cigar box lid), to see if the edges were evenly curved so that they touched the surface all the way around. After doing that, he held the two sides together, and when he found that they did not fit together perfectly, shaped them a little more until they fitted exactly.

Tom examined the canteen he was using as a model to see how the spout was joined to the body of the flask. He marked off the proper width for the spout, and then with a length of steel wire fastened the two sides tightly together and reinforced this binding with heavy quarter-inch wire, which was doubled around the flask in two directions. Scraps of silver, borax, and water were spread along the seam, and Tom soldered the two pieces together, turning the flask as he proceeded. When the two sides were firmly joined, the wire was snipped. All of this work took up the whole of the day, and not until the next morning did he file a notch where the spout was to be joined to the body. At this point, Tom was interrupted in his work by Sam Begay, his brother-in-law, who came into the hogan and said that he and his father were about to brand the cattle which belonged to the family. Tom went out to help him, remarking that summer was no time to work silver, as there was too much to be done outdoors.

After the calves had been branded, Tom returned to his work in the hogan, taking up the filing once more. A semicircular cut three-eighths of an inch wide was made in the edge through the seam joining the two sides. He inserted a rivet in the opening and bent the silver out on each side, so that the cut, which had been a pointed oval, was changed to a circle; then with small pliers he finished this part of the work.

In the afternoon Tom melted together and pounded out one and one-half slugs, from which he intended to make the spout and the stopper. He measured this piece to the correct width, and computed the length from a pattern made out of a piece of scrap silver which he fitted into the opening of the canteen. This pattern was rolled out, and its length was measured off on the other piece. The piece from which the actual spout was to be made was wrapped around a ring-bar to make it perfectly round. After the seam of the spout was soldered, Tom tried to insert it in the hole of the flask, but it was a bit too big, and he had to file the hole to a slightly larger size before he could fit the spout in and solder it to the body of the canteen.

Filing on the seam around the outside of the canteen followed. A braid of silver wire was to be attached here; therefore, any excess bits of solder left from fastening the two sides together had to be removed. However, instead of making the silver braid next, Tom fashioned the stopper which was to fit inside the spout. It was made in just the same way as the spout, except that it was smaller. Tom did not have the same difficulty that Charlie Bitsui had had in fitting the stopper into the spout; and after only a little filing, the stopper was the right size. Out of the same piece of silver from which both spout and stopper came, Tom made a small round top, on which he stamped a design composed of crescents harmonizing with those on the body of the flask, and soldered it to the stopper. He filed around the outside of the die-work, leaving a scalloped edge. Then he cut four slits with his jig saw into the edge of the stopper so that it would have some play, and not stick to the spout when it was pushed in and pulled out.

Finally Tom melted one and one-quarter slugs of silver and poured the molten metal into a small oblong ingot mold. Then he started to pound out the piece of metal from which he was going to make the braid. It took him over half an hour to lengthen this piece, which was three inches by an inch and one-quarter, and three-eighths of an inch thick, to a piece twelve inches long and less than one-quarter of an inch wide, with the same thickness. When he had finished, he took a drawplate off the shelf and placed it between four long spikes which were driven into a log near the door of his hogan. He then tied a rope around his waist and looped the other end around a large pair of metal-worker's pliers (draw tongs). He inserted the bar of silver in the largest square hole in the drawbar and grasped the other end with the pliers. Next he placed a sheep pelt on the floor and sat down on it, bracing his feet against the door post, with his legs slightly flexed at the knees [Plate 13A]. Then he pushed back, straightening out his knees, and as he pushed, he slid across the ground on the sheep pelt, and the silver was drawn through the hole in the bar. Then the silver bar was inserted progressively in the next smaller opening. Before this operation was completed, the wire had been pulled through seventeen different holes, each one smaller than the one before. As the silver lengthened, pulling became easier, so the rope was discarded, and Tom was able to pull the silver through with just the force of his arms, no longer needing to use the strength of his entire body. It took him fifteen minutes to pull the silver through this plate.

Then Tom took another drawplate, which had round holes, and placed it in the holder. The first plate, which he had just used, progressed from gauge one to gauge thirty; on the second plate Tom pulled the square wire through round holes starting with gauge one and going through gauge thirty-four. Then the wire was sufficiently small to be made into a braid. Three equal lengths were cut from the long piece, each long enough to go around the outside of the canteen. Tom wrapped some wire around both ends of this bundle of three strands and heated the wire slightly. He then picked up two pairs of pliers, handed one pair to Sam Begay, who grasped one end of the wires while Tom held the other. They each twisted the pliers, turning them in opposite directions, but at first the wire did not twist evenly, and it had to be untwisted and braided again. The second time it came out smoothly, without a single flaw. Tom took the braid and, holding it up to the sides of the canteen, measured the exact amount that he wanted. Once more he filed, then polished, the edge along which the braid was to be attached. The braid was next bound with the steel wire to the body of the flask, and soldered into place. By the time the wire was attached to the flask, it was getting too dark to do any more work; therefore, Tom stopped for the day, which was the second full day he had spent in making this piece.

The next morning when I arrived at the hogan to watch Tom finish the work, I was surprised to find that he did not have the canteen. He told me that his wife had taken it to her mother's hogan to show it to her parents and had left it there. They had wanted to see the peculiar piece of silver that Tom was making and to show it to other relatives. As this was the first canteen that most of the Navajo around Pine Springs had ever seen, it was quite a novelty. Tom sent his wife for the canteen rather than go himself, because his mother-in-law was there, and a Navajo man and his mother-in-law never look at each other or have any sort of contact.

When Tom had the canteen once more, he made a small loop which he soldered to the top of the stopper. When he noticed that the braid was soldered on one side of the spout a bit crookedly, he applied the heat of his torch to that place, and sprinkled a bit of borax on it in order to melt the solder so that he could straighten the braid and resolder it. Then he filed around the braid to make it slightly flat on the outside. Another small loop was made and fastened to the braid one and one-half inches from the spout. Then Tom was ready to make the chain, which he fashioned from a single strand of the wire which he had made the day before. He snipped it into small pieces, and with a pair of snub-nose pliers bent each piece into a figure eight, attaching one link to the next as he went along.

That finished all of the construction work on the canteen, and it was ready to be blanched, brushed, oxydized, and polished. Tom remarked that this was the most difficult piece of silver he had ever made, that he had never done so much soldering on one piece before.

Although I had given Tom the canteen made by Charlie Bitsui as a model, I had told him to put on it a design of his own choice. His piece varied in other respects, also, from the original: The top to the stopper was constructed differently—the original canteen having a stopper with a convex top and a fluted design; Tom had made his canteen larger than the model and slightly flatter, the sides being less convex; and the braid he made was heavier than that on the model. Tom was loath to copy a piece of silver. Even when I gave him pieces and asked him to copy them as exactly as possible, he would make some minor variations in the form or the design. This is true of all Navajo smiths. Each piece they prefer to make slightly different from any other piece.

CHAPTER V

The Modern Craftsman: 2

TOM BURNSIDES had agreed to teach me how to work silver, so one morning I arrived at his hogan ready to start work. When he wanted to know what I would like to make, I asked him what would be best for a beginner, and he advised me to make a bracelet. Then he asked me whether I wanted to begin with silver or learn first how to work copper or lead. He said that many Navajo smiths worked at copper or lead before they started on silver, because those metals were cheaper and easier to work. When I told him that I wanted the feel of working silver, he gave me one and one-half slugs and told me to melt them. I placed the silver in the crucible and lighted the torch. Tom said that a small amount of silver may be melted with the torch; the forge is usually used only when melting three or more slugs at a time. I held the muzzle of the torch, slanting at an angle, to one side of the crucible; but Tom told me that the torch should be held above the crucible so that the heat would spread evenly·over the whole surface of the silver. Then he placed the ingot mold near the crucible, propping it up against a tool, explaining again that the mold must be hot when the silver is poured in, or the metal will cool too rapidly, and crack when it is pounded.

When the silver had heated for a few moments, Tom told me to put a pinch of borax on it, and after I had sprinkled the flux in the crucible, the silver melted more rapidly. I picked up the pliers with which I intended to grasp the crucible, but Tom told me to wait, saying that the metal was not sufficiently melted. This time he greased the ingot mold with a bit of sheep tallow, so that the metal would not stick to the rock. Then Tom said that the silver was ready, and I grasped the crucible with the pliers; but in the meanwhile I had let the nozzle of the torch direct the flame out of the crucible, and in a fraction of a second a thin film formed on the surface of the metal. Tom told me not to pour it, saying that

73

it must be heated again. He said that the torch must be directed at the silver until it is poured or this film would form. Therefore, I heated it a few seconds more, and again the metal was molten. Then I removed the crucible from the wire stand, and poured the silver. Some of the metal ran into the mold, some of it spilled over the outside, and some of it adhered to the crucible. I had not poured rapidly enough, and Tom told me that once more I had let the flame shoot out away from the crucible. Holding the pliers and pouring the metal with the one hand while holding the torch in exact position with the other hand was too much for me.

As a result I had to start all over again. In my first effort I had wasted some silver which could not be recovered, for every time silver is poured, a small part of it goes off in ash. The next time I was more successful. All of the silver ran out. But I did make one mistake: As I poured the silver, I moved the crucible back and forth over the ingot, thinking that the metal would spread evenly. The result of this precaution was the pouring of more silver at one end than at the other; and when the metal solidified, the bar was thicker at one end than at the other. Tom told me that the crucible should have been held in one place.

After the silver had cooled for about ten minutes, Tom told me that it was ready to pound. Gripping one end of the bar with pliers, I held the bar over the anvil and pounded down on the metal. I had given it just two blows with the hammer when the silver flew out from the pliers and landed three feet away. Tom laughed. I hammered once more. Tom instructed me to strike the blows at an angle so that the edge, and not the flat end of the hammer head, would hit the metal. After half a dozen blows, the silver again flew out from the pliers, this time hitting me in the head. Hammering had always looked very easy. As I had watched smiths at work, I had realized that it was tiring work and that it took a certain amount of strength, but I thought there was no trick to it. One just pounded.

Before that first day was over, I learned that there is a great deal of skill in hammering properly. One doesn't just pound. Every stroke has to be directed. If he does not hammer evenly, the silver spreads more at one place than at another, and twice as much time and effort is spent in trying to get the bar back into shape. Holding the silver with the pliers is most difficult at first. With every blow there is a jar on the hand in which the pliers are held. This sets the beginner on edge. If he grips the silver too tightly, he tires himself out, mars the metal where the tool grips, and does not allow sufficient "give," a failure which causes the metal to fly out of the pliers. If he does not hold it tightly enough, the metal flies out anyway. Only experience teaches just how hard to grip the silver.

After pounding for a while on the one side, I turned the bar over and pounded on the other, as I had seen Tom do many times. Then he told me to heat the metal again. This I did. Then I pounded once more, this time holding the thin edge of the bar upright to receive the hammer blows. This was even more difficult. The bar continually slipped from the pliers. But I had beginner's luck in that I managed to keep all the edges of the bar straight. However, I had more troubles ahead. The silver began to crack under the blows of the hammer. I asked Tom why this was, and he said that I had allowed the silver to get too cold before I had reheated it, that it should be heated more frequently. As I pounded, the cracks grew larger. I put down the hammer, stopped work, and asked Tom if I shouldn't begin again. I knew that the cracks would show on the finished bracelet, no matter how well it was soldered. Tom told me to go ahead and finish the bracelet. He said that when Navajo learned to make silver, the older smiths who were instructing them always told them to finish each piece they started, no matter what mistakes were made. In this way, he said, they learned how to make silver, but if they started in again every time they soldered badly or pounded wrong, they never got anywhere and never would learn how to make jewelry. I asked Tom if the Navajo didn't learn to do one thing at a time, by helping the experienced smith first with just his pounding, and then when that was learned, by helping with soldering, and so on, until all of the different processes were learned. Tom smiled when I asked him this and replied that Navajo never learned anything that way. He repeated that the only way smiths learned was by finishing each piece. Tom said that the Navajo learn by watching and then doing, following as exactly as possible what they have seen their teachers do.

After I had worked for more than an hour, the bar had lengthened sufficiently and was fairly uniform in thickness. Tom evened it for me in one or two places, and then with the dividers drew a line down one edge. He filed along this edge down to the line. He handed the silver back to me and told me to do the same thing to the other side. I found that the hardest part of the filing is holding the narrow piece of silver with one hand while filing with the other. This work took me half an hour, and when I had finished, I compared the edge that I had filed with the one Tom had filed—his edge was perfectly smooth, while mine was rough in places.

When I got the edge as smooth as I could, Tom asked me which dies I wanted to use to mark the silver. I selected one die which was long and thin, with a series of small crescents on it, and another shorter one with a chevron design. As I planned to mark a single line of these down the center of the bracelet, I made two construction lines to guide me in the placing of the dies. I selected the small one first, placed it on the silver, and holding it as steady as possible, I hit it with the hammer. I hit it too hard, and the die made too deep a mark in the silver. I then took the larger die and, holding it steady, I pounded again, remembering this time not to pound hard. One end of the crescent pattern showed up well, while the other end did not leave a mark. Tom told me that I must hit harder when I used a larger die, and that I had hit the die at one end rather than in the middle, so that the stamp went into the silver deeper at that end of the die.

By this time my legs were so cramped I couldn't straighten them out. I had been sitting at the anvil for several hours, with my legs crossed tailor-fashion. I tried sitting with my legs out in front of me, but soon found that that was too hard on my back, which had no support, so once more I folded my legs beneath me, and again they became so cramped that I couldn't feel them any more; they were numb. I asked Tom if his legs didn't get tired when he sat that way all day long. He said that when he was first learning, they got a little sore, but that he got over that after a while, and that his back used to get more tired than his legs. He said that his back still got tired if he worked silver for a whole day. He told me that one time the winter before he had bought some whiskey and had taken a swallow of it every now and then while he was working, and that this had made him feel so good that he didn't notice the pain in his back.

I marked the dies all along the bracelet. The line of designs was anything but straight; some of the chevrons were tipped out of line, and the crescents were both crooked and unevenly stamped. But I followed Tom's directions and finished the piece. Next the bracelet had to be bent to fit the wrist. I heated the silver for just a moment, and Tom showed me how to bend the silver around the butt end of the hammer while holding the hammer handle between my ankles as I sat cross-legged. He bent the silver a little in the middle of the bracelet first, and then he bent it at one side and in the back. He gave it to me to bend on the other side. This is the way the smiths instruct the younger men, by showing them how something is done, then asking them to do the same thing. Next Tom showed me how to blanch the silver in the acid, leaving it in the solution for only a minute. I finished the bracelet by brushing it with the wire brush and buffing it on the wheel.

This first bracelet that I made was a peculiar object. It was not uniform in either thickness or width; there were scratches and hammer marks along the surface; the die-work was crooked; and there was a large crack at one side. I told Tom that I didn't think it was very good, and he said that I should melt it and start on another bracelet the next day.

The next morning I started making another bracelet, somewhat heavier than the first one. I succeeded in pouring the silver correctly; the ingot produced was of even thickness. This made the pounding easier than on the other bracelet. My pounding on this second one was somewhat better, although the silver still slipped out from the pliers. No cracks appeared in the bar this time. When the silver bar was sufficiently long, Tom trimmed the edges, this time with a pair of shears rather than a file. He then marked construction lines on the bracelet, selected a die and stamped the silver. He pounded the silver several times with the die, and then handed the die to me and told me to finish the die-work. I was able to stamp all but one or two of the designs evenly along the construction line in this second attempt at handling the dies. But I pounded them too hard, making the silver spread along the edge, so that it was crooked. Therefore, I had to file down the edge to make it even again. Tom took the file from me and finished both edges. He soldered one of the end pieces and asked me to solder the other one. I found it difficult to spread the solder evenly along the seam. I did manage, however, to solder the two pieces together, but I left one small crack, which Tom mended. After that I spent a good hour filing off the solder where it had over-flowed the seam, and filing and papering the edges and the under side of the bracelet. Tom told me that I should take off the scratches left by the coarse emery paper by rubbing the metal with some fine emery cloth. This time Tom bent the silver over the hammer head.

The finished bracelet was many times better than the one I had made on the day before. Of course, this time Tom had done at least half of the work, but nevertheless I felt encouraged with my progress. Tom thought the bracelet sufficiently good to sell to the trader, and he didn't want me to melt it. Several days later I saw the trader's son wearing the bracelet. I did not ask the trader whether he had given it to him because he liked it, or because he was afraid that he could not sell it. I imagine in any case that he was surprised when Tom brought such a bracelet into the post.

Although there were no major blemishes on this bracelet and the die-work was presentable, there were all sorts of minor flaws which clearly tagged the silver as the work of a beginner. It was, in the first place, too thin to have the nice solid feeling which all good silver jewelry should have. Then, the proportions of the bracelet were not pleasing; it was too narrow and the dies were a bit too large for it. There were also minor blemishes, such as small scratches and inaccuracies in the stamping. Flaws such as these can only be overcome by experience in working at the craft.

Charlie Bitsui works for one of the trading posts in Zuñi, where he lives for the greater part of the year. Charlie's hogan is

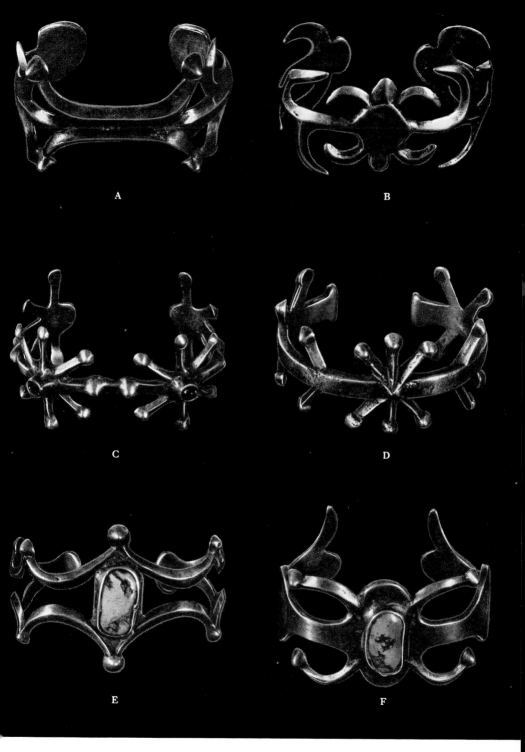

A

B

C

D

E

F

PLATE 9

EARLY NAVAJO BRACELETS (CAST)

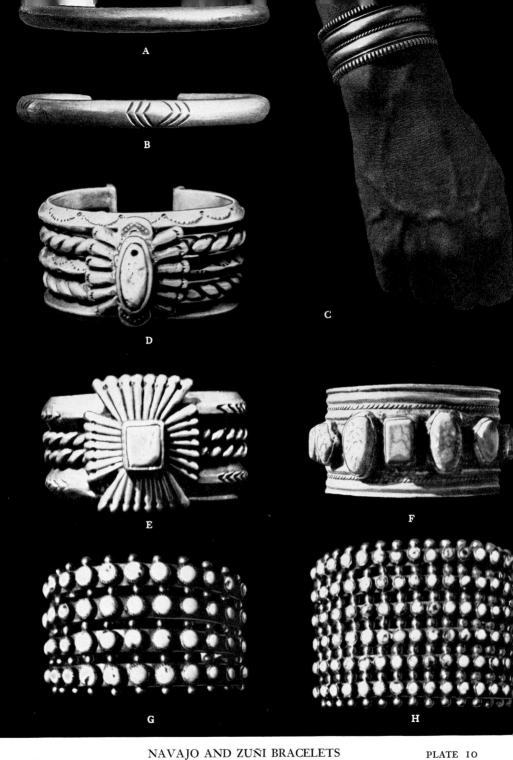

NAVAJO AND ZUÑI BRACELETS   PLATE 10

A–B. Early Navajo
    D–E. Old Navajo   C. Modern Navajo (U. S. Indian School)
        G–H. Modern Zuñi   F. Old Zuñi

twenty-five miles north of Zuñi, near Manuelito. It was here that Charlie learned the craft from his grandfather (his mother's father) over twelve years ago. He became a good silversmith, and as the years passed, he spent more and more of his time at his silver work. Eight years ago he came to Zuñi to work. His sister's husband, Ike Wilson, was already a well-known Navajo craftsman in the pueblo.[1]

Charlie lives in a modernized hogan which is owned by the trader, Charles Kelsey, for whose trading post Charlie does his work. This hogan is very different from the one in which Tom lives. It has a wooden floor, windows, and a long workbench, large enough for several smiths. When I was there, one end of the bench was usually occupied by a Navajo boy about fifteen years old, whose name is Francis Yazzie. He is a relative of Charlie's, the son of his sister's daughter, and was learning the craft from Charlie, who paid him ten dollars a month for helping him with his work. The bench at which they worked is well equipped. In the front there are drawers in which tools are kept and in which scraps of silver and silver dust are stored. The top of the bench is covered with tin. There are two anvils, each mounted on logs like those belonging to Tom Burnsides, but the wooden bases of these are higher, so that the smiths can pound their silver while sitting in chairs.

There are individual differences in the way silversmiths work. In many respects Charlie's work differs from Tom's. While the finished pieces that each makes conform to Navajo traditional patterns, there are differences in their technique. There are differences in the way they handle their tools, in the way they pound the silver, and in the way they melt it. These variations are due to differences in the way the smiths originally learned from their Navajo teachers. Each smith developed his own style of working, and once a pattern was formed, it was adhered to. Muscular co-ordinations became fixed as habits. When Charlie wrapped a piece of wire around two pieces of silver which were to be

[1] Ike Wilson's father, Son of White Haired Man, was the first Navajo silversmith to live in the village and work for a trader (Charles Kelsey). This was over twenty years ago. His hogan was between Zuñi and Gallup near Cousins Trading Post.

soldered together, he always held one end of the wire in his mouth, leaving one hand free to hold the silver. Tom never used his mouth, but rested the silver against something while he tied the wire. This is only one of many differences in their working methods. There are probably as many differences in the muscular habits of silver-smiths as there are individuals who follow the craft. Another reason for this variation in technique from smith to smith is that every one has a different set of tools. Some smiths, Tom for example, have many more than the older smiths, like Charlie Houck, who lives south of Pine Springs [Plate 13B]. Still other smiths, like Charlie Bitsui, who work in regions where silver has become more commercialized, have a good many more implements than Tom. Different tools demand different techniques in the handling of the metal. Charlie Houck follows the method used in the nineteenth century. He works without a torch, heating all of his silver with charcoal, and he uses a blowpipe to direct the flame of the fire at his silver when he solders. Tom uses a gasoline torch, but he works on the floor of his hogan. Charlie Bitsui has a bench at which to work and an apprentice to help him.

I watched Charlie make a canteen. This canteen is the one which Tom used as a model. Charlie used for a model an old canteen obtained from the pawn rack of the Ramah Trading Company, a few miles east of Zuñi, and he had also made one of them before, some years ago. Charlie did not melt the silver and pound it out, but gave that job to Francis Yazzie, for he was busy finishing a ring which he was repairing for a Zuñi. Charlie did not have a forge like Tom's, but a small makeshift one was constructed by placing coals around the large ingot stone which had a depression in which the metal was melted. Coals were taken from the near-by cook stove and set up around this stone. Then the torch was used to heat the silver. The coals caught the heat and acted as the sides of a miniature furnace in melting the metal. It took Francis about three hours to pound out the two pieces which were to be used for the sides of the canteen. This was about twice as long as it took Tom, who had considerably more strength, as well as experience. When Charlie had finished the ring, he lent Francis a hand. Soon the silver was thin enough and roughly circular in shape. Charlie took a piece of tin from a trunk and placed the piece of silver upon it. Charlie's wife, who was acting as interpreter, explained that he had made this pattern for the canteen he had made previously.

Charlie marked construction lines to guide his die-work much as Tom had done. But the die-work was very different. Charlie hammered many designs into the silver, and before he had finished with the stamps, there was not a square inch left without design. This was typical of Charlie's work; silver which he made for the trader tended to be elaborate, almost too much so. Sense of design varies considerably from one smith to the next. Tom used design sparingly. He liked to do file work, in which the patterns are straight, formal, and reserved. On the other hand, Charlie took great pleasure in stamping with his dies, of which he had many, and he could not resist using them on every occasion.

Nor was Charlie quite so careful in his work as Tom. One of his dies went too deep, tearing a hole in the silver. It was patched underneath with a bit of solder and scrap silver, a rather simple job given to Francis. That is the way a master craftsman uses his apprentice. He gives him the work of melting and pounding the metal. Likewise, the easy routine work, such as blanching, brushing, polishing, filing, and papering, fell to Francis. Die-working and difficult jobs of soldering Charlie always did himself. While Francis was patching, Charlie left the hogan, reappearing a few minutes later with some steel wire. He said that he had borrowed it from Sam Jackson, his younger brother, who worked in a shed several hundred yards away. Charlie often borrowed tools, and tools were borrowed from him. If he did not have the kind of die that he wanted or if he had run out of borax or some other supply, he would go to Ike Wilson's or to Allen Chee's. Allen is his cousin, who also works for the traders at Zuñi. It was always one of these relatives from whom Charlie borrowed or to whom he lent tools. I never saw him exchange tools with the other Navajo smiths in the village.

Charlie used a different method from Tom's for twisting the wire for the braid. He instructed Francis in doing this. One end of the strands was inserted in the bit of a hand drill, the other end was held in a pair of pliers by Charlie's wife. Then as the handle of the drill was turned, the silver wire turned, forming a tight twist. Charlie applied this braid to the two sides of the canteen, which he had soldered together, in much the same way as Tom applied the braid to his canteen.

In making the top for the stopper, Charlie used a tool that Tom did not have, a steel bar (female die) in which there are circular depressions of various sizes used in button and bead making. Silver pounded down into the depressions comes out in a hemispherical form. This tool, which belonged to Sam Jackson, had been purchased from the trading post.[2]

When all of the construction work was completed, Charlie blanched the silver by placing it in a copper bowl filled with a mixture of rock salt and water. Rock salt and almogen, also used for this purpose, are both found in the surrounding region; the rock salt coming from Salt Lake, south of Zuñi. In this one respect Charlie used a more primitive method than Tom, who blanched with nitric acid, for the Navajo smiths sixty years ago, in the days of Washington Matthews, whitened their silver in the same way. This mixture was allowed to come to a boil, the silver was dropped in, and after a few moments fished out with a copper hook. Iron or steel must not come in contact with the silver while it is in this solution, or a chemical change will take place which will tinge the silver red.

The finished canteen made by Charlie can not compare with the one made by Tom, even though it was made under more favorable working conditions. In two places Charlie had to patch the silver where a die had gone too deep. The die-work was not only less attractive in pattern, but the dies were not applied as precisely,

2 Tom, however, had made his own bead mold. He had heated a blunt rivet in his forge until it was red hot and then had plunged it into water, tempering the metal in this way. Then he pounded it down into another piece of iron, which was red hot. When the depression was deep enough, this piece was also tempered. This is an example of the way a silversmith works: if he does not have a tool, he makes his own. Silver may be made with a minimum of tools, as it was fifty years ago, or it may be produced with an extensive supply such as that of Charlie's. Although a certain number of tools is required to make silver in many forms, the quality of the silver depends more on the way the tools are used than on the tools themselves.

and the soldering was not filed off as neatly as on Tom's canteen. The fact that one was better than the other was not due to any difference in the abilities of these two smiths, but to an economic factor. The Navajo silversmiths who work at Zuñi are professionals; they earn their living wholly by their craft. Charlie earns an average of one hundred dollars a month. In order to derive good incomes, these smiths must fill the orders that the traders give them, and frequently have to rush their work. This does not mean that good silver is not produced by them, for it is. The blemishes on the canteen that Charlie made were minor ones which did not detract from the total effect of the piece, but it did not have the perfection, the precision in every detail that characterized Tom's work. To make silver as good as that he turned out, unlimited time is essential. Smiths who do not have to earn their livelihood from their art, and who work silver during the winter months for the most part, have the time to lavish on perfecting their work. Such perfection has always been a quality of the best Navajo silver, new or old.

I watched Charlie make other pieces. One of them was a squash-blossom bead. Two small hemispheres were made by pounding silver down into the steel bead mold. The rough edges were filed off. Then Charlie punched a small hole in each hemisphere, using the end of a file which he had sharpened. These two hemispheres were then strung on a piece of wire and soldered together. (When Tom made a bead, he held the two parts together with a pair of tweezers while soldering.) Next Charlie took a small rectangular piece of silver, one inch by one-half inch, and drew a line across it, dividing it into two parts of one-half inch each. One of these parts was divided again and cut into three equal pieces, the cuts extending up to the center line just mentioned. The other half of the whole piece was trimmed off at each corner. Then Charlie bent the piece around the handle of a small file and soldered where the two edges came together, thus making a small tube. After that he bent back the three pieces made by the cutting. These formed the "petals" of the bead. With a pair of small pliers the petals were not only bent outward, but each was given a concave surface, so that each petal had a pleasing curve. A third part was made in a triangular shape with a long prong extending out from one side. This prong was filed down to a fine point and pushed through the hole in the bead. The point extended out on the other side of the bead and was soldered to the tubular part on the end of which were the petals. Then Charlie drilled a hole through the triangular piece; the string of the necklace would be laced through the hole. It took him almost an hour to make this one bead. After seeing just this one squash-blossom made in three separate parts, I was able to appreciate better the tremendous amount of labor which goes into the making of a whole necklace containing dozens of these beads; and I could understand that silversmiths do not like to make strings of beads because the work is very monotonous.

One morning I watched Charlie make some rings. He had received an order from the trader for two dozen of them, not an unusually large order for him. Navajo silversmiths at Zuñi spend all of their time while they are in the village at the craft. They work silver for five or six days intensively, and then they go to their homes on the reservation for several days. During the summer, these smiths are continually going off to squaw-dances where they remain for several days. When they are working silver, they frequently make a great number of rings or bracelets or boxes at one time. In this way, they can make many more pieces in a given period of time.

When I entered Charlie's shop, he was making the shanks for this lot of rings by fastening together with steel wire three pieces of silver wire, each about two inches long. The steel wire was bound one-half inch from each end of the three strands. The ends of the two outer strands were then bent away from the center one. Next Charlie soldered the three strands of silver together in the middle, placing silver solder on the inside of the binding wire. This solder flushed evenly along the silver and joined the three pieces into one. He removed the bindings at each side, and bent the entire piece around a ring-bar. The solid part was to be the back of the ring, and the three separate pieces which spread out fanlike were to be the prongs. Most Navajo rings are made with these prongs on the side. Sometimes there are three, other times four or five. When Tom makes a ring, he uses one piece of silver which he divides at each end to form the prongs. Charlie did not follow these processes through in sequence with each ring. Instead, he performed the first step on all of the rings, and then went on to the second process, and so on.

On this day Charlie's wife was sitting at the end of the bench,[3] helping him with the rings. She told me that Charlie had taught her how to make silver two years before, and that she was able to make rings, bracelets, and conchas by herself. Usually, however, she just helped her husband with his work, and only on rare occasions made any pieces herself from start to finish. She said that Charlie had also taught his three sisters how to make silver, and two of them had taught their husbands the craft. These women and their husbands all made silver for the traders at Zuñi. Charlie's wife then was cutting little snips of silver. She took a piece of charred wood which had many small pits in the surface and placed a snip of silver in each one of these small depressions. Then she took the torch and directed the flame at the bits of silver and sprinkled borax on each. As the metal in the depressions melted, each bit formed a small ball about an eighth of an inch in circumference. About a hundred small silver balls were made in this way and allowed to cool. In the meanwhile Charlie was still making the shanks for the rings and filing them off. Francis Yazzie, the young smith, was pounding out slugs of silver for bracelets, which the trader had also ordered from Charlie. Charlie's wife started to make bezels for the rings. From a strip of silver that was very thin and about one-eighth of an inch wide, she measured and cut off lengths to go around each stone. She shaped them to fit around the stones and placed each one on a thin piece of metal, called a plate, which was slightly larger than the stones themselves. She soldered the seams of the bezels and then soldered each of the bezels on the plates upon which they were placed. She did not rest her silver upon an asbestos pad as Tom Burnsides did. She used a block of sandstone upon which she rested a heavy metal gridiron.

[3] This is Charlie's second wife. The first wife did not want to live at Zuñi. She wanted to be with her sheep, at her hogan between Manuelito and Two-Wells. She told Charlie that he could have her daughter by a former marriage for a wife to live with him at Zuñi.

Charlie's wife took some of the bezels, mounted now on the plates, and soldered lengths of fine, twisted wire around the bases. This wire, consisting of two strands of fine wire wound tightly together, is an ornamental device that is used by the Zuñi smiths in the making of jewelry, and the Navajo have taken it over from them. Following this twisted wire, she trimmed the plate, which had been soldered fast. Charlie soldered each mounted bezel to a shank, and then soldered a single, small silver ball to each of the prongs. These silver balls are known to the curio dealers as raindrops. The rings were then blanched and polished by Francis Yazzie before Charlie set the stones in them.

This is the way many silversmiths work who make silver for the traders in such centers as Zuñi, where silver has been highly commercialized. Another is Smith Lake, and a third, Manuelito. The batch of rings that Charlie and his wife made were well done, but they were all alike, and there was no individuality in any one piece. This was because all of the rings had been made at the same time. If one ring had been completed before the next one was begun, there would have been more variety in the finished jewelry. This method of silver-working is in marked contrast to the methods used by such smiths as Tom Burnsides and Atsidi Nez. They finish one piece before going on to the next. Mass production such as this is used in turning out silver which is to be sold for a cheap price. Larger and more elaborate pieces, which have more design work on them, are not made in this way. With them attention is given to each individual piece.

CHAPTER VI

Silver in Navajo Culture

WHEN a Navajo man wants to learn how to make silver, he goes to a relative for instruction. Only if there are no silversmiths among his blood relatives or among his relatives by marriage, will he turn to an outsider for instruction. This seldom happens, as most Navajo have at least one relative who knows the art. If a man's father knows the craft, he will be the one from whom he learns. If the father does not make silver, the man will go to a brother, or failing that, he will seek instruction from another close relative, a mother's brother, or a mother's father, or even a mother's mother's brother. Less often will he learn from a cousin or a father's brother.

The silversmiths learn from relatives by marriage less frequently, but if they do, no particular relative is favored to a marked degree: a wife's brother, a sister's husband or his brother, may be sought out. There is a tendency to learn the craft from a relative that is living in the same hogan group of the person desirous of learning the art; that is, a man is likely to learn from a related smith in the immediate vicinity rather than going to a more distant hogan.

If a young man has a father who is a silversmith, he will begin to help him with the work when he is about fourteen years old. By that time he will be strong enough to help hammer out the silver and do other bits of work that require only a limited amount of skill. If the father is a smith, the son does not make a choice of whether or not he wants to learn silversmithing, for his helping is a routine activity, just as fetching wood and water or herding the sheep. As he grows older and becomes more experienced in working the metal, his father gives him more work to do, and within a period of a year or two he is able to make silver by himself and sell it at the trading post. Because he finds this work profitable, yielding an income in the form of credit at the store, with an occasional cash payment, he continues to work at the art.

Many Navajo women know how to make silver, but it has been only in the last thirty years that they have learned, and most of them live in the centers where there has been considerable commercialization of the craft. Only a few of the women who make silver carry on the art as independent craftsmen, getting silver and turquoise from the traders and being paid by them for their work. Mary Burnsides was an independent worker. She said: "I learned to make silver from my husband, Goodluck. I used to watch him at his work, and I ground turquoise for him to put in his jewelry. I picked up the art from him and made some silver for myself. I remember the first piece that I made was a ring. I made more and more silver, and pretty soon I sold some to the Navajo living around here. They bought buttons, bracelets, rings, and beads from me. I never made any conchas because it takes so much pounding to make them. They paid for their jewelry in sheep or in cash. I also made shell beads which I sold to the Navajo, and I ground turquoise, too. I did most of this silver-work at night. During the daytime I wove at my rugs and watched after the sheep when there was no one else to do it. I earned more money by weaving than by silver. I made about two hundred dollars a year from my rugs. One time I went to Gallup, and I bought some glass beads that looked like turquoise.[1] I set these in buttons and rings and took them up to Ganado. I sold them for goats and sheep. The Navajo knew that these weren't turquoise, but they thought that they looked pretty so they bought lots of them. I stopped doing silver work seven years ago because it hurt my eyes."

The majority of the women work at the craft as assistants to the men [Plate 23B]. Usually they help their husbands by grinding and polishing the turquoise, setting the stones, and doing other tasks similar to those performed by Charlie Bitsui's wife.[2] But on

---

[1] These may have been frosted glass beads of a turquoise color, made in Czechoslovakia. A number of years ago large lots of these were sold in the Southwest. Contrary to the opinions of many people, the Navajo are never fooled by fake turquoise. They buy these imitations because, as Mary said, they consider them pretty.

[2] The Navajo women (and men) use the same method for grinding and polishing turquoise as the Zuñi. With steel snippers a stone is broken from the

occasion women also help their fathers or their brothers with the silver. It is from one of these three relatives that the women learn the craft, and the husband is usually the teacher. The Navajo smiths who work at the craft during the whole year, those whom I have called professional smiths, are the ones who teach their wives to make silver. In regions like Zuñi, Smith Lake, and Manuelito, the traders keep the smiths busy with orders for the greater part of the year. The more silver a smith can turn out, the greater his income; therefore, it is to his economic advantage to teach the art not only to his sons, but also to his daughters and his wife. They will increase the family income in direct proportion to the amount of silver they make. Women whose husbands make only a small amount of silver are not apt to learn the art.

Table 1 shows from whom fifty-two Navajo silversmiths learned the craft.

TABLE I

2 Learned from nonrelatives
50 Learned from relatives

		from consanguine relatives			*from affinal relatives*
40 men	16 :	fathers	2 :	wife's brothers	
	5 :	brothers	1 :	wife's father	
	1 :	father's brother	1 :	father's mother's sister's husband	
	3 :	mother's brothers			
	3 :	mother's fathers	1 :	brother's wife's brother	
	1 :	cousin			
	3 :	mother's mother's brothers	3 :	sister's husband's brothers	
10 women	3 :	brothers	5 :	husbands	
	2 :	fathers			

If a Navajo learns how to make silver from a relative, he does not pay for his instruction. He asks a relative to teach him to make silver, and in return he assists the master smith with his work. The

matrix, mounted on a lapidary's stick with wax, and ground into shape by a carborundum wheel.

advantages are mutual—the apprentice learns a craft which will yield an income to him in the future, and while he learns, the experienced smith is enabled to increase his own income by turning out more silver. Or, to state this the other way around, the experienced smith asks one of his relatives to help him with his work, and in return for this help, he is willing to teach the craft to the assistant. This state of affairs exists in the regions where silver has been extensively commercialized and where a smith needs help with his work. In fact, such smiths often retain the services of their apprentices after they have gained skill in the art. A smith is considered skilled in the craft when he has mastered the art of soldering. Charlie Bitsui paid Francis Yazzie ten dollars a month for helping him. Peter Roans learned from his cross-cousin, John Hoxie, and when he became skilled, he was given money enough to buy clothes at the post, and in addition scrap silver and turquoise. Suski helped his father, Chai Begay, and in return his father made occasional gifts of small amounts of money. The novices often work in this way for a master smith for several years. In the meanwhile, they save their money and buy their own tools. It is often two years, and sometimes longer, before a smith has a sufficient number of tools to set up his own shop and work independently.

There is no payment either from the apprentice to the master, or from the master to the apprentice if they are relatives, except when the novice is retained as a helper after he has gained skill as a silversmith. However, there is a payment made to the master craftsman if the apprentice is not a relative. The payment varies according to the length of the teaching period. As much as forty dollars, or the equivalent in goods, may be demanded by the experienced smith if the teaching extends over a long period of time. If the novice merely watches the other smith or works with him for a short time, a small amount will be paid, a dollar or more, or perhaps a bracelet.

Many silversmiths have learned the craft just by watching other smiths at their work. When I asked Charlie Houck from whom he had learned the art, he replied: "No one taught me, I just learned myself. I watched other fellows make silver, then I went ahead and made some myself. I was able to do everything but solder and I learned how to do that from Red Mexican." Many smiths have learned the art in just that way, with no formal instruction of any sort, but it is considered dishonest if one smith watches another without telling him that he wants to learn. I asked Atsidi Yazzie how he learned. He said: "I didn't learn from any one person. I just picked it up by watching different smiths at work. I stole the art from some of those smiths. I watched Atsidi Chon make silver, but he didn't know that I was learning while I was watching him. Then when he went away for a day or so I would go over to his hogan near Klagetoh and use his tools and solder to make some buttons and other things out of my own dimes and quarters."

Chai Begay, an old smith who lives near Danoff, was the first silversmith to work the metal among the southern Navajo, who live in the region of Zuñi. He said: "I learned how to make silver when I was living up at Mariano Lake. Fifty years ago I moved down here. At that time there were no silversmiths anywhere around here. Some younger fellows used to watch me at my work, and they stole the art from me. Now there are a lot of smiths around here."

Many silversmiths do not like other Navajo to watch them while they are working because they do not want their art stolen. They guard their method of making solder as if it were a trade secret. There are many ways of making it, different proportions of ingredients being used on silver of various fineness.

There are a number of interesting parallels between the learning of silversmithing and the learning of ceremonials. Clyde Kluckhohn has written in a paper on Navajo ceremonial practice of the Ramah-Atarque region:[3] "To questions of this sort, 'From whom should a Navajo learn a ceremonial?' replies followed this general pattern, 'From anyone, usually from a relative or a friend.'

"The particular persons from whom ceremonials are most often learned are the father and the maternal uncle. To these only no fees are paid.

[3] Clyde Kluckhohn, "Some Personal and Social Aspects of Navaho Ceremonial Practice," *The Harvard Theological Review*, Vol. XXXII, No. 1. (January, 1939), pages 58–66.

"Payment for instruction, like payment for ceremonials, is not rigidly standardized but varies with kinship, friendship or other factors.

"There is a good deal of informal learning of songs, medicines, and parts of ceremonial behaviors. . . . In general, however, anyone who attempts to conduct ceremonials without having entered into a somewhat formalized teacher-learner relationship meets with disapproval on the part of recognized practitioners and distrust on the part of people generally."

It is interesting to note that learning something for nothing is frowned upon by singers as well as silversmiths.

I asked Tom Burnsides if there were any restrictions on the behavior of silversmiths comparable to the taboos observed by the Navajo women when they made pottery and baskets. Tom said that there was only one—no one should be watching the silversmith when he is pouring the silver into the casting or ingot molds, or when he is doing delicate soldering. He said that if some one is watching, the metal will not pour correctly, and the solder will not stick to the silver, and the work will have to be done over again. When I asked Eski Sosi if I could watch him make silver he said that the last time he let someone watch him, the silver would not melt the way it should and he was not able to pour it. Silversmiths do let the apprentices whom they are teaching watch them while they are doing this part of the work, which requires such intense concentration. It is an interesting note on the behavior of smiths and gives another reason for their dislike of being watched. I do not think that this is a taboo, for it lacks supernatural sanctions and is not strictly adhered to. However, silversmiths feel definitely uncomfortable when some stranger is watching them. The presence of a watcher seems to distract the attention of the smiths from their work so that they ruin the silver. An old chanter by the name of Red Moustache told me that many silversmiths have the reputation of being disagreeable and evil-tempered because they get angry when someone comes to watch them at work.

The craft of silversmithing runs in family lines. There are certain families in which there are many more silversmiths than in others. This situation is due mainly to the influence of the traders.

They give their best smiths large quantities of silver to make into jewelry and encourage these smiths to teach the art to other members of their families. In this way the traders are able to centralize their silver business, and instead of scattering their silver to isolated smiths spread over a large territory, they can dole it out to related smiths in a small community. Because of this encouragement from the traders, there are in different regions certain families in which there are many smiths. Chai Begay is the nucleus of such an "outfit" of smiths in the region of Danoff. There are a dozen smiths closely related to him, by either blood or marriage, who have learned the craft from him. Near Crystal there is a group of smiths descended from Atsidi Sani and his brothers. Four of these are Andrew, John, Henry, and Fred Peshlakai, all of whom are brothers. Around Lupton there is the Goodluck outfit; at Pine Springs, the Burnsides; at Smith Lake, the Largos; and in the region of Manuelito, the family to which Charlie Bitsui belongs. Charlie and his brother, Sam Jackson, learned to make silver from their mother's father. A younger brother, called Ki Jackson, learned from the older brothers. There are four sisters in this family, all of whom make silver, and each one of them is married to a silversmith. Sam and Ki Jackson and Charlie Bitsui have all taught their wives to help them with their work. Charlie's wife also comes from a family of silversmiths; two of her father's brothers and her own older brother make silver.

The fact that silversmiths learn the craft from blood relatives more frequently than they learn from affinal relatives and the fact that they seldom learn from nonrelatives has also been effective in the grouping of silversmiths in certain family lines. Since more silversmiths learn the art from their fathers than from any other relative, the craft tends to follow the male line of the family. There are families living in the regions mentioned above that have few if any smiths. Perhaps a reason for this is that there were no old smiths in these families to teach the craft to their kin. The occasional smiths in such families are younger men who have learned from an affinal relative or outsiders.

Every Navajo silversmith makes silver for his fellow tribesmen as well as for sale to the traders, although, to be sure, this represents a minor portion of the silver made on the reservation today. When a Navajo man or woman wants a piece of jewelry, he goes to a silversmith, perferably a relative, and describes the type of piece he desires. The silversmith then makes the jewelry according to specifications. The buyer usually furnishes the turquoise and silver for the bracelets, rings, conchas, or whatever he happens to want. Any silver or turquoise that the smith has on hand is apt to belong to the trader for whom he works; he seldom has a supply of his own. The Navajo buyer pays the smith only for the labor which he expends in making jewelry from the furnished supplies. Of course, if the smith makes the jewelry from his own silver and turquoise, the buyer is charged just that much more. This is the case when he sells a piece that is already made. The payment for the work is in various forms, frequently in cash, sometimes in kind. Sheep, goats, or calves are common forms of payment, and by this exchange many smiths have built up large flocks. Lacking cash, the buyers often secure on credit at the trading post some desired object for the smith. Turquoise or silver may be given for the jewelry, or the buyer may render some service to the smith, such as working in his fields or herding his sheep.

Often silversmiths make jewelry with their own supplies in payment of a debt. Very frequently they pay for sings which are held for members of their families with bracelets, necklaces, conchas, or other pieces. Table II lists some of the silver that Tom Burnsides made for various Navajo. In each case, if there is a known relationship between the smith and the buyer, it is stated.

TABLE II

Type of jewelry	Buyer	Relation to Tom	Form of payment
Bracelet, rings, and buttons	Nazbah Burnsides	sister	Made for gifts.
3 bracelets	Mr. Liar		Two of these still not paid for; third made as payment for sing Mr. Liar performed over Tom's wife when she had a baby.
Ring and bracelet	name unknown	wife's sister	Made in return for help rendered around hogan at time of wife's lying-in.

94

PLATE II

TOBACCO CANTEENS

A. Mexican (brass)   B. Old Navajo (silver)
C. Modern Navajo (silver)   D. Mexican (rawhide)

ILLUSTRATIONS OF DESIGN DIFFUSION   PLATE 12

A. Zuñi ceremonial head ornament. B. Navajo squash-blossom necklace. C. Pomegranate. D. North African pin (Kabyle). E. North African amulet. F. *Islamic ring*. G. Navajo najahe (pendant). H. Navajo headstall (detail). I. Navajo buttons (cast)

Concha belt	Jack Kahn	mother's sister's daughter's husband	$8.50 cash, buyer supplied silver.
3 rings and 3 buttons	Sam Begay's wife	wife's brother's wife	1 sheep.
2 rings	Juan Tsosi	wife's brother	Made in return for help given in making silver.
1 bracelet	John John's daughter		$2.00 cash, buyer furnished silver and stones.
6 buttons 2 rings 2 bracelets	name unknown	wife's mother's sister's daughter	3 sheep.
1 bracelet 1 ring	Mr. Cowboy	wife's mother's brother	Made in return for working in cornfield.

Table III lists the silver John Burnsides made for relatives and friends.

TABLE III

Type of jewelry	Buyer	Relation to John	Form of payment
Bracelet and concha belt	Mable Burnsides	sister	1 shawl for bracelet. $9.00 Stetson hat for belt. Buyer supplied silver for belt.
Bracelet and buttons	Mary Burnsides	mother	Turquoise ground by the buyer.
3 rings	Lucy Burnsides	sister	Shell beads made by the buyer.
1 bracelet	Mr. White-hair	brother's father-in-law	Made in return for plowing his cornfield.
Bracelet and buttons	Mr. Broken Dam's wife	wife's sister	1 sheep, buyer's silver and turquoise.
Concha belt and 2 rings	name unknown	wife's sister's son	1 cow.
Bracelet and buttons	Sam Belu's niece		Made in return for helping around hogan.
Buttons	Grant Belu's wife		1 sheep.
Bracelet and buttons	Mr. Donkey's daughter	sister's father-in-law's daughter	1 double saddle blanket.
Bracelet and two rings	Nazbah Roans	sister	1 sheep, 1 goat. (Buyer's silver, smith's turquoise.)
3 bracelets and buttons	Joe Walker's wife		19 sheep.
2 bracelets	Mr. Gambler's wife		$6.00 cash and 6 sheep. Buyer furnished materials for one bracelet.

95

One of my informants said to me: "Sometimes a silversmith makes a nice bracelet which catches the eye of some girl and she wants it, but maybe she doesn't have any money to buy it. Then sometimes the smith tells the girl that he will let her have it if she will give herself to him." The informant added: "This happens most often among the younger unmarried smiths. Of course they don't say anything about it, but everyone knows that silversmiths do that."

I asked this same informant about the transaction between a smith and a buyer. He told me: "If a Navajo smith has a bracelet on his arm and another Navajo comes along and sees it, he might say, 'That's a nice bracelet; how much would I have to offer to get a bracelet like that?' The silversmith might say, 'If you like this bracelet how much do you think you could give me? I don't think that you have enough money, you know that it is expensive.' Then the other fellow might say, 'I will give you twenty dollars for it.' The silversmith would tell him how long it took him to make it and what a hard job it was. Then he would say, 'I want thirty dollars for it because the materials and the time cost a lot of money.' The buyer will say, 'I will pay you whatever you say because you know how much it cost you to make it.' The Navajo buying the bracelet would then take it and he would feel proud because he had paid so much money for it. A smith is doing the Navajo a favor when he sells him jewelry for a high price, because then the buyer can boast of how much he paid. He wouldn't be able to do this if he sold it to him for a cheap price. When a smith sells jewelry to a trader it isn't like that. He sells the silver for whatever the trader offers him for it. He meets the trader's price. He doesn't care about what the white man thinks of the silver. Silversmiths stamp designs on the silver which they sell to the white man that they wouldn't put on the jewelry if they were selling it to other Navajo. The Navajo won't buy silver made just any old way."

The Navajo also buy silver jewelry at the trading posts. Every trader has a showcase full of silver. On the southern part of the reservation this jewelry is made by the smiths who work for that particular trading post, but on the northern part of the reservation, where there are very few silversmiths, the jewelry is shipped from Gallup by the mercantile companies which supply the trading posts with goods.

The Navajo sell and trade their silver to other Indians of the Southwest. Most of this trade is with the Pueblo Indians. The western Navajo carry on a trade with the Hopi. The central and the southern Navajo trade their dies and some of their silver to the Zuñi, especially when they go to the pueblo in December to see Shalako. The central and eastern Navajo trade silver to the Acoma, Laguna, Jemez, Santa Ana, and other eastern Pueblos. The Santo Domingo come out to the Navajo reservation and trade turquoise for silver jewelry and Navajo blankets.

A small amount of silver is traded by the western Navajo to the Walapai and Havasupai when they come in to the annual Pow-wow held in Flagstaff on the Fourth of July. Considerably more silver is traded to the southern Ute and to the Apache. The Navajo living in the vicinity of the "four corners" trade their silver for Ute beadwork and buckskin. At the annual Shiprock fair held in October, Navajo men may be seen wearing beaded belts and gloves with elaborate beading on the gauntlets. At this same fair, Ute are in evidence wearing Navajo bracelets and rings. The trading posts at Towaoc, Colorado, on the southern Ute reservation, carry Navajo rings, buttons, and bracelets, which are shipped from Gallup. The Jicarilla Apache move down to the southern edge of their reservation in the winter and are in contact with the neighboring Navajo. The Navajo give them rings, bracelets, and buttons in return for goats and buckskin. Since the government reduced the number of Navajo goats as a measure in the soil conservation program, these Apache goats have been a favorite article of trade. The Jicarilla like to stud their wide, leather riding belts with these Navajo buttons.

The White Mountain Apache wear more silver than any of the other tribes mentioned above. There are four stores at Fort Apache and at White River that sell silver which is obtained from dealers in Gallup. The total sale per year of Navajo silver in these stores amounts to about four hundred dollars. Almost every Apache woman owns at least one Navajo bracelet and possibly a ring. There is also some direct trading between these Apache and the Navajo. Holbrook and Flagstaff are the main loci of this trade. On rare occasions a Navajo smith comes down to the Apache reservation and sells some of his jewelry. Tom Burnsides made some silver tweezers for the trader at the post at Pine Springs who had received an order from a trader at White River for them.

Navajo values regarding their jewelry are economic for the most part. The first thing that a Navajo says when complimenting another person on a piece of jewelry that he is wearing is, "That's pretty; how much did you pay for it?" The Navajo wear as much jewelry as they do in order to display their wealth. This wealth display is especially obvious at any large gathering, at a squaw-dance, a Yeibichai, or at the Ceremonial in Gallup. At that time every Navajo will wear as much of his silver as he is able. He will wear all of the jewelry he has at his hogan, and he will redeem silver which is in pawn at the trading post if he can possibly get the necessary cash to do so. Each person owns his own jewelry, but members of a family borrow each other's silver and turquoise. Many times I saw Tom Burnsides and his wife wearing the same silver on different occasions. For the most part, the Navajo invest their money in two different forms, in sheep and goats and in jewelry. A Navajo obtains the same satisfaction in appearing at a squaw-dance bedecked in silver and turquoise as he does when he gathers his sheep and goats together at the sheep dip where other Navajo have come with their flocks. This display of wealth is not a personal matter as much as it is a family matter. It is not "see how much money I have," but "see how much money we have in our family." In a similar fashion, members of a Navajo family herd their sheep together, although every animal is owned by individual members of the family.

Navajo women wear more jewelry than the men, and usually it is the women who are the actual owners of the sheep. A Navajo man wearing a concha belt, a turquoise necklace and ear pendants, silver moccasin buttons, a ketoh, a bracelet, and two or three rings would be considered wealthy. But a wealthy woman would wear a concha belt, a turquoise necklace, or a silver one (and sometimes both), several dozen buttons on her blouse—at the collar, up the front, and along the sleeves, as many as six or seven rings, just as many bracelets, and earrings set with stones. If she were wearing moccasins, they too would be decorated with silver.

Silver is worn for its decorative effect as well as for its display value. Bracelets, rings, and necklaces have become an essential part of a Navajo's dress. I asked Grey Moustache if he would let me take his photograph. He declined, saying: "No, I won't let you do that. I don't have any of my turquoise and silver on. People who see it will say, 'Why that Navajo doesn't have anything at all.' I would feel like a chicken with all its feathers plucked out."

If a Navajo has all of his jewelry in pawn and is going somewhere, he will borrow his relatives' jewelry because he would feel undressed and conspicuous if he were not wearing any. A singer's assistant at a Mountain Chant held at Window Rock borrowed a concha belt from a white man because he did not have one. I saw Yeibichai dancers borrow belts and bracelets from each other on the last night of a ceremony at Shiprock, and at another ceremony at Danoff.

When the silver is not being worn, it is either stored away in trunks and boxes in the hogans or pawned at the trading posts. Smaller pieces, such as rings, and one or two bracelets are worn from day to day, but the larger pieces, such as the concha belts, are worn only on special occasions. Silver and turquoise of all types are pawned at the posts. Thus the Navajo's jewelry serves three functions: as decoration, to display his wealth, and as collateral against which he can borrow at the trading post.

What happens to a Navajo's silver when he dies? The Navajo are notoriously afraid of their dead and it has been said that all of a dead man's jewelry is buried with him. It is certain that much of the old silver has disappeared in this way. But all of a person's jewelry is not buried. One of my informants explained: "If a person dies with a lot of silver on, some of it is taken off. A dead person is never buried with all his jewelry. The jewelry that is taken from the dead body is sung over to purify it. One of the Evil Way ceremonies is given. Motion-in-the-hand is done to decide which of these ceremonies should be held. On the first night the silver is washed in soap and water, and pollen is sprinkled over it. The jewelry is placed next to the person who has inherited the silver. That person must be sung over too. If there are several people who have been left silver, they all go into the hogan, and the jewelry is placed next to each one. On the second night, which is the last night, the Blessing Way songs are sung and prayers are said. After that a person can wear the jewelry that has been taken from a dead man without any fear of evil spirits.

"If a man dying of a sickness has a lot of jewelry and other property, he will usually take his silver off and distribute it to his relatives. If there is a lot of silver in pawn when a man dies, the family will redeem it. But it must be sung over before it is worn. Henry Taliman's brother-in-law died last winter. He left all of his silver to his younger brother. He also left a medicine pouch for Evil Way, a silver belt, horses, sheep, and some other property. Little Medicine Man, from the other side of Oak Springs, sang Big Star Way. I did motion-in-the-hand. When my grandfather died, he left cattle, sheep, farm tools, and some silver and turquoise. This property was sung over by Tall Medicine Man. He did Moving Up Way."

The æsthetic function of silver is of a secondary nature. Navajo admire beauty of craftsmanship; a heavy piece of silver, well marked with dies and set with good stones of a dark color, excites admiration. Sloppily made, poorly constructed silver is rarely worn by them although they may sell much of it for white consumption.

Standards of beauty are undergoing a change today, just as they have in the past. Silver judged beautiful forty years ago was very massive and heavy with bold, simple designs. Twenty years later jewelry was more elaborate in form and beginning to look baroque. Recently there has been a strong influence from the pueblo of Zuñi. At this time most Navajo prefer silver with many sets, and even with bent wire work. I showed the filed bracelet with no turquoise sets that Tom made to his aunt, Mary Burnsides, and I asked her what she thought of it. She said, "It looks old-fashioned; it ought to have some turquoise in it." The ketoh which Tom made was offered for sale by the trader, Bill Stewart, to Mr. Blacksheep, who wanted one. But he didn't like it, and said that he wanted one with more stones in it.

Silver is not worn in a tarnished state. The Navajo keep their silver polished, so that it looks shiny and new. Rings and bracelets that are only slightly tarnished by contact with the skin are brightened by vigorous brushing in yucca suds and water. If the silver is too dark to be polished with a cloth or a buffing wheel, they take it to a smith, who removes the turquoise and reblanches the silver. This gives it the appearance of having just been made. There is an economic reason for this as well as an æsthetic one: If the silver looks new, people are likely to compliment the owner on it and ask him how much he paid for it.

Apparently the designs which the Navajo smiths stamp on silver are not symbolic. I showed a piece of copper stamped with various designs to five different silversmiths and asked them what they were. All five of them laughed at this question and their attitude seemed to indicate that the designs were meaningless to them. Their reaction was like that of a white man if he were asked what the circles on his necktie meant. Each one hesitated before answering, and sometimes no answer was given until my interpreter asked them once more, this time inquiring what the designs looked like, what they suggested to them. Table IV shows that no one design was called exactly the same thing by all of the smiths. There was a uniformity of opinion on only two of these designs; the one called "cloud" and the one called "lightning." These two designs resemble figures depicted in the sandpaintings, in which medium they have a symbolic significance. Furthermore, I am sure that the smiths questioned were not holding back any design name because of religious reasons, since they named these two designs more readily than the others. All but one person agreed on one of the other figures which they called "trees growing between hills," and on another which they called "leaf." In all of these cases I am sure that the silversmiths meant that the designs suggested these forms to them, rather than that they were symbolic of the objects named, with the possible exception of "cloud" and "lightning." But even here I think that these designs stamped on metal only reminded them of the designs in the sandpaintings. They are not symbolic of cloud and lightning as they are when they are used in the sandpaintings; they have no religious significance. The first four designs are much more common than the others, and these showed the least uniformity in name. It is these designs, and others similar to them, that are the oldest of the stamp designs which were derived from the Mexican leather stamps. The first seven of these designs were made with dies which belonged to Tom Burnsides. It is interesting to note that he, the maker of these dies, had a less definite idea of their meaning than three of the other smiths.

John Six is a silversmith who lives a few miles south of the trading post at Pine Springs. He makes several hundred dollars'

TABLE IV

Tom Burnsides	John Burnsides	Isadore Burnsides	Husky Burnsides	John Six
1. ?	mountain	half moon	mountain	quarter moon
2. rug design	tooth	?	cloud	peak of rock
3. green grass	bushes	?	sun rays	blossoms of small plant
4. ?	eye	?	half moon	weeds
5. cloud	rising cloud	?	rain cloud	like cloud in sandpainting of Male Shooting Way Chant
6. ?	lightning	lightning	lightning	lightning
7. trees be-tween hills	trees and hills	?	mountains with trees	clouds on horizon
8. leaf	not asked	leaf	feather	leaf
9. leaf	not asked	?	mountain peak	mountain peak with trees
10. worm	not asked	?	feather	hind part of snake
11. rainbow	not asked	rainbow	waves on water	mountain ridge

worth of silver a year for this post. He is an expert at making dies, and he sells many of them to the various silversmiths who live in the region. Many silversmiths dislike making dies themselves because it is very hard on the eyes, and they prefer buying them to straining their eyes, which are overtaxed by working silver as it is. Die-making takes skill and requires a good deal of time even in the making of a fairly simple die. The designs are cut into the ends of pieces of scrap iron with extremely fine files, and then the dies are tempered by heating and sudden cooling in water, so that the design will hold up under the strain of hammering. There are certain smiths, like John Six, who have developed a skill in the making of these stamps, and they make a specialty of selling them to other smiths. John said that he was paid a dollar and a half for a large die, and for one of the smallest size he was paid fifty cents. He has made many dies for Joe Thomas, the most prolific silversmith in the region.

An analysis of the stamp designs based on the impressions of the dies made by six different silversmiths and on the dies used in the shops in two of the Indian schools reveals that the form of these stamps falls into four basic types [Table v]. These types are: the crescent; the triangle (with or without a base); the circle, with lines radiating from the center; and long narrow designs with parallel edges. All four of these design types have a number of variations. The crescent varies from a shallow or deep curve a quarter of an inch in length to a shallow crescent several inches long. The triangles and circles also vary in size. Some of the crescents have smooth edges, others have saw-tooth edges with a line in the center; still others have lines cut from one edge to the other in a radiating pattern. There is a similar variety in individual stamps of the other types.

Of these basic types the crescent is by far the most common An average of the dies belonging to these six smiths and two shops was taken. There were twenty-three dies of the crescent type, eleven of the triangular type, four of the circular type, and three of the type with the straight edges. All of these types have their origin in the Mexican leather stamps.

The silversmiths on the reservation use very few naturalistic designs. Of these the arrow and a generalized bird design, which were originally introduced by the traders, are the most popular. Certain curio dealers in the Southwest have printed folders picturing designs such as swastikas, thunderbirds, arrows, and horses, which are stamped on Navajo silver, and they have attributed definite symbolic meanings to these designs. This is sales promotion rather than fact.

Many smiths have taken up singing; there are old singers on the reservation who knew silversmithing in the past. Long Moustache, of Klagetoh, and Sam Tilden are the best known of these. Grey Moustache, of Sunrise Springs, knows some prayers and minor ceremonials, and Atsidi Sani was a singer. The smith needs a lucrative avocation, for he can do accurate work for only twenty years or a little more, then his eyes begin to grow weak and he can no longer see well enough to work silver. Eyestrain may be called the occupational disease of silversmithing. Many smiths ruin their eyes because they work in their hogans at night with only the light of kerosene or gasoline lanterns.

Tom Burnsides remarked to me: "You can't do good silver work for very long. It all depends on how long your eyes last. After my eyes get too weak to do silver, I can do medicine work. I am going to begin to learn Apache Wind Way from my father-in-law, Whitehair, some time soon."[4]

For over twenty-five years the traders have encouraged the Navajo smiths to make thin, light bracelets in the form of snakes, with turquoise sets for eyes. These have always been a popular type of souvenir. But because of the Navajo's fear of snakes (an animal that figures prominently in Navajo religion, and which is believed to cause illness), many smiths will not make bracelets of this type. Charles Newcomb, the trader who has a post at Prewitt, said of Charlie Peacock, an old smith who works for the traders in the region: "He is the only one around here that will make snake bracelets. He says he doesn't care if he makes them because he is going blind anyway."

[4] For descriptive accounts and analyses of Navajo Wind Way and Apache Wind Way (Chiricahua), see Kluckhohn and Wyman, *An Introduction to Navaho Chant Practice, Memoirs* of the American Anthropological Association, No. 53 (Menasha, Wisconsin, 1940).

TABLE V

105

A singer who lives just south of Gallup told me: "I learned to make silver fifteen years ago. I made lots of jewelry, but my eyes weren't strong and they got even weaker. My father said to me, 'After your eyes begin to trouble you, the traders won't buy what you make because you won't be able to stamp it straight. If you go blind, you lose your job, but if you know how to sing you still have a job because you can smell the different medicines.' So I learned some chants from my father who was a medicine man. I learned to do Navajo Wind Way, Apache Wind Way, and Blessing Way from him. Now I earn a good deal with my singing, but I still do a little silver work in the winter time."

John Burnsides is a silversmith thirty-five years old who is also a singer. He began to learn singing over ten years ago. He does Apache Wind Way, which he learned from Whitehair. He does excerpts of several other chants: Navajo Wind Way, Moving Up Way, and Big Star Way. He helps other singers perform the full versions of these sings, and at the present time he is learning the Female Shooting Chant from Yellow Crutches, a well-known singer who lives in the region. In addition to these ceremonies, John does motion-in-the-hand, a method of diagnosing diseases. John is still a novice. Apache Wind Way is the only ceremonial of which he does a complete version by himself. He lacks either the necessary paraphernalia to do the other sings in their entirety or a complete knowledge of those chants.

I asked him to tell me of some of the chants which he had performed. He replied: "John Sam's son had a bad dream. He dreamed that he saw coming towards him his dead mother who had just died in that same hogan. I sung Moving Up Way over him for two nights. Another time I was working at my silver here in my house when I was called over to Oak Springs to find out what was the matter with the silversmith, Juan Yazzie. He had been having pains in his head and in his eyes. He had gone to an American doctor, who had told him that there wasn't anything wrong with him. I did motion-in-the-hand and my hand shook towards me when I thought of Apache Wind Way. I sung that over him for two nights and he got well. Another time my wife was sick. She had had four children, and all of them had died.

That caused her sickness. I did motion-in-the-hand and my hand told me that she should have Moving Up Way. Tall Medicine Man did the singing. Singing often interrupts my silver work. So I just put it aside until the sing is over, when I take it up again. Once in a while I dream about the designs I have put on my silver, and sometimes I see bracelets and rings that I am going to make."

Less than one-fifth of John's total income, which in 1937 amounted to more than one thousand dollars, is derived from his medicine activities. By far the greater part of his income is derived from his silver work, with which his wife and his two sons help him. I asked John whether he was planning to do more singing or silversmithing in the future. He answered: "It all depends on my eyes. If my eyes get weak, I will earn more from singing than I do from silver."

CHAPTER VII

Economics of the Craft

ON the Navajo reservation the pawn rack plays an important part in the economics of the tribe. In every post there is one of these racks where silver jewelry, turquoise necklaces, and other items are stored. In some of the older posts the necklaces and concha belts hang over long bars suspended overhead, with the bracelets and rings hanging on nails at the rear of the counter. In the more modern trading posts all of this silver is kept in a safe in the rear of the store. Each article bears a tag on which is listed the name of the owner, when it was pawned, and how much credit or cash was advanced on the particular article. Other objects are also pawned on occasion. I have seen guns, chaps, spurs, saddle-blankets, and even saddles in pawn. Additional articles commonly pawned are mocassins, Paiute woven baskets which are used in the sings, and buckskins.

The amount of cash or credit advanced on any article depends on both the intrinsic value of the object, in the case of jewelry the amount of turquoise and silver, and the owner's credit rating in the store. If the Indian has the reputation of paying his account in full at fairly regular intervals, the trader may give him more than the actual worth of the pawn. Usually, however, the intrinsic value is much greater than the amount given by the trader. The traders always allow more on pawn which is taken out in trade than on that for which cash is advanced, in order to protect themselves in the event the Navajo does not redeem his jewelry. Some pieces stay on the rack for as long as five or six years before they are redeemed. Pawn is redeemed with cash. The law requires the traders to hold pawn for only thirty days, but there is not a single trader who would dare foreclose as soon as that. If a Navajo comes back to the store and finds that his silver has been sold, he will very likely not trade at that post again, and he might run off leaving a sizable bill behind him. The Navajo seldom fail to redeem their jewelry, although it may take them a long while to do so.[1] They place too high a value on it to let it go for so little. "Dead" pawn, that which will probably not be redeemed, the traders sell at a considerable profit to Navajo and to white men.

The pawn moves in and out of the trading post at regular seasonal intervals. The Navajo pay their store accounts twice a year. Sheep are the basis of Navajo economy. In the spring after they have sold their wool crops to the traders and in the fall after the lambs are sold, they come in to settle their accounts. If the amount of the wool or lamb sales exceeds his bill, the Navajo will redeem his pawn. Thus in the summer and early fall the pawn racks are comparatively empty. Much of the jewelry is kept out of pawn during the summer months while the squaw-dances are being performed. In November some of the jewelry is brought into the post again, and during the winter more and more accumulates. In this way the pawn helps tide the Navajo over from one season to the next. A Navajo does not pawn all of his silver at one trading post. If he has obtained credit or possibly cash on pawn from one trader, he may also go to another post and pawn several more pieces.

TABLE VI

Trading Post	Object pawned	Amount pawned for	Owner's valuation	Date pawned
Pine Springs	pin	$ 1.00	$ 3.00	June 1938
"	bracelet	4.50	5.00	May "
"	4 buttons	2.25	4.00	July "
"	2 strands of turquoise beads	2.00	4.00	" "
White Mounds	2 baskets	4.00	5.00	Jan. "
"	4 rings	2.50	3.00	?
A. C. White (near Houck)	moccasins	2.00	10.00	?
		$18.25	$34.00	

[1] The pawn rack has been an essential part of the Navajo trading post for over sixty years. Lieutenant Bourke wrote in his journal on April 25, 1881: "No amount of money will persuade an Indian to surrender one of these necklaces (turquoise), and when pressed for cash, they will pawn them at the trader's, but the pledge is always redeemed promptly at the expiration of the term specified". (Bloom, *op. cit.*, Vol. XI, No. 1, January, 1936).

Frequently the silver belonging to one person may be scattered over an area of fifty miles.

Table VI lists the silver that Tom Burnsides had in pawn in the month of August, 1938. Table VII shows John Burnsides' pawn in the same month.

TABLE VII

Trading Post	Object pawned	Amount pawned for	Owner's valuation	Date pawned
Pine Springs	bracelet	$ 10.00		over a year
"	bracelet	8.00	All of	ago
"	bracelet	7.00	these	"
"	bracelet	6.00	bracelets	"
"	bracelet	11.00	together	"
"	bracelet	3.50	valued at	"
"	bracelet	2.00	over $100.00	"
"	bracelet	2.00		"
"	bracelet	3.00		"
"	bracelet	7.25		"
"	bracelet	1.00		"
"	bracelet	1.00		"
"	turquoise beads	8.00	$ 30.00	last winter
"	turquoise beads	6.00	25.00	"
"	large turquoise and shell beads	15.00	200.00	a year ago
"	6 rings	9.50	15.00	last fall
"	6 buttons	5.00	30.00	"
"	moccasins	2.00	3.00	last winter
White Mounds	bracelet	2.00	5.00	month ago
"	rifle	2.00	9.00	December
"	buckskin	9.00	15.00	"
Lupton	2 bracelets	2.00	5.00	two years ago
Gallup	bracelet	5.00	10.00	"
"	ring	3.00	5.00	last fall
White Mounds	wagon	35.00	90.00	a month ago
"	silver beads	15.00	100.00	three months ago
"	turquoise beads	25.00	200.00	seven months ago
"	turquoise beads	10.00	35.00	four months ago
		$215.25	$877.00	

PLATE 13

A. Tom Burnsides drawing silver wire   B. Charlie Houck, an old Navajo smith

C. Navajo homemade blowtorch   D. Navajo wearing pouch

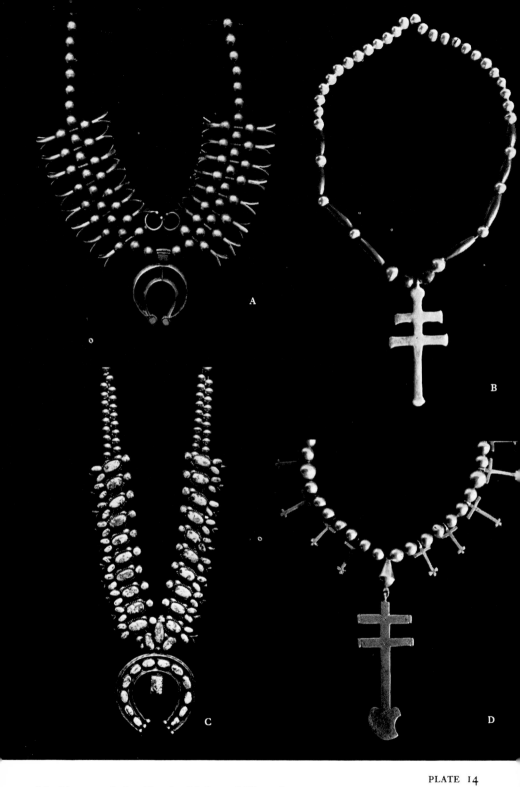

PLATE 14

A. Necklace made by Slender Maker of Silver for
   Chee Dodge
C. Zuñi turquoise squash-blossom necklace
B. Old Pueblo necklace
D. Old Pueblo cross necklace

In addition to the items listed in Table vii, last winter John had "pawned" a bracelet to Calvin Sherley, the assistant at the day school at Pine Springs, for eight dollars. John said it is worth fifteen dollars.

A large amount of the trader's business is tied up in his pawn rack. In the spring of 1938 the trading post at Pine Springs had advanced close to $3,000 on pawned objects. The White Mounds Trading Post at Houck had $2,500 out on pawn that same summer.

Table viii lists the pawn of a trading post in the region of Ramah, New Mexico, in July, 1937 (Ramah is a small town forty miles south of Gallup).

TABLE VIII

Name of owner	Object pawned	Amount pawned for	Date pawned
Boots Stinson	bracelet	$ 2.30	March '37
Rafael's daughter	bracelet	2.75	May '36
Lee Kino	bracelet	7.50	?
Jolly Pino	bracelet	3.00	April '31
Nora Pino	bracelet	2.00	Feb. '36
Jake Kino	turquoise necklace	7.30	Feb. '37
Mrs. Jesus	bracelet	?	Feb. '35
Max Miller	bracelet	?	Jan. '37
Frank Jesus' mother	coral necklace	1.50	April '36
Slim Franks' wife	coral necklace	1.50	April '37
Frank Jesus' wife	turquoise earrings	1.50	Jan. '35
Mrs. Red Eye	turquoise necklace	1.00	June '37
Mrs. Marganto	shell beads	.50	?
Vicente Coho	silver bridle conchas	5.00	?
Frank Martin's wife	turquoise necklace	6.10	July '36
Julian Carrizzo	turquoise & coral necklace	5.00	Feb. '37
Jake Kino's wife	turquoise bracelet	.90	Oct. '29
Slim Frank Navajo	turquoise necklace	held as security on harness	March '36
Frank Martin's wife	turquoise necklace	1.00	March '37
Boots Stinson	turquoise necklace	5.00	Feb. '37
Frank Cracho's mother	coral and silver necklace	2.00	March '37
Rafael's sister	2 turquoise necklaces	4.50	Jan. '36
Abram Natan	turquoise necklace	?	Oct. '33
Miss Naspar Beaver	silver necklace	1.50	Feb. '31

Name of owner	Object pawned	Amount pawned for	Date pawned
Mariano Chatto's wife	ring	.50	June '37
Antonio Rafael's daughter	buckskin	4.00	May '37
Rafael's daughter	basket	2.50	July '37
Jake's oldest daughter	buckskin	6.00	July '37
Manuel Pino's sister	ring	2.50	July '37
Amisola	turquoise necklace	7.50	Dec. '30
Mrs. Patogai	bracelet	1.00	?
Dick Pino	ring	.20	May '35
John Pino's sister	ring	.50	March '35
Irene Miller	bracelet	3.00	April '37
Dorothy Pino	bracelet	2.50	March '37
Thomas Martin	bracelet	2.50	Feb. '37
Mariano Chatto's wife	bracelet	5.00	Feb. '37
Jake's girl	bracelet and beads	3.00	March '37
José Martin's wife	bracelet	2.75	Feb. '37
Felipe's wife	bracelet	1.00	June '37
Jolly Pino's mother	necklace	10.50	July '37
Lemon Jim	bracelet	6.00	Feb. '36
		$122.80	

There is a great range in the incomes silversmiths derive from their work. Many smiths, living far from the centers of commercialization, make less than fifty dollars' worth of silver a year, counting both that which they make for the Navajo and that which they sell at the trading posts. There are a few silversmiths who make as much as $1,500 a year. A survey made of the arts and crafts in New Mexico reveals that the average net annual income for all silversmiths is $383.[2] This figure is based on a sampling of fifty-two smiths. Ike Wilson and his wife have an income of close to $2,000 a year from their silver. Chai Begay, with the help of his family, makes about $1,500 worth of jewelry. These figures represent clear profit, the amount that is paid to them for making up the silver. Many silversmiths make around $1,000 a year. Charlie Bitsui and Billy Goodluck make approximately that amount. Smiths that make as much as that work at the craft the

[2] Arthur L. Campa and Cornelius C. Knipers, *Arts and Crafts in New Mexico: A Survey of the Present Status of Handicrafts in New Mexico*, unpublished manuscript at the University of New Mexico.

year around. But the majority of silversmiths earn from $300 to $500 a year. Tom Burnsides belongs to this group. His income from the craft, counting sales to the traders and to the Navajo, is around $350 a year.

John Burnsides is typical of the silversmiths who earn around $1,000 a year. John works silver throughout the year, but it is from November to April that he does the greater part of his work. In late spring there is the shearing of the family's sheep to be tended to, and the cornfield must be planted and cultivated. During the summer there is a long series of squaw-dances which interrupt his work, and in the early fall there is harvesting, and, in the years that there is a crop, piñon nuts must be gathered. Therefore, it is not until late fall that John is able to settle down to steady work again. The Navajo do not like to work in their hogans during the hot weather, and even if their other activities do not demand all of their time, they prefer not to work on silver during this season.

John Burnsides keeps an account of the amount of silver which he makes. Most of it is sold to the trader at Houck, and a smaller part of it, in 1938, was sold to the post at Pine Springs. In January he had listed $192.60; in February, $211.30; in March, $133.10; in April, $148.75; and in May, only $33.00. The figures for the months from May to November totaled less than $100.00.

John has two sons who help him at this work. One of them is a boy about twelve years old, and the other one is fourteen. John's wife grinds out turquoise and also does some of the silver work. In addition to this, she earns about $150 a year from her weaving.

John invests part of his earnings in turquoise and silver and the rest in sheep. It is interesting to note that he had listed as part of his earned income the value of the silver which he had made for himself. He had an entry of $19.00 as part of his income, which he said was the value of some bracelets he had made for himself. There was another entry of $25.00 for a belt he had made for himself, and $6.00 for rings. Much of this silver John pawns at the different trading posts, and some of it he sells.

The trading post plays a very important part in the economics of the craft. The traders are the middlemen, the link between the smiths and the outside world. It is at the posts that the smiths obtain their tools (frequently being charged exorbitant prices for them), and it is here that they get their silver and turquoise. Usually the metal and the stones are not bought outright by the smiths; they are farmed out to them. The trader has a number of smiths who work for him, and he doles silver and turquoise out to them and pays them for their work in making the silver into jewelry. The price that is fairly uniform all over the reservation is fifty cents per ounce worked, with ten or fifteen cents extra for every turquoise set. As a result of this price system, many Navajo make silver of a mediocre quality, silver that is just good enough to be accepted by the trader. Why should a smith spend a long time making silver that is perfectly finished and good in design if he is paid the same for silver that he can make in half the time? A few of the traders have realized that quality and not quantity should be the criterion of value, and by paying a bonus for good work, they have secured better silver. Unfortunately, there are very few traders who follow this practice. The silversmiths are paid by most of them in credit slips which allow them to purchase goods at the store for the amount stated, and only occasionally is payment made in cash. There is nothing surprising about this fact when one realizes that trading posts have always functioned on a barter basis rather than on a cash purchasing basis. Navajo rugs are also bought by their weight and paid for in the same manner.

Bill Stewart, the trader at Pine Springs, made some interesting comments on the silversmiths who did work for him. "The best way to get good silver made for you is to give out the turquoise and the silver to the smiths and then just forget about them. Don't ask the smiths when they come into the store when they are going to bring in the work, because if you rush them, they will bring in a lot of junk that is no good at all. I know this because I tried it, and I got a lot of bad silver. The slower a silversmith is, the better he is. Now take Atsidi Nez for example; he keeps the silver for a long time, sometimes for several months. But then some day comes along when he doesn't have anything else to do, and he will sit down and make a couple of fine bracelets. That's the way it goes. I figure that the smiths who work for me keep the silver for an average of a month and a half before they bring in the finished jewelry. The smiths who make silver only on occasion do the best work. There is more art in their work than that which is made by smiths who depend on silver for a living. It isn't so standardized and commercial looking."

But the traders do not always get the best of the bargain. Frequently the Navajo will not bring the jewelry back to the trader to whom it belongs but will take it to another trading post and sell it for whatever cash they can get. They do not return either the silver and turquoise or the finished jewelry to the right owner; but if they do this, it is many months before they can get materials to make jewelry to replace that which they sold.

There were fourteen silversmiths working for this post at Pine Springs in 1938 (Appendix II–B), but during previous years when business conditions had been better, there were as many as twenty-five who made silver for this post. The trader sells the finished pieces in Gallup to one of the large mercantile companies from which he buys silver and turquoise and other supplies. The work done here represents a very small volume of silver when compared to that produced at some of the more important centers of the craft. During the same summer (1938) there were sixty smiths working for Mike Kirk's post at Manuelito, which is between Gallup and Pine Springs. In that same year, during the winter, when the smiths make more silver, there were seventy-nine craftsmen working for this one post. Smith Lake, which is northeast of Gallup, is the second largest of the silver centers. In the spring of 1938 there were 120 smiths who were selling their silver to the trader at the post there. Another large center of Navajo silver production is Zuñi. Gallup is a large center for direct sale of silver from the Navajo smiths as well as from the surrounding trading posts. Gallup, including the trading posts that lie within a ten-mile radius of it, has the greatest concentration of silversmiths in the Southwest.

Silversmithing is carried on as a commercial enterprise only on the southeastern part of the Navajo reservation. Very little silver is made on the western and northern edges for the non-Navajo market; in fact, there are very few smiths in those regions who make silver even for their own people. Much of the silver these Navajo wear they obtain in trade from Navajo of other regions or from the trading posts which import silver from the wholesale centers to the south. There never have been many silversmiths in this region, for the art has flourished principally on the eastern edge of the reservation, where it was first learned from the Mexicans. There are virtually no silversmiths who make silver in any quantity living north of an imaginary line drawn from Tuba City to Chin Lee, and west of a line from Chin Lee to Ganado. There is a sparse population of smiths south from Tuba City, and north from Holbrook. In the last twenty years the few silversmiths who lived in the region of Chin Lee have moved toward Gallup, where their silver can be more readily sold. There have been a number of trading posts on the reservation that have built up a large silver business and attracted silversmiths from other regions. Generally speaking, however, there has been a drift towards the railroad and Gallup. Two notable exceptions are Zuñi and Smith Lake, which have attracted smiths from the Two Wells and Thoreau regions respectively.

We have followed the silver made by John Burnsides and other silversmiths of the region to the trading post at Pine Springs and from there to a wholesale house in Gallup. In a similar fashion the work of hundreds of smiths, made for trading posts ranging from Drolet's and Newcomb's in the north to posts at Zuñi in the south, and from those around Crown Point in the east to Ganado in the west, all comes to Gallup, where it is sold to three large wholesale companies and many dealers and stores. The individual trading posts sell some of their silver directly to retailers at some distance and a small part directly to the consumer, but the greatest part of it goes into Gallup. Here large quantities are sold to tourists, and from here it is shipped all over the country. Large amounts are shipped to Phoenix and other winter resorts in southern Arizona. Quantities of it are sent to Los Angeles, Pasadena, San Francisco, and other cities on the west coast. Summer resorts in Colorado import large quantities, and some silver finds its way to stores in the cities of the Middle West and on the eastern seaboard.

The traders on the Navajo reservation and the wholesale

traders of Gallup engage in keen competition with the manufacturers of silver in Albuquerque and Santa Fé. In these cities there are firms that employ Indian labor to turn out silver made with punches, drop presses, and other elaborate mechanical devices. Silversmiths work at long benches and make jewelry in a regular assembly-line manner. One smith makes the shanks of rings; another applies the plate and the bezel and possibly fastens on the raindrops; a third files and finishes the piece. These shops turn out a tremendous quantity of cheap silver and a much smaller amount of more expensive silver, heavy in weight and patterned on traditional Navajo designs. Silver can be produced at a much lower figure by these methods and the manufacturers are able to undersell the Gallup dealers. In order to meet this competition, the wholesalers who handle silver made on the reservation by more primitive methods have had to resort to lowering the standards of the jewelry which they buy and sell. As a result the craft has suffered from the standpoint of design and workmanship. A great quantity of silver is sold that is very light, flimsy, and at best only something to give to an aunt who stayed at home. Only a minor part of the production is of a truly artistic nature, following the old Navajo designs.

There are approximately six hundred Navajo silversmiths working on the reservation, or just over its southern and eastern boundaries. It is almost impossible to estimate the total sale of this silver in dollars. A survey of the trading posts on the reservation and in Gallup conducted by the Soil Conservation Service of the Department of Agriculture reveals that in 1936, which was an off-year for silversmithing because of market conditions, there was a total of $49,360 paid to the Navajo smiths for their labor in making silver and for silver which was sold to the traders outright. It is interesting to note that the same survey gave $288,840 as the amount paid the Navajo women for their rugs. The silver figure is very conservative. When the traders and dealers of Zuñi, Flagstaff, Holbrook, and those just over the southeastern border of the reservation are taken into account, the production of a more typical year should amount to about $100,000. This figure applies only to the money or credit the Navajo derive from the craft.

PART II

The Pueblos

CHAPTER VIII

History of Zuñi Silver

LIKE the Navajo, the Zuñi made their jewelry of brass and copper before they learned the art of silversmithing. The use of these metals goes back thirty or forty years before the introduction of silver, that is, to about 1830–40. Rings, bracelets, buttons, and bow-guard mountings were made from the yellow metal of old pots and pans, which had been melted and pounded into the proper shape. Later, brass and copper were obtained in the more convenient form of wire, which was supplied to the Zuñi by the traders.

Mexicans used to bring these metals to Zuñi and ask the smiths to make jewelry out of them. According to several of my Zuñi informants,[1] because the Mexicans believed that brass and copper warded off rheumatism, they always wore a piece of the metal somewhere on their person. The Zuñi frequently made crosses for the Mexicans, which they wore about their necks. Evidently this copper and brass jewelry was highly prized by the Mexicans, for they would pay a Zuñi smith a sheep for his work.

This copper and brass jewelry, like that of the Navajo, was crude in workmanship and simple in design; what decoration it had consisted of file marks scratched on to form geometric patterns. When silver came in, the use of these yellow metals gradually died out; however, some copper was worked until fifteen years ago, but most of the jewelry made from it has been discarded, and today the old pieces of copper and brass are very scarce.

At Zuñi, again as on the Navajo reservation, the craft of the blacksmith is an older one than that of the silversmith. The first blacksmith was a man called Kiwashinakwe, which in English means Ax-maker. The craft, in his day, consisted of making and mending axes and hoes. Possibly it was this blacksmith's shop which Captain Sitgreaves visited when he was in the village in

[1] Bill Lewis, Lonkwine, Lanyade, and Keneshde (Unaiede).

1852. In the report of his visit to Zuñi, he reproduced a drawing of a blacksmith shop, which was made by the artist, R. H. Kern.[2]

With the introduction of the wagon, blacksmithing became a more important craft at Zuñi. In 1889[3] Douglas D. Graham, the government farmer at Zuñi, obtained a forge and a full set of tools for the blacksmith, Kuwishti, who heretofore had had only crude implements to carry on the craft. He set up his forge on the south side of the river, just across the road from Kelsey's trading post.[4] Kuwishti died some years ago, but at the present time a shop is run by his maternal nephew, who does a considerable business mending wagon wheels.

The Zuñi learned the art of silversmithing from the Navajo. The Zuñi who was the first in the pueblo to learn the craft, a man by the name of Lanyade, is still living [Plate 21A]. Today he is an old man, about ninety-five years of age. I talked with Lanyade for many hours; he tells this story of how he learned the craft:[5]

"When I was a young man about thirty years old [1872], a Navajo came to Zuñi who knew how to make silver. This man's Navajo name was Atsidi Chon.[6] I had traveled through the Navajo country a good many times, on my way to the Hopi villages, and I knew how to speak their language. We became good friends, this man and I, and he came over to my house and lived.

"At that time no one in Zuñi knew how to make silver, and we had never seen anyone make it. We had seen the Mexicans and

[2] I am indebted to Dr. F. W. Hodge for this information regarding Sitgreaves' visit to Zuñi. See his article, "How Old is Southwestern Indian Silverwork?" *El Palacio*, Vol. XXV, Nos. 14–17 (October 6–27, 1928), pages 224–32. A reproduction of Kern's drawing of the blacksmith's shop accompanies the article.

[3] This is the date given by Hodge in the article mentioned in note 2 above.

[4] In her article, "The Zuñi Indians," in the *Twenty-third Annual Report, 1901–1902*, Bureau of American Ethnology (Washington, 1904), page 377, Mrs. Stevenson reproduces a drawing of a silversmith's shop. Mrs. Margaret Lewis, of Zuñi, on seeing this picture, informed me that it is the shop "of Kuwishti, silver worker and also the village blacksmith. This shop is located where the Vanderwagon store now is." By the time Mrs. Stevenson made her report, Kuwishti was working in silver.

[5] My statement that Lanyade was the first Zuñi silversmith, as well as the important facts in his account, were checked with three other informants—Keneshde, Lonkwine, and Juan Deleosa.

[6] This man, Ugly Smith, is the silversmith who is mentioned in Chapter I. His clan was Standing House, and his hogan was near Klagetoh.

the Navajo wearing it, and we had bought some pieces of it from them. But those silver buttons and bracelets were very expensive, and only a few people in the village had any. Atsidi Chon came to the village just a few years after the Navajo returned from the East [*c.* 1872], where they had been held as captives by the government.[7]

"We became good friends and so he let me watch him make silver. I was the only one that ever saw him at work, because he used to shut himself up in my house when he worked. He didn't want any of the Zuñi men to see him make silver, because if they watched him they would learn how, and then he wouldn't be able to sell them the silver that he made. I told him that I would give him a good horse if he would teach me how to work with the silver. So he taught me how, and I was the only Zuñi to learn from him.

"Atsidi Chon made objects of silver that we never had before he came here. He made bridles and concha belts. The conchas were the kind that had a hole in the center, through which the leather was laced. He sold a belt like that for a team of good horses. He made the first silver mounting for a bow-guard. Before that our bow-guards were decorated with pieces of tin[8] or copper. Atsidi also made crosses for us. He had never made these before and he copied them from our copper crosses.

"This Navajo brought the first dies to Zuñi. None of us had seen dies before. Those men in the village that made jewelry of copper and brass filed on the designs. We had never seen designs stamped on to a piece of metal. He taught me how to make dies like this, but while he was here in the village I used his tools. It was after he left that I made my own bellows and dies. Atsidi Chon lived here at Zuñi for a year. When he came down to the village from the Navajo reservation, he brought only the horse he rode on, but when he went back to the reservation, he drove ahead of

[7] Atsidi Chon probably came to Zuñi during the early seventies, since Lanyade said that he came there seven years before Frank Cushing arrived in the village in 1879.

[8] James Stevenson, "Illustrated Catalogue of Collections Obtained from the Pueblos of Zuñi, New Mexico, and Walpi, Arizona, in 1881," *Third Annual Report, 1881–82*, Bureau of American Ethnology (Washington, 1884), page 586. Therein is listed "small scale bow-guards of leather ornamented with plates of tin. . . ."

him many horses and sheep. All of these he had bought with his silver.

"After Atsidi left the village, I made myself a pair of bellows like his. I made these out of buffalo skin which my father's youngest brother gave to me. He had traded a Santo Domingo some grain for this hide. The Santo Domingo had bought it from a Comanche. I made the hoops for the bellows out of oak. At this time [1873] I also made a few dies and some other tools, and I set up a shop where I made silver for the Zuñi.

"I used to get some of my silver pesos over at Albuquerque. There was a trader there that we called "Red Headed." I traded him mantas, which I got from the Hopi, and buckskins, for American pesos. One buckskin would buy from five to ten pesos. I also got pesos here in the village. In the early days American dollars were used by all the silversmiths. But about fifty years ago, after Graham had been here for some years, we began to use Mexican pesos. The government told us that we were not to melt up any more American pesos, and from that time on [c. 1890], silversmiths here in the village used Mexican pesos, which Graham got for us. The Mexican pesos were softer and more easily worked than the American pesos.

"I made many different things out of the pesos. I made conchas with holes in the middle, like those that Atsidi Chon had made. I made plain hollow beads, and bow-guards, and buttons. I sold a great many bracelets that were triangular in shape. The earrings which I made were large hoops of silver with a hollow bead at the bottom. I also made some which were flat and shaped like a crescent moon. Zuñi women in those days didn't have any of the fancy earrings with sets of turquoise. All of the silver I made was without turquoise; I had never seen it set in silver. Atsidi Chon had never made any silver with sets while he was here. I didn't see any until many years after.

"I traded my silver to the Navajo as well as to the Zuñi. At that time there were no Navajo smiths south of Gallup. I would sell a Navajo a silver bridle for a horse, or for a good calf. Later on I made a trip up to the Hopi reservation where I stayed and made silver. I sold my silver to the Hopi for mantas, sashes, and kilts. At about that same time [*c.* 1900] I went over to Laguna and Isleta, where I made up silver. I made some for Pablo Abeita [Plate 10F].[9] While I was at Isleta I sold the Hopi mantas for cattle.

"During those first years, just after I had learned to make silver from Atsidi Chon, I wouldn't let anyone watch me at work. I was just like that Navajo. I didn't want anyone else to learn because then I wouldn't be able to sell as much of my silver. At that time my shop was up on the road just this side [north] of the bridge.

"Finally I did teach one man to make silver. That man was a friend of mine by the name of Balawade. Until then the only jewelry he could make was of copper or brass. It was from him that some of the other Zuñi learned how to make silver jewelry. Balawade, and the men that learned to make silver from him,[10] were all older than myself. They had made copper and brass jewelry before I taught them to work with silver. I had never known how to work those metals.

"It was about seven years after Atsidi Chon left the village that the white man, Cushing,[11] came here to live. When he came here, Balawade and I were the only ones that worked silver. It was later on that those other older men learned. Both Balawade and myself made up silver for Cushing. Balawade made the silver buttons for him which he wore on the side of his leggings.[12]

---

[9] When I was at Isleta, Pablo Abeita showed me the silver that Lanyade had made for him. This silver, which is still worn by his wife, consists of a necklace of heavy, plain beads, and three bracelets, two of which were triangular on the sides and square across the front, with simple but effective die-work; the third was set with crudely cut turquoise.

[10] The older men who learned to make silver from Balawade, either directly, or indirectly, are: Yachilthle, Lawiaocelo, Hacecenane, Kiwianade, and Kwaisedemon.

[11] Frank H. Cushing was sent to Zuñi in 1879 by the Bureau of Ethnology and lived in the village for the next five years.

[12] "The splendid deerskin costume which Cushing wore during much of the time he was at Zuñi was elaborately ornamented with silver buttons of Navaho manufacture: These gave rise to the Navaho equivalent of 'Many Buttons,' by which sobriquet Cushing was known to members of that tribe." (Hodge, *op. cit.*, Vol. XXV, No. 14-17, page 231). From what Lanyade said, it seems that these buttons were made by Zuñi smiths and not by the Navajo.

"I made several pieces of silver for Cushing.[13] I made conchas with holes in the middle, as well as the kind which had the solid center. He paid me twelve dollars apiece in American money for those belts. I also made bracelets and rings for him. He paid me about three dollars each for those small things. I earned a good deal from my work. Sometimes I was paid in cash, but usually I was paid in livestock or in goods.

"About thirty-five years ago, Mrs. Stevenson, that white woman who used to live here, bought my tools and my bellows and took them to Washington with her.[14] She paid me fifty dollars for them. I took the money and went up to Albuquerque, where I bought a harness for my team, and a small pair of bellows, the kind that they sell in the stores. After she left the village, I didn't do much silver work. I spent most of my time after that on my farm."

Until Mrs. Stevenson bought his tools, Lanyade evidently spent the greater part of his time making silver. For him, the occupation was more than a part-time one, just as it is for many Zuñi today. This does not mean that he did not work in the fields and participate in the religious life of the pueblo, but those pursuits were secondary. Lanyade continued to make silver occasionally up to ten years ago. Although he is ninety-five years old, he works out in his fields for many hours each day. Because of his inactivity as a silver craftsman during the last thirty-five years, many of the

[13] I was able to find only one mention of silver at Zuñi in the published work of Cushing. In his magazine article, "My Adventures at Zuñi" (*The Century Magazine*, February, 1883), he said, in describing a dance that took place in the village on the day of his arrival in 1879: "Only the upper portions of their painted faces and occasional patches of their silver bedecked persons were exposed. . . . The arms were bedecked with green bands, fluttering turkey plumes, silver bangles, and wrist-guards of the same material." He did not mention that there were Zuñi silversmiths in the village when he was there. This negative evidence does not prove that there were no smiths there at that time, since only a very small part of Cushing's material was published. Evidence of silversmiths in the village is to be found in Mrs. Stevenson's statement: "Mr. Stevenson, during his first visit to the Zuñis in 1879 inaugurated many changes for the better. Window panes, candles, lamps, and silversmith's implements were introduced." (*Twenty-third Annual Report, 1901–1902*, Bureau of American Ethnology, page 379.)

[14] Matilda Coxe Stevenson, the research worker from the Bureau of Ethnology, probably bought the tools before she left the village in 1902. These tools were accessioned in the National Museum in 1905.

PLATE 15

A. Old Navajo buttons
B. Modern Navajo pins
E. Old Navajo button

C. Modern Navajo buttons
D. Old Navajo buttons
F. Navajo rings

PLATE 16

EVELYN TONY, NAVAJO

people in the village under forty years of age do not know that Lanyade was at one time the leading silversmith in the pueblo, and the first Zuñi to learn the craft.

It has been stated that the Zuñi learned the art of silversmithing from the Mexicans; in fact, that is the popular belief of the traders, curio-dealers, and residents of the Southwest. However, these people have confused influence and later development with origin. Furthermore, they have made the mistake of comparing the design of Mexican silver with that the Zuñi smiths made after they learned to set turquoise, instead of with the Zuñi silver which was made in the seventies of the last century. While there is a similarity in the design of recent Zuñi silver and that of the Mexican, there was little resemblance between the two types at an earlier date. After the Zuñi smith learned to set turquoise, his craft became more complex in design with the passing of each year. Today, Zuñi silver, studded with turquoise surrounded by minute bezels of delicately bent wire, does have the same total effect in design, the same rococo quality, as that of the Mexican. But in the seventies and the early eighties Zuñi silver was simple in pattern and massive, like the Navajo silver from which it was copied. Lanyade, Balawade, and the other Zuñi smiths followed the forms and the technique introduced to Zuñi by Atsidi Chon, the Navajo smith. Lieutenant Bourke was at Zuñi in 1881, and in his journal described the silver worn by the natives of the pueblo: "Their necklaces are made of beads of malachite, of seashells, silver buttons and balls, made by themselves. Their finger rings are of silver and their earrings and bangles of the same material cannot be distinguished from those made by the Navajoes."[15]

To be sure, there was a Mexican influence in the Zuñi craft. There was continual contact between the Eastern pueblos and Zuñi. Laguna and Isleta smiths visited Zuñi, and Zuñi smiths went to these villages. In fact, Lanyade said that he made silver for the Isletans. These pueblos were in even more immediate contact with the Mexicans than was the pueblo of Zuñi. The silver which they made had a Mexican flavor at an early date, and this influence diffused to Zuñi. There also was some direct diffusion from the

[15] Bloom (ed.), *op. cit.*, Vol. XI, No. 2 (April, 1936), pages 196–97.

Mexicans to the Zuñi, as evidenced by goods traded for Mexican-made jewelry.

The Zuñi learned from the Navajo the technique of working silver. There was Mexican jewelry in the pueblo before Atsidi Chon taught Lanyade the craft. But it takes more technical ability to make silver in the fancy Mexican patterns than the first Zuñi smiths possessed. And what is more important, it takes finer tools than the Zuñi had in the early seventies to make silver of that sort. With the introduction of more tools and with their increasing dexterity in working the metal, Zuñi smiths were able to depart from the simple, early Navajo patterns taught to them by Atsidi Chon. Then they began to make silver in Mexican patterns.

Matilda Coxe Stevenson, writing in 1910, said: "The first setting of turquoise and silver occurred about 1880, done by a Navajo in a ring, which he presented to the writer."[16] It seems likely that the Zuñi did not set their silver with turquoise as early as that, or Mrs. Stevenson, with her keen eye for detail, would have noted the fact. It seems to have been about 1890 when the Zuñi first mounted the stone in their jewelry.

Keneshde, one of the elders of the village, who used to make silver, told of how he learned the art and of the first time he set turquoise:

"When I was a boy about fifteen years old, I used to help Kwaisedemon, who was my grandfather, make silver. He was my father's father, and at that time he was an old man. It was hard work for him to pound out the silver, so I used to do that for him. In return for my helping him, he showed me how to work the metal into the form of buttons and earrings.

"Fifty years ago [*c.* 1890], when I was about twenty-five years old, I made a trip with some other men over to Santo Domingo to trade. We wanted to get indigo more than anything else. A good-sized lump, or a box of that dye, cost six dollars. While we were at Santo Domingo, we asked the men where they

---

[16] From Mrs. Stevenson's unpublished manuscript, *Pueblo Clothing and Ornament*. I am indebted to Mr. F. H. Douglas for permitting me to study the notes which he had taken on this manuscript.

got the turquoise that they wore. In those days the Santo Domingo didn't sell polished turquoise beads at Zuñi the way they do today,[17] but once in a while one of them would come over to Zuñi with turquoise in the matrix. We wanted to know where they got this fine blue stone, because fifty years ago turquoise was rare, and you couldn't just go into a trading post or a store in one of the towns and buy it. They told us that we would have to go to see the governor in Santa Fé if we wanted to get turquoise from the mine where they got theirs, which was just east of Santo Domingo.

"We went on to Santa Fé and saw the governor. He told us that we would have to get permission from the owner of the mine. We saw that man, who was called Mankey, and he told us that for five dollars he would let us go down into the mine and get some of the stone. I was the only one who went down because all the others were afraid. I took a chisel with me and I knocked off a great big piece. I was the first Zuñi to get turquoise out of that mine.[18]

"I brought this turquoise back to Zuñi. It was at that time [*c.* 1890] that I thought that turquoise would look nice on the silver. So I took four pieces of the stone, which I had polished, and I put them on the silver, and soldered a rim around each one. I knew how to make solder, as my grandfather had taught me how to solder the two sides of a bead together. I had never seen turquoise set on silver before, as none of the Zuñi or Navajo that I

[17] Lonkwine told me that the Santo Domingo began to bring turquoise beads to Zuñi about twenty years ago, after mines in Colorado and Nevada were opened, and the stones were more plentiful. He said that he and his brothers used to go to the Navajo reservation where they obtained Navajo blankets. Then they would take these blankets to Santo Domingo and trade them for turquoise. This they brought back to Zuñi, and during the winter months they made beads from the rough stones. During the following summer Lonkwine and his brothers would go to the Navajo reservation again. This time they sold the beads for sheep and for more blankets, with which they could buy more rough turquoise. In this way they also built up a good-sized flock of sheep.

[18] The mine referred to is the Cerillos mine, fifteen miles to the east of Santo Domingo. The person Keneshde refers to as Mankey was possibly Benjamin F. Pankey, of Santa Fé. Miss Ruth Watson, of Taos, who is writing a history of southwestern turquoise mines, informs me that "he was a politico well-known in Santa Fé. . . . [he] may easily have had financial interest in those mines during the 1880's."

knew had their jewelry fixed that way. I sold this bracelet for ten dollars cash to a Navajo that lived near Lupton. His wives and his daughters wanted bracelets just like that one, so I made some for them too.

"One day Balawade came into my house. He said, 'I have heard that you have been fastening turquoise to silver bracelets. Will you show me how to do it?' So I showed him how to make the rim around the stone. Then those other old smiths, Yachilthle, Kwianade, and Lawiacelo learned from him. It wasn't long before all the smiths in Zuñi were setting turquoise in their silver."

In 1880 Balawade, Lawiacelo, Yachilthle, Kwianade, and Kwaisedemon all worked in the same shop, which was located near Hekyapawa kiva, which today is just east of the main road that leads down to the bridge. Some years after Cushing left the village, Balawade and Lawiacelo set up a separate shop on the other side of the river. When all of these men had worked in the one shop, they had shared the same set of tools. After Cushing left, he sent tools back to Balawade, who had been a very close friend of his. I suspect that it was the possession of his own set of tools which led Balawade to set up a separate shop. It was quite natural that those friends who had shared the same shop with Balawade should have learned to set silver from him.

Whether the setting of turquoise spread to the rest of the pueblo from the independent invention of Keneshde, or diffused to the pueblo from the Navajo, is a moot question. One must remember that at this time there were probably no Navajo smiths living in the vicinity of Zuñi, as there are today. Therefore, if it was a Navajo from whom the technique was learned, he must have come down to Zuñi from the reservation. There is also the possibility that the other Zuñi smiths saw some Navajo silver set with turquoise, and copied it.

This same man, Keneshde, still has in his possession an old pair of buffalo-hide bellows [Plate 21B]. These are very rare; in fact, this bellows is the only one of its type that I saw in the Southwest. Keneshde obtained the buffalo hide for them at Santo Domingo, which was where Lanyade obtained the skin for his bellows. The three uprights and the ribs are of oak, from a tree felled on the Zuñi Mountains twenty miles east of the pueblo. Thongs draw in the hide between the ribs, forming three compartments on each side of the center upright. On this bellows, the air spout, made of rawhide, is mounted on the center upright, and there is one intake at each end of the leather bag. An iron bar passes through holes drilled in the upper end of the wooden supports and keeps the air bags in line. The top of one of these uprights serves as a handle by which the bellows is drawn in and out. The other one of the two uprights is fastened in a stationary position.

This bellows is quite different in construction from the old Navajo bellows, if one may judge from a photograph of one. In the Navajo bellows, the intake is at the opposite end from the outlet, and on a line with it, while in Keneshde's bellows, the intakes are in a transverse position. There is an advantage in Keneshde's construction in that he has made a double bellows which may be worked by pulling only one handle, while the other hand is left free for manipulating the crucible and the silver, and at the same time there is the steady passage of air that only a double bellows will give. The Navajo smith built a double bellows by placing the two air chambers side by side, instead of one adjoining the other in a single construction. By pulling and pushing the two handles of the bellows alternately a steady draft issued from a bifurcated spout. Two hands were required to work a bellows of this type, and thus, in order to pour or even heat the silver at the same time, the smith must have a helper to carry on one of the two tasks.

The first Zuñi silver set with turquoise, which was made during the nineties, was different in appearance from the silver made in the pueblo today. It resembles the type of jewelry the Navajo have always prized—heavy in construction with a few well-matched pieces of massive stone. This is particularly true of bracelet construction. At that time from one to half a dozen stones were set in one piece of silver. Today a popular type of Zuñi bracelet has as many as one-hundred and fifty sets [Plate 10G–H].

One reason for the sparing use of turquoise was the limited supply of the stones. The Zuñi have always had turquoise (many pieces of it were unearthed in the excavations at Hawikuh), but they have not always had it in the quantity that they have today. The older residents of the village say that the stone was scarce until mines operated by the white man in the surrounding states began to ship stones to the traders about the turn of the century.

Six large pieces of turquoise will make thirty or more smaller sets. Why did not the Zuñi smiths cut up the stones then, as they do now? Because the turquoise were of a fine and very hard grade, and the larger a hard blue stone is, the greater the value. If it were cut into smaller pieces, the value would decrease. The many small stones which one sees in the modern Zuñi bracelets are often odds and ends which are left in the matrix after the large pieces have been removed.

Tools again play an important part in the determination of the art form. As with the Navajo, the changes in the form and design of the silver are closely correlated with the progressive introduction of better tools by the traders. It is an arduous task to grind down and polish 150 pieces of hard blue turquoise with only a slab of rock and the palm of the hand for tools. It is considerably easier to make the same bracelet with the use of an emery wheel, sealing wax, and lapidary's sticks. Therefore, the introduction of wheels to Zuñi was a stimulus to the production of multi-set jewelry.

The introduction of fine pliers, the drawplate, and more recently, the roller, has also been a boon to the smith who wanted to stud his silver with as much turquoise as possible. Pliers are essential in making the minute bezels which surround the sets. A drawplate is necessary for the production of fine wire, which as time went on was used more and more as a decorative element outside of the bezel, one of the elements in the construction of Zuñi silver that heightens its remembrance to Mexican silver. It is difficult work to make small bezels, as the silver has to be very thin and uniform in thickness, and it requires patience to pound it out by hand to the required thinness. Therefore, when the traders brought rollers into the village, the production of the multi-set silver became just that much easier, and in many cases, the silver became just that much more tawdry. Thus, the introduction of these tools also had a disastrous effect on the design of much of the silver.

During the early nineties, when Keneshde first set turquoise, the Zuñi were wearing articles of jewelry similar to those that they wore in 1879. Mrs. Stevenson mentions that the following objects, made of silver, were worn in 1879, when she arrived at the pueblo. The men wore concha belts, bow-guards with silver trim, moccasin and legging buttons, and earrings in the form of a hoop. The women wore silver beads with crescent pendants, bangles, and rings.[19] In fact, all of the basic forms of silver which are worn in the pueblo now were worn in 1879. While the basic forms of jewelry made during the nineties were the same as those made a decade earlier, with the introduction of turquoise the pattern and design of many of these forms changed.

Many of the buttons, which had been plain in design, often without any ornamentation, were made larger and studded with turquoise. Up to this time, buttons were worn for the most part by the men; now the women began to wear those that were set with stones. These brooches, for that is what the buttons had become, provided effective decoration when worn against the blue-black of the wool dress.

Before turquoise was set in silver, the earring, like the button, was part of the Zuñi man's costume. When the women did wear earrings, they were similar in design to those worn by the men. Often they were in the form of silver hoops, just like the men's earrings, only smaller, and sometimes they were hammered flat, and were wider at the bottom than at the top. [Plate 20c]. With the increasing use of turquoise in silver, the picture changes. By 1910 the earring had become the most important item in the Zuñi woman's decorative apparel. It was the only article of silver that was worn all of the time. Beads, bracelets, and brooches were donned for dress occasions, but were not worn while the woman was doing the daily chores around the house and village. Earrings, however, were worn as continually as the manta or the moccasin; rarely was a woman without these large silver ornaments, set with many turquoise and bordered by delicately twisted wire.

[19] Stevenson, *Pueblo Clothing and Ornament.*

The finest workmanship of the Zuñi smith is displayed in these earrings [Plate 20 B & E]. Delicately balanced and pleasing in form, many of them are just as fine as old Navajo silver, although their beauty and appeal is different. It takes a gifted smith to make a fine pair of earrings, an artist with a good sense of design and a sure hand. A less expert smith is able to make a concha, or a bracelet, which requires experience and patience more than anything else; but he must have more than these if he wishes to fashion beautiful earrings.

As turquoise became more common, the Zuñi men discarded their annular-shaped silver earrings, and like the Navajo, began to wear turquoise ear-drops fastened through the lobe of the ear with a bit of string. In the eighties, nearly every man in the pueblo wore the silver ear ornaments. Today there are only three men in the village who still wear these old hoop-shaped rings.

In 1910, twenty years after the first turquoise was set, Zuñi silver looked very different from the simple forms of jewelry made in 1880. If Cushing had lived longer and had visited the pueblo of Zuñi at that time, he would have been surprised by the complete change in the character of the silver. Not only had the buttons, bracelets, and earrings changed in style; all Zuñi jewelry was different. Bow-guards, which had been flat plates of silver, were now encrusted with the stones. Conchas, at one time dependent on die-work for ornamentation, now had a set in the center and frequently a rim of stones around the outside. The other pieces—squash-blossoms [Plate 14C], finger rings, and buckles—all were ornamented with the blue stone.

We have seen that the change in the style of Zuñi silver was brought about by two factors: the setting of turquoise and the introduction of modern tools by the traders, tools which facilitated the setting of the stones. A third factor, commercialization of Zuñi silver by the traders, was of negligible importance in 1910. However, with increasing tourist trade and the corresponding growth of the Indian curio industry, commercialization of Zuñi silver became the most important factor of all in the change in Zuñi silver.

Commercialization of Southwestern Indian silver as a whole

began on the Navajo reservation, because it was the logical place for the wholesale houses to standardize the native craft for tourist consumption. There were many more Navajo smiths than there were Pueblo; and there were more trading posts on the Navajo reservation that offered points of contact with the native silver-smiths than at Zuñi, where there were only three trading posts from which silver could be bought, and only a few smiths from whom these traders could buy jewelry. The 1920's saw the tremendous development of Southern California as a resort center. Up to then most of the travel had been by train, but now automobiles began to cross the Southwest. As the decade passed, the highways of the nation, as well as those of New Mexico and Arizona (which, to be sure, were few and far between), became more and more crowded with tourists. Wherever there are tourists, there are souvenirs. And by 1930 an Indian-made ring or bracelet had become one of the most popular curios.

At that time the demand for Indian-made silver had become so great that it exceeded the production of the Navajo smiths. The commercial craft spread to the pueblos, and to Zuñi in particular, where there was a large group of potential craftsmen.

Until about 1920 all the silver that the Zuñi smiths made was sold, or traded, to the members of their own pueblo, to the Indians of the other pueblos, or to the Navajo. A finished piece of silver might, on occasion, be sold to a white man visiting the village, but silver was not fashioned for white consumption. The smith had the Indian in mind when he made jewelry, and he made his wares to meet the approval of that consumer. About 1920 the traders at Zuñi began to buy silver from the natives of the village for sale to the tourists. The next step was taken when the traders encouraged the smiths to make and sell to them silver that was suitable for the tourist trade.

This had a tremendous effect on the craft. The smith now had the tourist in mind when designing jewelry, and not the Indian. Much of his silver became the Indian's idea of the trader's idea of what the white man thought was Indian design. Not only did the design of silver change, but the whole economic life of the pueblo was affected by the growing demand for Zuñi silver. In

1920 there were not more than eight Zuñi silversmiths who made silver in appreciable quantities.[20] In 1938 there were ninety smiths in that pueblo, not counting ten Navajo smiths who worked there. In a village the size of Zuñi the change brought about by the growth of this handicraft amounted to what might be called an economic revolution.

[20] Of these eight smiths in 1920, the most outstanding ones were: Lanyade, Aiuli (Horace's father), Juan Deleosa, and Kuwishti. In the summer of 1939 there were thirty-five Navajo smiths in Zuñi.

CHAPTER IX

The Zuñi Silversmith of Today

FROM this group of ninety smiths at Zuñi two will be studied in detail here, in order to see how a craftsman carries on his work today.

Horace Aiuli is typical of that group of Zuñi smiths who might be termed professional. He is an artist who depends wholly on his craft for his livelihood. The other group may be called the semiprofessional smiths, who, like the artists of that status in our own culture, depend on other sources for the major part of their income, but supplement that amount with the proceeds of their craft. In Zuñi there are no amateur silversmiths who work at the art simply because they enjoy doing so. Among Indian silversmiths there is no "art for art's sake."

Horace, a man in his late thirties, is the son of a silversmith and the grandson of a smith. His father's father, Hatsetsenane, Sneezing Man, was one of the first generation of Zuñi smiths. Horace learned the art from his father in 1924, a few years after he had returned from school in Phoenix, where he had learned the trade of blacksmithing. Because he was unable to find employment as a blacksmith at Zuñi, since the one smithy there was sufficient for the needs of the village, he turned to silversmithing and has been at it ever since. At the present time he is one of the two or three best artisans in the pueblo, and his ability as a craftsman is recognized by the natives as well as the white people. The traders at Zuñi are always glad to have him turn out silver for them. He also teaches the craft to the boys attending the government day school during the nine months of the school term.

Horace lives to the northwest of the old part of the pueblo, just beyond the point where the main road turns south toward the bridge. His house is a three-room structure, with one large room and two smaller ones. One of the small rooms, banked with windows on the south wall, is the workshop. The modern Zuñi, unlike his forefathers, wants to have light in his house, or at least in part of it, although the back rooms are frequently as dark as they were in the old days before window and door sashes were introduced into Zuñi building.

The shop is well furnished with a complete set of tools. The most conspicuous of these is the anvil, which, like the Navajo's, is a short length of railroad track cleated into a stump. Horace has a manufactured anvil as well, on which he does the finer work [Plate 22A]. Next to his anvil, by the window, is the workbench. This offers a contrast to many Navajo shops, where, if the smith works in his hogan, the floor is the only place to sit, and tools are stored in orange crates. The silversmith's workbench is no innovation at Zuñi. Long before Horace learned the craft, the smiths in that pueblo had used benches.[1] A small vise is clamped on one corner of the bench, the top of which is covered with an assortment of tools, similar to that of the modern Navajo smith of the Gallup region. There is a gasoline torch, hammers, metal-shears, and steel screen and charred rock, upon which the silver is heated. Dividers, rule, files, and pincers, standard equipment in any silversmith's shop, are scattered across the bench top. A drawplate rests on the window ledge.

For a forge Horace uses the corner fireplace, a part of every pueblo house. Here he places an old kettle, with a hole knocked in the front. The crucible is put into the kettle and surrounded with charcoal.[2] A pair of bellows bought at the trading post is held up to the hole to provide the necessary draft. Here Horace's method differs from that of many Zuñi smiths, who do not use a metal container, but simply rest the crucible in the coals piled up on the floor of the small fireplace, and hold the bellows to a metal

[1] Hodge quotes Washington Matthews: "The appliances and the processes of the smith are much the same among the Navaho and the Pueblo. But the Pueblo artisan living in a spacious house builds a permanent forge on a frame, at such a height that he can work standing, while his less fortunate Navaho confrere . . . constructs a temporary forge on the ground." (*Op. cit.,* page 225.)

[2] Horace says that the smiths used to get their charcoal from the ovens in which the Zuñi women bake bread. But when the demand for silver became great and many men in the village took up the art, the women began to gather the coals after baking and sell them for fifty cents a bag.

pipe which is inserted in the adobe rim which walls in the floor of the fireplace.

On the day of my visit Horace was at work carving a stone mold. He was dressed in his work clothes, an old shirt and a worn pair of trousers. On a warm day he may remove his shirt while working over the hot flame of his torch. I have yet to see a silversmith at work in his best clothes or his ceremonial garb, his neck festooned with necklaces, his arms covered with bracelets, and concha belts spread out on the floor, in the way smiths are usually photographed. Horace's wife, from San Felipe, was in the next room beading rabbits' feet. Their two small sons were playing in front of the house. At closer view it could be seen that Horace was carving a Knife-Wing monster in the stone [Plate 22B]. Knife-Wing, a god of the zenith, is one of the Zuñi animal spirits. However, when his image is made in silver, it has no religious significance, but becomes merely decorative, as do the Navajo supernaturals when they are woven into a rug. The design Horace was carving into the rock was to be a mold for a brooch, ordered by one of the traders to be sold to a white man. Horace was the first smith in the village to represent Knife-Wing in silver, in 1928. The first one he made was cut and filed out of wrought silver. The traders liked it so much that they asked him to make more. Two years later he tried to make a cast one, and as this proved to be an easier method, he continued to use that process.[3]

[3] Frank Hamilton Cushing, "Zuñi Fetishes," *Second Annual Report, 1880–81*, Bureau of American Ethnology (Washington, 1883). "Knife-feathered Monster, A-tchi-ala-to-pa . . . is the hero of hundreds of folklore tales, and the tutelar deity of several societies of Zuñi. He is represented possessing a human form, furnished with flint knife-feathered pinions, and tail. His dress consists of the conventional terraced cap (representative of his dwelling place among the clouds). . . . His weapons are the great Flint-Knife of War, the Bow of the Skies (the Rain-bow), and the arrow of lightning, and his guardians or warriors are the Great Mountain Lion of the North and Upper regions. He was doubtless the original War God of the Zuñis, although now secondary in the order of war, to the two Children of the Sun. . . . Anciently he was inimical to man, stealing and carrying away to his city in the skies the women of all nations until subdued by other gods and men of magic powers."

For further references see Ruth Benedict, *Zuñi Mythology*, Columbia University *Contributions to Anthropology*, XXI, (New York, 1935, 2 vols.), I, 43–49, 272–73; II, 91–98, 279–80. Also see Ruth Bunzel, "Introduction to Zuñi Cere-

The pieces of stone on the bench came from a place called White Hill, which is just to the south of the reservation in the Atarque country. Horace said that Juan Deleosa, one of the older smiths in the village, got his stone there, and told him where to find it. Horace and his friend, Tom Wiakwe, who is one of the best turquoise-workers in the pueblo, went after it and brought back several large pieces of the rock. The stone is pumiceous tuff, like the volcanic rock Tom Burnsides, the Navajo smith, dug out of the hillside south of Houck.

As Horace makes the mold, he first marks construction lines on the stone with a pencil, then he draws Knife-Wing freehand within the marked area. His next step is to carve out the stone within the borders of the design. After that he will make a groove in the stone from the edge to that part which has been carved out. This will serve as a channel through which the molten silver will be poured. On top of this stone will be placed another one which will fit tightly against the carved side and serve as a cover. The carved surface and the groove leading down to it will be covered with an even coat of carbon. This will not be charcoal, the substance that some smiths use, but carbon produced by the smoke of hot coals smothered with peach pits. This smoke deposits a heavy black layer of carbon on the stone, which is better, according to Horace, than the powdered charcoal. Horace probably will not get to the actual pouring of the silver until afternoon. The next morning will be spent in filing down the rough edges and smoothing off the whole surface of the brooch with emery paper. After this he may set several pieces of turquoise in the pin.

On another day, Horace might be making some spoons or ash trays for one of the traders. He is one of the few Zuñi smiths

---

monialism," *Forty-seventh Annual Report, 1929–30*, Bureau of American Ethnology (Washington, 1932), page 528.

It was Horace who told me that he was the first in the village to make Knife-Wing Monster. Later, I received contrary evidence in a letter from Mrs. Lewis, of Zuñi, who said: "In 1932 Kelsey had Ike Wilson (Navajo) make the first Knife bird. It was taken from a design from a letterhead of Fred Harvey's. The first ones were plain and later on he began to inlay them with the turquoise." Mr. Schweizer, of the Fred Harvey Company, told me that the design on the letterhead was copied from a reproduction in one of the Zuñi reports published by the Bureau of American Ethnology.

who make large pieces of hammered ware decorated with die-work rather than turquoise. Most of the smiths dislike doing this type of work, and would rather spend their time in making the more delicate pieces, with turquoise sets and twisted wire.

Horace is a versatile and skilled smith. He is able to do set work, as well as cast and wrought die-marked silver. He makes many bracelets which have a single row of small stones set in a narrow band of silver. After the metal foundation and all of the small housings for the stones have been made, Horace grinds down and polishes the turquoise, a separate piece for each housing. The stones are supplied to him by the trader for whom he is working at the time, and these small sets, of course, are usually made from scraps of stone which remain in the matrix after the larger stones have been removed. With a pair of pliers the soft matrix is snipped away from the small bits of blue stone which are mounted with wax on the end of short sticks, such as any lapidary uses. Horace then holds the stick up against the side of a hand-turned carborundum wheel and twirls it, while he presses the stone against the wheel, grinding it evenly on all sides. It takes about seven minutes to grind down each stone to the proper dimensions. When they are all uniform in size and shape, he removes the carborundum wheel and attaches a wooden one covered with emery paper. The sticks with their tiny caps of blue stone are held up once more, and this time the surfaces of the stones are polished to a smooth texture.

It takes Horace over an hour to make the sets for just the one small bracelet. When the turquoise has been removed from the sticks, and the wax has been scraped off the back of each set, the stones will be ready for matching and setting. The darkest stones are placed in the middle of the bracelet, for they are the ones which will retain their blue color the longest. Before they are set in the housings, a small cardboard cushion must be placed inside of each bezel. This prevents the stone from cracking when the rim is pressed up to the sides of the set and keeps the turquoise firmly in position.

In a week or so Horace will take the finished brooch, the bracelets, and the rings to the trading post. The trader will pay him about two dollars and a half for his work on the brooch, and fifty cents an ounce for the bracelets and rings, plus ten cents for each small set and fifteen cents for the larger ones. Depending on Horace's credit and the financial state of the store, he may be paid in cash or in trade. If payment is in trade and he does not want to buy anything at this time, a due bill will be given to him, with which he can buy goods at another time. The trader will also give Horace more silver slugs and turquoise to work up. Possibly he will want him to make some small squash-blossom beads, or perhaps a concha belt.

Cash is scarce in Zuñi today, and for that reason Horace frequently goes to Gallup, where he buys silver slugs of his own. When jewelry has been made of these, he will attempt to sell it in Gallup for cash. Horace, like the other members of his tribe, is no longer content with credit in the trading posts. He wants money to buy what he pleases, where he pleases, and when he pleases.

Several years ago Horace realized about $900 a year from his craft. In 1938, this figure was off about one-third because of market conditions. He used to sell nearly all of his silver to the traders at Zuñi, but now he takes almost half of it to Gallup.

When business was good, he employed helpers in his shop. One of these was his mother's brother. Two others were cousins and fellow clansmen. These men, Raymond and Jerry Watson, who learned the craft from Horace, are well-known silversmiths in the village now. Horace said that he used to pay them five dollars "every once in a while" in return for their assistance during their period of apprenticeship. Other men, prominent as smiths at the present time, learned from Horace some years ago. One of these is Okweene Neese, and another is Benny Hamona. These men are brothers of Horace's first wife. They used to come to their sister's house, where Horace lived, and during their visits they learned the art from him. They did not help him in his shop but just "picked up" the art by watching him, and occasionally asking him for instruction. Because they were such close relatives, they did not pay him for the instruction, as a nonrelative might be obliged to do.

It was seven years ago when Okweene Neese learned to make

PLATE 17

TOM BURNSIDES, NAVAJO

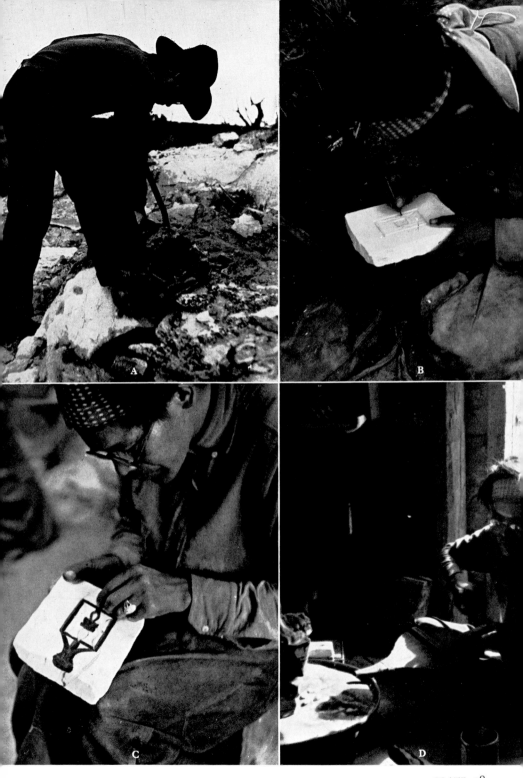

PLATE 18

STEPS IN MAKING A KETOH (BOW-GUARD)

A. Obtaining the stone   B. Carving the mold

C. Coating groove with charcoal   D. Heating the silver

silver from Horace. For several years after that he did not have enough tools to set up his own shop; therefore, he used those belonging to Horace, and those of his friends, Dishde and Teshlakai. A silversmith's equipment is expensive. Okweene spent over $200 on his, buying one tool at a time. He makes some of his dies and, like other Zuñi smiths, buys many from Navajo smiths. He showed me a large die with an intricate pattern, for which he paid a Navajo three dollars. Smaller ones he has bought for seventy-five cents. He says that he still does not have a complete set of tools. There are a few small ones, such as snub-nose pliers, which would enable him to do better work.

Okweene says that he has been doing expert work for only the last two years, for it takes most smiths five or six years to perfect their art. At the present time he is one of the best artisans in the pueblo. His work, unlike that of Horace, tends to be elaborate. There is not a man in the village who can make a better pair of fancy earrings than he. His work is not only good in design but it is well put together. Zuñi jewelry is light in weight, and the silver serves merely as a plastic base to hold the many turquoise sets in position. Sometimes the thin silver of the pieces made for the tourist trade will crack, or the stones will work loose from the bezels. This never happens when Okweene makes a ring or a bracelet.

His house is a bit to the east of Horace's, and to the north of the old village. It is a small, two-room house, with a typical American front porch, an innovation in house construction at Zuñi. Okweene works in both of the rooms. In the one, an old storage room, are his anvil and forge; in the other is a work table where he fashions the wrought silver into the finished product. This room also serves as combined kitchen and living quarters for his wife and his daughter. By doing the heavy work in another room, he spares them from the constant clang of the hammer and the heat of the forge.

It is interesting to watch Okweene make a pair of earrings, which he creates with such an adept hand. He melts a slug of silver under the heat of his torch, and then pours the molten silver into a small, open, rock mold, oblong in shape. When the metal has cooled, he divides the bar into equal halves with a cold chisel. One of these halves he pounds out into a long, thin bar, square in cross-section. The other half he pounds into a thin square. It is a half-an-hour's job to do this pounding. When the long bar is rod-like in proportions, Okweene inserts one end in a drawplate and pulls it through the largest hole. He has devised a very ingenious apparatus to make the drawing easy. Four nails are driven at the end of a long heavy plank. The drawplate is placed between these. Okweene has driven wooden cleats at regular intervals down the length of the board, parallel to the drawplate. He grasps the end of the silver bar, which extends through the plate, with a large pair of metal-worker's pliers. Encircling the handle of this tool is a steel chain, which is attached to a crowbar. This serves as a lever and the cleats, which hold one end of the crowbar in place, act as a series of fulcrums when Okweene pulls back on the bar and draws the silver through the hole in the plate. When he has pulled the silver through the one hole he inserts it in the next, repeating the process. As the silver lengthens he moves the crowbar back from one cleat to the next. This homemade apparatus facilitates the drawing of silver wire, which, when made in the way Tom Burnsides makes his wire, is a strenuous as well as a tedious task. Nor is this as expensive an apparatus as the commercially manufactured ones which many of the other Zuñi smiths use.

When the wire has been drawn to a fine gauge, Okweene takes it, as well as the thin square of silver made from the other half of the silver bar, to the other room where he does the more delicate work of fashioning the earrings.

The next step is to cut out of the flat square of silver the ovals which are to be the mountings for the stones. The bezels are cut out of this same piece and soldered to the mounting. He then forms the triangular rim which provides the framework for the whole earring, and to which the bezels of the sets are attached. This is stamped transversely with a tiny die, as are the small round pieces which are placed at each side of the bottom set. On these round pieces and on the triangular rim, raindrops are fastened. These have been made in the usual way, by heating small snips of silver on a block of charred wood. It requires a good deal of patience to fasten these small balls of silver into position, as they must be put on precisely, in a uniform line, and on the same level. The only tools Okweene has for this work are a pair of pincers and a steady hand. After that, larger raindrops will be placed on the four sides of the bottom set. Then short lengths of the wire are cut off, bent to form small loops, and fastened in place. Seven more short lengths of the wire are snipped off and bent with a pair of jeweler's pliers to a circular shape. These are soldered, one at the base of the triangle, and one at the apex. A longer length of wire is tempered to give it the proper elasticity and shaped into the clasp which will hold the ring to the lobe of the ear.

Next comes the hardest job of all—making the tiny squash-blossoms which are to dangle at the bottom of the earrings. It is quite a trick to make large squash-blossom beads, but it is a much more difficult task to make them in this microscopic size. Only a smith with considerable experience and even more patience is able to make such minute ones. Each dangle is composed of three separate pieces soldered securely together. It takes many hours for Okweene to finish this exacting work. When the dangles are fastened, all the silver of the earrings will be in place, and the metal, covered with a black film, known as "fire coat," will be blanched in acid and brushed until it has a high sheen. Last of all, the stones will be set in the mounting and the earrings will be ready for sale to the trader. It takes him almost three days to make this single pair of earrings.

There are only two Zuñi who peddle their silver in the manner of the Santo Domingo smiths. One of these is Tom Pakwine, the other is Okweene. The latter has a pickup truck which he drives to the various fiestas and celebrations during the summer and fall. I saw him at the Fourth of July celebration at Flagstaff in 1938. He told me that he had made one hundred rings, working on them day and night for several weeks before the event so that he would have them ready for sale. These rings he sold for one dollar each. White people were the principal buyers. He also had some bracelets and bow-guards which he sold to the Navajo. For these he was paid in rugs. A month later Okweene took these rugs up to one of the wholesale trading houses in Gallup and sold them. On this one trip to Flagstaff he realized a profit of about seventy-five dollars in return for his labor.

In November, 1937, he made a trip with his wife to the White Mountain Apache reservation, to visit her brother, who is employed at Fort Apache by the Indian Service. Okweene thought that the Apache might buy his silver and took some along. He sold several rings and bracelets, getting three times as much for them as he would have received from the traders in his pueblo. It was at that time that Okweene came into possession of the buckle which he now wears. He tells this story of how he obtained the belt: "When I was at Fort Apache trading, one of the Apache men came up to me and said, 'I would like to buy that ring you are wearing. How much will it cost me?' I told him five dollars. He said, 'I don't have five dollars to give you for it, but I will give you this beaded belt with the silver buckle on it for that ring.' So I traded him. I was wearing that belt in Gallup one day and a tourist came up to me and asked me if I would sell the beaded belt. I sold it to him for seven dollars without the buckle. I wanted to keep that for myself. It is a good Navajo buckle. But I thought that it would look better if it had some turquoise, so I set these two stones in it." This is a good illustration of the Zuñi's opinion of unset Navajo silver. From this story one would think that Okweene was a Santo Domingo, for he drove a hard bargain.

During the last week of August Okweene may be seen in Gallup at the Inter-tribal Ceremonial. He will sell some of his silver to the Navajo who have come to town by the thousands. The Navajo like Zuñi-made silver, with its many sets, and they place a high value on it when the jewelry is as well made as that of Okweene. Some of his silver will be on display in the exhibition hall where the traders from the pueblo are displaying the silver made at Zuñi. A few weeks later there will be a fiesta at Laguna where he will take some rings and bracelets to sell to the Indians of that pueblo, to those from Acoma, and to residents of the Rio Grande villages who have come to trade. More silver will be sold to the ever-present Navajo, who will come from the eastern end of their reservation and from the region of Ramah.

In the course of a year Okweene makes about six hundred dollars working for the traders at Zuñi, and a hundred more making silver for other Zuñi. His trading outside of the pueblo brings two to three hundred dollars, making his income just short of a thousand dollars a year. But in order to make that much he often has to work long into the night, running grave risk of injuring his eyes. His wife, to whom he has taught the fundamentals of the craft, helps him on occasion, when he is rushed with a large order of rings and bracelets. Remarking on his worldly goods, Okweene said, "My wife and I have fifty-five sheep and ten goats, my auto, and this new house. Seven years ago we didn't have anything."

CHAPTER X

Design of Zuñi Silver

THE Zuñi have known the art of carving turquoise for hundreds of years. Small bits of blue stone were carved into the form of animals, similar in shape to the large fetishes. Frequently the animal spirits, Mountain Lion and Bear, were formed in small bits of turquoise and worn between the nuggets of the necklaces. These necklaces, with an occasional animal form, are worn at the present time by the men and women of the village, who have inherited them as heirlooms which have been handed down from one generation to the next for centuries.

There is an interesting outgrowth of this art which has sprung up within the last twenty years. It is an art form which depends on the artistry of two different craftsmen, the turquoise-worker, who carves the stone, and the silversmith, who mounts the stone in silver. The traders import shell, usually spiney oyster, which is also fashioned by the lapidaries and set in silver. Jet is also provided by the traders for this purpose.

Two of the most expert turquoise-workers in the village are Ted Wiakwe and Leekya. They are provided with turquoise by the trader, and he pays them by the piece for their work. Then the trader has one of the silversmiths mount the stone on silver. While the work is done by the two Indian craftsmen, these pieces are really the result of the labor of three men, the lapidary, the smith, and the trader, for the trader is the one who suggests the form of the finished piece to the craftsmen. Some of the designs have been copied from the illustrations in the annual reports of The Bureau of American Ethnology.

Knife-Wing has become a popular design [Plate 22c]. Wholesale traders and curio dealers, to whom traders sell silver made at Zuñi, found a ready market for the silver decorated with these figures, known to the white man as thunderbirds. As a result, the traders have encouraged the lapidaries to cut shell, jet, and turquoise into small units, which when assembled and set in bezels, one for each unit, form the design of Knife-Wing. These are frequently set in box tops, the boxes being made by the Navajo smiths who work in the village.

Another Zuñi animal design which is employed by the turquoise worker is Dragon-Fly. I photographed two brooches in which the stones were carved by Ted Wiakwe, and the silver mountings were the work of Okweene Neese [Plate 22D]. These pieces were made for one of the traders and will be sold outside of the village. However, the silversmiths themselves like to use these animal forms, and as they possess a certain degree of skill in turquoise-working, acquired from grinding and polishing, they will on occasion carve the stone to the required shape and set it in silver. I saw a bow-guard, set with a shell Dragon-Fly, which was made by Okweene Neese. It was one of the pieces that he took to the Fourth of July celebration at Flagstaff.

The Knife-Wings and Dragon-Flies set in silver are flat-relief work. There is some turquoise carving in the round, copied after the old necklace fetish designs. The traders commission Ted Wiakwe and Leekya, who make a specialty of this type of work, to carve small animal forms, which are fastened to the box tops made by the Navajo smiths. There is one smith in the pueblo, Juan Deleosa, who makes these fetish animal forms of silver. These are small in size, one figure being no more than one-half inch long, and delicately molded. These small bits of silver are cast in a mold which differs from the usual molds in that both the top and the bottom stones are carved. This gives a cast which is in the round, and not flat on one surface. Juan files down the silver, polishes it, and, as a final touch, provides the tiny animal with a mouth and eyes.

The technique of casting is not a recent development. It was known to Lanyade and the other smiths of the last century.[1] It

[1] Lanyade described a method of casting which he used over fifty years ago to make cast crosses and najahes. Soft rock (evidently sandstone) was heated and pounded into fine particles. The sand thus produced was put in a shallow wooden or metal box. Sugar was dissolved in water and the liquid was poured over the sand. Then a wooden form or a piece of silver was pressed down into the sand. This form had approximately the same shape the finished piece was to have, and

has never been a popular technique, however. There are not more than six smiths in the pueblo at the present time who do cast work in any quantity. The best of these are Horace Aiuli and Juan Deleosa.

Juan, now over sixty years of age, is one of the oldest active silversmiths at Zuñi. He is a specialist at casting, and does little work of any other type. Juan learned the technique of casting from a Navajo. In watching this Navajo at work, he failed to see him grease his stone, so the first casts he made did not turn out well, as the silver stuck to the stone. After some experimentation, Juan had the idea of moistening the mold with kerosene, which prevented the silver from adhering to the surface of the stone. Juan still uses kerosene for this purpose, and if he does not happen to have any of it on hand, he uses machine oil. He says that either one of these is better than lard or tallow, and just as good as charcoal or lampblack.

Juan uses hard stones for his molds as well as the soft pumiceous tuff. While it is much more difficult to carve the mold out of hard rock, once the mold is made, it will last indefinitely, whereas the tuff mold will crack after less than a dozen pourings.

In addition to the usual types of cast bracelets, bow-guards, and conchas, Juan makes crucifixes. He made his first crucifix some thirty years ago for Father Arnold, of the re-established mission at Zuñi, and it was wrought. But after he learned the technique of casting, he began to make crucifixes in this way. These molded crucifixes show technical virtuosity in the treatment of the figure of Christ. With crude tools Juan is able to render the most exact detail, giving the figure a naturalistic appearance.

A question frequently asked is: "How can Zuñi silver be dis-

---

served as a positive mold by which the negative mold was made in the sand. A groove leading to the depressed area was made in the sand. A lid of rock was put over the top, and the molten silver was poured in. This was as much as I was able to learn about the process. The function of the sugar solution puzzles me. Evidently it cemented the particles of sand together. Possibly it prevented the sand from adhering to the silver. Another old smith by the name of Chumohe told me that the Zuñi smiths also made molds of adobe, but he had never heard of sugarwater being used.

tinguished from Navajo silver?" The differences are obvious if one is speaking of Zuñi silver as a whole compared to Navajo silver as a whole. But it is impossible to say with any degree of accuracy that a particular piece of silver was made at Zuñi. One reason for this is that the Navajo in recent years have copied Zuñi patterns in jewelry, and the traders at Zuñi have encouraged certain smiths there to make silver in Navajo style. Therefore, it is only possible to say of a particular piece of silver: "That is typical of the jewelry made by the Zuñi smiths;" or, "That looks like Navajo silver."

The most prominent characteristic of Zuñi silver is the turquoise sets. Rarely does the smith of that pueblo make a piece of silver with no sets, and seldom is a piece made with only a few sets. That is the first element to be considered in distinguishing the two types of silver. Next in importance is the weight of the silver. Navajo silver tends to be heavier than that made in the pueblo— I am speaking of the silver that the Zuñi and the Navajo make for their own use. The silver that is made by both of these tribes for the tourist market is considerably lighter than that which the Indians wear. Silver to the Zuñi is primarily a plastic material in which turquoise may be held; silver in itself does not possess the beauty that it does in the eyes of their Navajo neighbors. As a result, the silver in a Zuñi bracelet is just heavy enough to provide a firm foundation for the stones. This is true of the bow-guards, thin plates of silver holding massive nuggets of turquoise, and the brooches, buckles, conchas, and other pieces. Compared with the Navajo silver it seems light and flimsy, but it is not without a beauty of its own. The blue-green stones, finely polished and sometimes carved in animal forms, are effectively set in balanced patterns against the silver background. Earrings and finger rings have a delicacy rivaled only by their Mexican prototypes.

A third distinguishing characteristic is die-work. One rarely sees a piece of Navajo silver without some stamped designs. Zuñi silver with die-work is almost as rare. If the pueblo jewelry is stamped with designs, the dies are used sparingly. If the Zuñi smith has no turquoise to put in his silver, he will not make any jewelry until he has the stones. The Navajo who has no turquoise, or at least only one or two pieces, will make the silver and decorate it with his dies. Turquoise is the decorative element in Zuñi silver, and for this reason die-work has never gained favor. Those dies that are used are obtained, for the most part, from the Navajo smiths.[2] Die-making is an art in itself, and one that only three or four Zuñi smiths understand. There have been a few smiths in the pueblo who have had this knowledge, ever since the time Atsidi Chon brought the first set of silver stamps to the village. The Navajo smith is just as proud of his collection of dies as he is of the silver he makes. To the Zuñi, the die is just another tool.

Boxes, ashtrays, tableware, and other pieces of silver made by the Indian smith for the white man's home are the work of the Navajo craftsman. Large pieces of hand-hammered silver depend on die-work for decoration. The Zuñi smith does not have as many dies, nor is he as skillful in applying them to the silver as the Navajo. The Zuñi smiths do little of this type of work for another reason—they do not like to hammer out large pieces of silver, but prefer to do the more delicate set and bent-wire work.

If we apply these differences in design to distinct pieces of silver, we will find that the Navajo concha is larger in circumference, heavier, and die-marked. The Zuñi concha is smaller and frequently has many sets. The Navajo bow-guard is usually made by the stone-casting technique. If it is hammered, it will be heavy and stamped, with perhaps one or two sets. Nearly all of the Zuñi bow-guards are of one hammered piece with many sets. A Navajo ring is simple in design; the Zuñi ring is complicated, with small twists of wire bordering the bezel. The Zuñi rarely make plain beads. The squash-blossom necklaces are lighter, smaller, and studded with stones.

Although there are these differences in the design of Navajo and Zuñi silver, the technique of making silver is fundamentally the same among both groups. There are a few minor points of difference. Many Navajo smiths work sitting on the floor of their

[2] The Zuñi pay the Navajo from twenty-five cents to three dollars apiece for dies, depending on the size. Many of these are obtained from Navajo who come to Shalako in December. Tom Luhe showed me a small arrow-shaped die which he had bought from a Navajo who had many stamps of various designs for sale at the 1937 Shalako. The price of this die was seventy-five cents.

hogans, just as the generations of smiths before them did; but in the regions where Navajo silversmithing has been commercialized, as it has been at Zuñi, the Navajo craftsman works at a bench similar to that of the Pueblo smith. What differences there are in the actual technique of making silver result from the Zuñi smiths' preoccupation with delicate set-work and the Navajo smiths' preference for silver more massive, with fewer sets and more die-work. There is merely a difference in emphasis on various phases of the technology, which as a whole, is carried on in the same way by both groups. The tools of the Navajo who works at Zuñi or on the southern reservation, where the craft has been commercialized, and those of the Pueblo craftsman are the same type. The gasoline torch is used for applying heat when soldering and when working with thin silver, and Pueblo and Navajo alike melt the slugs in a homemade forge, with bellows bought at the trading post.[3] Files, saws, hammers, and materials used for blanching and oxydizing are identical and are used in the same way.

The quality of the design and workmanship on a particular piece of silver is not determined solely by the skill of the Zuñi or the Navajo smith. The trader plays an important part. Some traders will accept poorly made silver. They will sell rings with loose sets, bracelets with cracks on the inside (because of incorrect annealing), or badly soldered beads. Other traders will not accept this kind of work; if a smith brings into the post a lot of silver made in that fashion, they will not buy it, but will tell him to take it back, melt it, and rework the silver.

Some traders will accept silver with any kind of design. A silversmith may stamp his jewelry with designs copied from cigarette packages, candy bar wrappers, or wallpaper designs in the mail order catalogue. If the trader thinks that he can sell the silver to someone who doesn't know Navajo or Zuñi design, he

[3] There is a man by the name of Simone living at the Zuñi farming village, Pescado, who makes silver in the old way with just a pair of bellows, a blowpipe, charcoal, and a small homemade forge. He learned the art of silversmithing some forty years ago (today he is a man over sixty), long before gasoline torches were introduced. He said that he tried to use a torch recently, but that it was "no good" because it burned up his silver. Many of the older Navajo smiths who have tried to use the gasoline torch have had the same experience. They find it easier to stick to their old ways and use a bellows and a blowpipe.

will be only too glad to buy such silver. There are some traders who have more foresight. They realize that the lowering of standards means keener competition from the manufacturers of imitation Indian silver. Silver which is well designed and beautifully finished by hand can only be imitated at considerable expense by machinery. But a cheap, badly made piece may be imitated at a "dime a dozen." These traders know that by encouraging good craftsmanship and traditional design they will be able to build up at their posts a quality of work which will find a market in the future, whereas the cheaply made silver will no longer be profitable in the face of competition with the manufacturer.

There is just as much variation in personal taste among the traders as there is among silversmiths or among the ultimate consumers. One trader will like the silver to be elaborate and baroque in design, while another trader may prefer silver that is severely simple. Some will encourage new designs, or the application of designs from other arts of the tribe, as in the case of the Zuñi Dragon-Fly and Knife-Wing. Others will tell the smiths to use only traditional jewelry designs. There are traders who tell the Zuñi smiths to copy the Navajo designs and ask the Navajo smiths to copy Zuñi silver, if that happens to be the type of silver which they need at the time. On the other hand, I have met traders who would not buy a Zuñi-style bracelet from a Navajo smith.

Frequently the silver is modified in form, because of this influence of the trader, through whose hands most of the silver passes which is sold to the white man. Even if there is little modification and change in form, there is a selective factor at play, which is economic. The silver has to sell. No traders are in the business for the sheer joy of trading with Indians or of dealing in fine handmade silver.

The importance of the role the trader plays in the production of silver is realized by examining the silver that the Indians themselves wear. The Zuñi's own standards of beauty in design and workmanship are manifest in the silver and turquoise he wears. The silver a Zuñi smith makes, either for himself or for another Zuñi, is not affected by the white man's standards, but simply by the values of the Zuñi people. The values of the individual Zuñi are influenced by the fellow members of his society. His tastes conform to the pattern of the group in which he lives. From an early age he has been conditioned by the group, who have taught him what is respected by the community. Conditioning is equally important in forming personal taste in our society. The only difference is a quantitative one. The individual in our society is subject to more influences which mold his opinion of what is beautiful. As an example, a man in our culture may admire the work of abstract painters, or he may enjoy only the work of the English eighteenth century portrait painters, or, what is even more likely, he may not enjoy looking at painting at all. But whatever happens to be the case, there will be plenty of others who will offer the security of sharing the same opinion. At Zuñi, society is not so complex. There are fewer influences to condition an individual's conception of what is beautiful and what is not. Standards of beauty are more universal. A woman decorates her pottery with certain designs because those designs are the only type she has ever seen on a Zuñi olla. A silversmith studs his jewelry with turquoise because every other person in the village considers that to be the most beautiful type of jewelry, and he was taught the value of turquoise at a very young age.

In the photographs I took of Leekya and his wife, they are dressed in the height of fashion [Plate 21D and 23 A&D]. In fact, their apparel and jewelry is the epitome of good taste. Their turquoise is the envy of every man ond woman in the village. In each ear Leekya wears two large pendants of the finest robin's-egg blue. There is over three thousand dollars' worth of turquoise draped around his neck. He made these beads himself. On his right wrist he wears a bracelet mounted with three massive stones, the middle one carved into the shape of a toad. A large ring is on his fourth finger. He wears more turquoise, which can not be seen in this picture; on the other wrist is a bracelet with a single stone over three inches wide, and on that hand is another ring. He also wears a concha belt which has a set in each plaque, and a dozen sets in the buckle.

His wife wears three pins with tremendous pieces of turquoise in each one. The largest stone of all hangs from the bottom of her necklace. From each ear hangs a ring composed of a large stone, raindrops, and dangles. Up the side of her manta is a series of large pins, such as every Zuñi woman wears if she can afford them; these are larger and have more sets than the usual manta pins. There are two bracelets on each arm. One of these is a cluster bracelet with elaborate bent-wire work on the side; another one has three sets, each one bordered by countless raindrops. Her fingers are covered with rings. Most of this jewelry was made by her husband, who is a smith as well as a turquoise worker.

In this picture it is the turquoise, not the silver, which attracts attention. The silver jewelry worn by the Navajo woman, Mable Burnsides, is quite different in its total effect [Plate 1]. The stones and the silver are balanced, one setting off the other; whereas in the jewelry of these two Zuñi, the silver sets off the stones, to be sure, but one can hardly say that the stones set off the silver.

Zuñi standards in jewelry are economic for the most part. The larger the turquoise is, the greater its value; the more valuable a piece of turquoise, the greater is its beauty in the eyes of the Zuñi. By this standard the pins which Leekya's wife wears are considered very beautiful. She is very proud to wear this jewelry because it indicates her wealth. As among the Navajo, display of wealth is an important motive in the wearing of jewelry.

Economic value is not the sole criterion of beauty, however. Craftsmanship, form, and design all play a part. The value of the turquoise in the earrings made by Okweene Neese is considerably less than that of the stones in the earrings which Leekya's wife wears. Nonetheless, these would be admired by the natives of the pueblo. The high quality of the craftsmanship would excite great approval. The complicated wire work on these earrings is pleasing. The intricacy of form in which turquoise and silver are interlaced in a complicated pattern is considered most beautiful.

Elaborate design is a characteristic of Zuñi art. The pottery designs of the ollas, and the ritual costumes of the Kachina dancers have this same rococo quality. It is a type of design in which the curved line plays an important part. The women decorate their pottery with animal forms, border scrolls, and rosettes, all curvilinear in outline. There is a similar feeling to that of the designs found on much of Zuñi silver. The myriad raindrops and the delicate braid, interspersed with tiny bits of turquoise and wire, have a total decorative effect not unlike the designs on the pottery.

The Franciscan fathers, who have been missionaries to Zuñi for many decades, introduced the Christian cross to the pueblo. The cross which became the most popular with the natives of the pueblo was the double-barred cross, the cross of Saint James, the patron saint of Spain. During the early years of the nineteenth century these were made of brass and copper by the men of the village. Silver crosses were obtained from the Mexican smiths with whom the Zuñi and the Indians of the Rio Grande pueblos traded. After the Zuñi learned the art of working silver, they made crosses for themselves.

There is a reason for the popularity of the double-barred cross. It is similar in outline to the traditional Pueblo representation of Dragon-Fly. An Indian tribe, or any ethnic group, tends to accept that object which has some meaning in the light of their own experience. Meaningless objects introduced to an Indian group by the white man are not readily accepted. But the double-barred cross, which the Zuñi immediately equated with their Dragon-Fly, was accepted at once by the members of the pueblo, and became popular as decorative apparel.

This association is evident today. Out of six people, four said that the double-barred cross was Dragon-Fly, and two said that it was not Dragon-Fly, but the Christian cross. A seventh person, Lanyade, said that he thought that these crosses represented Dragon-Fly, but he also said that as a boy he used to wear a necklace with one of these crosses on it to the mission church. Thus, at the present time, Zuñi who have been taught the significance of the cross in Catholic belief still continue to associate the form with Dragon-Fly.

Another example of a silver design which was borrowed by the Zuñi is the squash-blossom. Lanyade said that the Zuñi learned to make these beads from Atsidi Chon, the Navajo smith. Again there is a Zuñi design form with which the Navajo bead was equated. Head decorations made of wood and yarn were worn by the Zuñi ceremonial dancers [Plate 12A]. These were representative of the blossom of the squash plant, an important crop in Pueblo agriculture.[4]

Just how the term squash-blossom became popular in the usage of the white man, I do not know. But the fact remains that the Zuñi associate the form of these beads with squash. This does not mean that it is representative or symbolic of squash to the Zuñi mind; rather, its form suggests to his mind the blossom of that plant.

[4] In a curio shop in Taos I photographed a head decoration, said to be from Zuñi. The yarn sheath is orange, yellow, green, and white. The part within the sheath is of wood painted yellow and orange. It seems to be the headdress worn by the Zuñi dancing girls in the Owinahaiye war dance. Matilda Coxe Stevenson mentions this headdress: "A leather band encircles the head, the front of which is concealed by a long bang which covers the face. A horn of carved wood is attached to the left side of the leather band and an artificial blossom of the squash flower, woven of red and yellow yarn, to the right." (*Twenty-third Annual Report, 1881–82*, Bureau of American Ethnology, page 213.)

I am indebted to Dr. Elsie Clews Parsons for drawing my attention to this reference. A similar squash-blossom made of yarn and wood is worn by the Hopi Kachina dancers. Alexander M. Stephen in his journal (Elsie Clews Parsons [ed.], *Hopi Journal of Alexander M. Stephen* [New York, 1936, 2 vols.], Vol. I, page 214) in describing the dress of Malo Kachinihu, said: "The ear is a convention of Squash blossom. . . . A convention of colored yarns wound around stems radiating from a solid stamen." Accompanying the description is a sketch. Also see Ruth Bunzel, *op. cit.*, page 527.

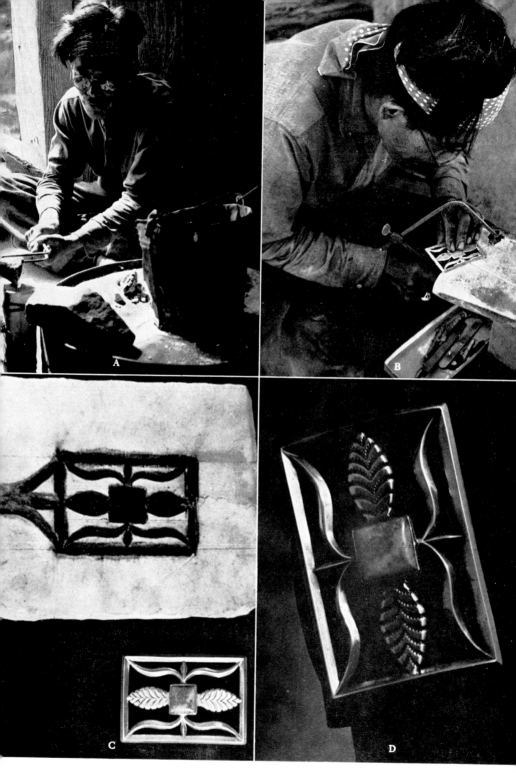

PLATE 19

STEPS IN MAKING A KETOH (continued)

A. Pouring the silver
C. Finished piece with mold

B. Sawing off rough edges
D. Ketoh mounted on leather

EARRINGS   PLATE 20

A. Old Navajo   D. (outside) Purchased at Acoma;
  B. Zuñi   (center) Mexican
    C. Early and Modern Zuñi   E. Zuñi

CHAPTER XI

Economics of the Craft

O NE of the most interesting phases in the study of an art is the relationship which exists between the art form and the culture of which it is a part. Within the last hundred and fifty years many of the arts in western civilization have been separated from the daily life of the people. Painting, sculpture, and the graphic arts, once a vital part of everyday life, have been relegated to the museum. There they are completely cut off from our homes and the activities which we consider important in our lives. Only a small portion of the population takes an interest in these arts. To the masses they are just as foreign and meaningless as the extinct dodo, which they view in the museum with the same curiosity.

The function of an art form in a particular culture may be studied to better advantage in a primitive culture, where the art has not been separated from the people. At Zuñi the art of the silversmith is not apart from the life of the people, but a phase of activity economically and socially related to the total activity of the pueblo.

At Zuñi silversmithing is a household affair. The craftsman works in his house, or rather in his wife's house, for the Pueblo man goes to live in the home of his bride when he is married. There, at one end of the room near the window, is the bench at which he works, while the room is crowded with relatives, young and old. At the other end of the room the silversmith's wife works at a table, making beaded rabbits' feet and small beaded dolls, which she sells to the trader. Usually there are other women sewing at the same table, sisters who share the house with her, sisters-in-law who have come to her house to work for the day, and perhaps a neighbor from a house near by.

Beadwork is a recent craft in the pueblo, less than ten years old. Every woman and girl old enough to sew works with the rabbits' feet and other beaded trinkets which are made for tourist consumption. Economically the craft has supplanted the art of the Zuñi potter. As a woman's craft, it is as important in the economy of the pueblo as pottery is at Acoma and basketry and pottery are in the Hopi villages.

There are other relatives who share this house with the silversmith. Besides his wife's sisters, who, with their mother, are the actual owners of the dwelling, there are many nieces and nephews, their fathers, and the unmarried younger brothers of his wife. Frequently there are several relatives of the generation of his mother-in-law, her husband, and possibly her sisters and their husbands.

These relatives do not all live in the same room. Each of his wife's sisters has her own room, or possibly two or three rooms, where her family lives. These rooms, separated by a wall, adjoin the rooms where he lives and works. In the old days, when Zuñi was a terraced pueblo, these rooms were built in three dimensional blocks, the floors of some rooms resting on the roofs of others. There are only one or two parts of the pueblo that retain this terraced construction. Houses are built with only one floor, and expansion is lateral and on a horizontal plane. When a woman's daughters marry and their husbands come to live with them, if the mother's quarters are crowded, new rooms will be constructed adjoining hers. This results in long rows of connected houses, each with its own doorway.

This matrilocal residence and system of house construction have had an effect on the craft of silversmithing. The art has become a function of the family, that is, of the household-compound owned by the women. This is the pattern that one would expect to develop at Zuñi. It is a pattern which is consistent with the rest of the culture. A. L. Kroeber emphasizes in his study of Zuñi the importance of the family. In the opening pages of his work he says: "The foundation of Zuñi society is the family. Life centers about the house. The clan is above all a ceremonial institution."[1] In another place the writer says: "In daily life it is common residence,

[1] Alfred Louis Kroeber, *Zuñi Kin and Clan, Anthropological Papers* of the American Museum of Natural History (New York, 1917), page 47.

and known blood common to individuals, and even friendship and neighborliness, that count. The clan is not thought of in ordinary personal relations of man to man, or man to woman. . . . Take away the clans, and the forms of Zuñi religion will be studded with vacancies, will even have to be made over in part; but the life and work of day to day, the contact of person with person will go on unaltered. The clans give color, variety, and interest to the life of the tribe. They serve an artistic need of the community. But they are only an ornamental excrescence upon Zuñi society, whose warp is the family of actual blood relations and whose woof is the house."[2]

Silversmithing is very much a part of the Zuñi work-a-day world. There is nothing ceremonial about the making of jewelry, and as a rule silversmiths do not hold ceremonial offices.[3] Its "warp and woof" are the family and the house. Clanship has little or no relationship to the craft.

The relationship between the art of the silversmith and the family and household is most clearly defined by the part they play in the learning of the craft. A Zuñi who wants to learn silversmithing turns to relatives for instruction in the art. They are the members of the village with whom he is the most intimate, with whom he associates in his daily life, and in whom he places his trust. The relatives with whom he associates most are the members of the family into which he was born. His father's family and his mother's family, in whose house he is brought up, will be his associates and friends for life. Even though the boy lives in the house of his bride after he is married, he will continue to see a good deal of his own family. After marriage, when the new residence is taken up, he

[2] *Ibid.*, pages 48–49.

[3] Mrs. Margaret Lewis, when asked the question, "What ceremonial offices were held by the older silversmiths [Lanyade, Keneshde, Juan Deleosa, Balawade, Kwaisedemon, etc.]," answered, "The older silversmiths did not have anything to do with the ceremonial life except the dancing—which all males have to take part in." In regard to the ceremonial offices held by the younger silversmiths, she said, "Only a few of the younger ones belong to the fraternities, but do not belong to the medicine part." Out of a list of twenty silversmiths, Mrs. Lewis noted the ceremonial affiliation of only four: Casi, Ant fraternity; Earnest Hamon, Ne'wekwe; Tom Paquin, Ne'wekwe; Nicholas Likiti, Ne'wekwe. Of the women smiths only Della Casi belonged to a fraternity, Ant fraternity.

will enlarge the circle of his friends to include the relatives of his wife. They will welcome him to their home, and a warm friendship will grow up with them, but it will not be as close a relationship as that which exists between himself and his family, or that which exists between his wife and her family. He will have the same regard for the husbands of his sisters, now living in his mother's house, as his wife's family has for him.

Thus, there are these two groups of relatives from which a Zuñi may choose when he wants to learn the craft of silversmithing: those of his own family, related to him by both his father and his mother, and the relatives of his wife on both sides of her family. On occasion a man may learn the art from a nonrelative, a school chum, or a man who belongs to the same kiva, with whom he has become friendly.

I know from whom thirty-two of the smiths in the village learned the craft. As may be seen in Table IX, the men tend to learn from a consanguine relative and the women from an affinal relative. The women learn the art at an older age than the men, usually after marriage.

TABLE IX

5 From nonrelatives
27 From relatives

	from consanguine relatives	*from affinal relatives*
6 women		4 : husbands
		1 : brother-in-law
		1 : both husband and brother-in-law
21 men	4 : brothers	5 : brothers-in-law
	3 : fathers	1 : sister-in-law
	2 : mother's brothers	
	1 : maternal grandfather	
	1 : paternal grandfather	
	4 : other members of family	

The term "apprenticeship" is misleading; it is too formalistic to describe correctly the teacher-student relationship. It is apt in that the student learns the craft in the shop of an experienced artisan, using that man's tools, as is done by apprentices in many crafts. But there is little formality in the Zuñi relationship. This becomes apparent when one asks the Zuñi smith from whom he learned the craft. He will answer, "Oh, I just picked it up." Then, if he is pressed, he will say: "I picked it up from my brother. I used to watch him make silver, and once in a while I helped him with his work." That is the way the Zuñi learns: by watching and then helping. The student, if he is a relative of the master smith, will not pay him for the privilege of watching and learning. The assistance which he offers in pounding out the silver and in doing other elementary tasks cancels any obligation to his teacher. It is an informal relationship, which is reciprocally valuable from the economic point of view. The one man teaches the other a handicraft which will yield a financial return, and this man, through his help, allows the teacher to make more silver, and thereby increase his income. If the master smith is one of the few "professional" smiths in the village, who depend completely on the craft for their livelihood, he may pay the novices who have become skilled to remain in his shop and help with the silver which he makes for the traders.[4] If a man who desires to learn the craft has no relatives experienced in silversmithing, he will turn to an outsider. In that case, a small fee will be paid by the novice for his instruction.

The length of time the beginner spends in the shop of the experienced silversmith depends not only upon his ability but also upon his financial state. If he has enough credit at the trading post to buy all of the necessary tools (the essential tools alone come to over a hundred dollars), then the period of instruction may be quite short, lasting about four months. Usually it lasts longer, and often it is two years before many of the younger smiths have been able to break away from their instructor and set up their own workbench.

Pueblo women have taken up silver-working in recent years.

[4] This was the case when the Watson brothers learned from Horace Aiuli.

The first woman to learn the art at Zuñi was Della Casi [Plate 23c]. She was taught the craft by her husband about twelve years ago. At that time there was a great demand for Indian-made silver, and there were not as many smiths in the village as there are today. Many of the younger silversmiths in the pueblo have "picked up" the craft in the last eight years, but before that the demand for jewelry was much greater than the producing capacity of the men who worked at the craft. The traders in the village supplied the artisans with as much silver and turquoise as they could make into jewelry.

For many years Zuñi women, during their spare time, have helped their husbands with silver work, lending a hand in that part of the work which requires more patience than strength. They would make the raindrops and solder them to the shank, twist the wire and mount it around the bezel, and set the stones in the finished jewelry. During the middle of the 1920's Della Casi, who had been helping her husband in this way, began to learn more and more of the craft, and soon she was a full-fledged smith in her own right. Her work greatly increased the income of her family, and in a few years several other women followed her example.

In 1938 there were nine women in the village who made silver for the traders at Zuñi. They have their own accounts on the traders' record books of the amount of silver and turquoise dealt out and the credit owed for the finished jewelry. There are probably the same number of women in the village who help their husbands with the working of the metal, some of whom are capable of turning out silver by themselves; but they do not have accounts of their own. Four years ago there were more women smiths than there are today. Many of the women who used to make silver have found beadwork a more lucrative craft. The traders can sell all of the beadwork that they turn out, as this type of work is done among the Zuñi only by women. Today there is a greater demand at Zuñi for these beaded rabbits' feet and beaded dolls than there is for silver, which is made by so many Navajo.

Twenty years ago the greatest part of a silversmith's income was derived from the jewelry he made for his fellow members in the pueblo. But that was before the traders began to commercialize the craft, and the farming out of silver and turquoise to the smiths developed. Now there are so many smiths in the village that the commissions any one smith receives from a resident of the pueblo are correspondingly small. A man or a woman who wants a bracelet made will ask a relative to make it before asking a non-relative. Since there is a smith in practically every family at Zuñi, the amount of silver any one smith makes for the Zuñi outside of his family is limited.

The smiths sell jewelry to a Zuñi for less than they will charge the traders. This is in contrast to the Navajo who sell jewelry to the members of the tribe, and even to relatives, for more than they will charge the traders. The Pueblo Indian does not place as high a value on the working of silver as the Navajo does. The Zuñi usually furnishes his own turquoise, and often the silver, to the smith; therefore, it makes no difference to him whether the smith charges him a small amount for making the jewelry. As long as the turquoise is well mounted, he is satisfied. And the smiths are, of course, loyal to their relatives and do the work for a modest payment.

The smiths also make silver for the other Pueblo Indians and for the Navajo, who place a premium on good Zuñi silver. Navajo, Acoma, Laguna, Santo Domingo, Isletans, and Hopi come to Shalako in great numbers. They come to trade as well as to see the ceremonies. It is at this time that many Hopi mantas and kilts are bartered. The Navajo women sell their rugs, and the silversmiths their dies, for Zuñi jewelry and agricultural produce. When the Zuñi sells his silver to one of these outsiders, the more he gets for it the better. If he sells a bracelet for thirty-five dollars to a Navajo, the deal is mutually satisfactory. Then the Navajo is able to say proudly to friends who ask him how much he paid for it, "I bought it for thirty-five dollars at Zuñi." And the Zuñi smith will boast to his friends: "I sold a bracelet to a Navajo for thirty-five dollars. He certainly was a sucker. I paid a Santo Domingo only twenty dollars for the stones, and there wasn't more than three dollars' worth of silver in it."

There are certain pieces of silver that the smiths make for themselves, or for other members of the village, which are rarely seen in the trading posts. These pieces may be seen to best advantage during the Zuñi ceremonies, especially during the summer Kachina dances. In the months of July and August, when most of the masked dances are held, the women are dressed in their finest array, watching the Koko (the Zuñi gods represented by the masked dancers) dance and sing in the plaza. They wear many rings, bracelets, earrings, manta pins, and necklaces which show off in bold contrast to the blue-black cloth. These pieces have larger turquoise sets than the silver which is sold to the traders.

The Kachina dancers in the plaza wear jewelry.[5] Bow-guards decorated with silver plaques and set with great nuggets of blue stone are as essential a part of the costume of the masked gods as the ritually prescribed fox skin and kilt. Turquoise necklaces, bracelets, moccasin buttons and concha belts are also worn by the dancers, for they possess wealth, and the silver and turquoise which they wear will bring riches to the pueblo, just as their presence will bring rain. Some of the men may be dressed as female Kachina, and the silver which they wear will be similar to the ornaments worn by the Zuñi women who are watching the dance from the housetops. If a man representing a god does not have the jewelry called for, he will borrow it, turning to a relative for this favor. Jewelry is also borrowed from the traders, who lend it to the dancers for the duration of the ceremony.

During 1937–38 there were sixty Zuñi smiths making jewelry for the traders in the village. This number includes nine women. But such a list does not include all of the men and women who make silver. There are probably ten smiths in the village who make a small amount and sell it in Gallup. There are at least twenty workers who have made silver in the past but who did not make any in that year. Including those smiths working in the small farming villages out from the pueblo, it would be a safe estimate to place the total number of Zuñi smiths at one hundred. Roughly, that is one smith out of every sixteen males and one woman smith out of every one hundred females. In other words, there is one

---

[5] For a detailed account of Kachina costumes, see Ruth Bunzel, "Zuñi Katcinas: An analytical Study," *Forty-seventh Annual Report, 1929-30*, Bureau of American Ethnology (Washington, 1932).

Zuñi smith out of every twenty-two persons in the village. This is quite different from the situation on the Navajo reservation. There, there is one silversmith to every one hundred Navajo.[6]

In Table x below are the average incomes of the forty-nine smiths on whom I have data. This is the income from the silver made for the traders at Zuñi. It does not take into account the jewelry made for traders in Gallup, or the amount made for direct sale to other Indians. As has been pointed out, the silver business in 1937–38 was off one-third from the amount bought and sold by the traders in the village during the previous years.

TABLE X

Average income of 49 smiths

	Men (40)	Women (9)	Both (49)
Average income for 1937–38	$238	$174	$227
Average income for typical year	$357	$261	$340

The eight smiths whom I have termed professional in Table xi realize up to $1,000 apiece when sales to traders outside of the village and direct sales to Indians are taken into account. In order to make this much from the craft, these men and the one woman, Della Casi, do little else.[7] They work the whole year around at their benches and do not take an active part in the cultivation of the fields, leaving that work to other members of their families. The families to which these smiths belong do not look down upon them for not working in the fields, for they contribute more than their share to the support of both their consanguine and their affinal relatives, who are proud to have them as members of their families. Money economy is becoming increasingly important at

[6] The United Pueblos Office, Albuquerque, census for Zuñi as of January 1, 1939: Total population, 2220; total males, 1234; total females, 936. Richard Van Valkenburgh, *A Short History of the Navajo People* (Window Rock, Arizona, 1938): Total population of Navajo for 1939, 45,000.

[7] Della Casi and her husband have the largest income of any single family in the village. Together they earn close to $2000 a year. They are the only smiths that I know of who have a shop separate from their house. They work in a one-room shed at the back of their house.

Zuñi. The credit and cash that these smiths derive from their steady work at the silver bench provide their relatives with goods from the store, which were once a luxury, but are now a necessity in the Zuñi household.

TABLE XI
Annual income of 49 smiths (1937–38)

	Men (40)	Women (9)
Smiths who work in winter only (earning less than $200)	18	6
Semiprofessional smiths (earning from $200–$400)	15	2
Professional smiths (earning more than $400)	7 (3—more than $600)	1 (more than $600)

The seventeen smiths whom I have termed semiprofessional depend on the proceeds of the craft for only part of their total income. They work in their shops during the whole of the year, but take time off for working in the fields.

The twenty-four craftsmen who earn two hundred dollars a year or less are the smiths who work only during the winter months. In the spring, summer, and fall they put away their tools and work in the fields from the planting to the harvesting season. In summing up the economic classification of the Zuñi silversmiths, it may be said that the craft is a full-time pursuit for only a very small percentage of the smiths. For most of the smiths the art offers a convenient method of deriving a cash and credit income from the traders, an income which supplements the sale of lambs, wool, and wheat, which are the important basis of the Zuñi money economy.

In addition to the hundred-odd Zuñi silversmiths, there are approximately a dozen Navajo smiths who live in the village and work the year around for two of the trading posts there. These smiths do a large business fashioning Navajo-style silver for the traders, and also make boxes, flatware, and other pieces of large, die-marked, hammered silverware of the type that few Zuñi smiths make.

At the present time there is a growing discontent at Zuñi because of the residence of these Navajo. This is not due to the ancient hostility of the two tribes, who for hundreds of years have fought and raided each other, as much as it is to the economic rivalry. The faction at Zuñi which is opposed to the Navajo smiths' living in the village is led by Zuñi silversmiths. They feel that every order a trader gives one of these Navajo smiths is just that much out of their own pockets. They think that if these Navajo were forced out of the village, they would receive more business from the traders.

One of the Zuñi smiths, however, expressed a very realistic view of the situation. He said the traders keep these smiths in the village to make silver boxes and other large pieces of die-marked work. Since the Zuñi smiths dislike doing this type of work, he reasoned, the traders will continue to hire Navajo to do it. The only way the Zuñi will be able to overcome this economic rivalry is by doing that type of work themselves, in which case the traders will no longer feel the necessity of keeping the Navajo smiths in the pueblo.

While this is an oversimplification of the problem, it is basically quite true. If the Zuñi did more of the Navajo-style work, they would increase their earnings. But what this Zuñi overlooked was the fact that if these Navajo were forced out of the pueblo, the traders would continue to buy Navajo silver from smiths who live in neighboring regions, just as they do today to some extent. I should say that it is much better for the future of the Zuñi craft for these Navajo to live in the pueblo where they are readily accessible to the traders, who farm out work to them, than it would be if the Zuñi had them removed from their reservation and started to imitate the Navajo ware. If that were the case, the Zuñi smiths would soon lose the identity which they have established by making silver distinct from that of the Navajo. The loss of that identity would bring about a corresponding economic loss.

A small part of the money and credit the silversmiths earn

from the traders is used for buying their own silver and turquoise. (One must remember that the silver and the turquoise which the Zuñi smiths work for the traders belong to the trading posts and not to themselves.) But the Zuñi who buys silver and turquoise does not think of the money with which he has purchased the metal and the stones as being spent. Rather, he regards that money as being invested, just as we think of the purchase of stocks and bonds as an investment rather than an expenditure. What is more, the Zuñi's investment is more stable than many of the investments which we make, since turquoise and silver are not subject to such marked depreciation, because of market conditions, as are stocks and bonds. Money used for the purchase of silver and turquoise is not spent, but is invested in a durable form which can always be sold for the amount of the original investment.

The desire of the Zuñi to display his wealth in personal adornment accounts for about one-fourth of a silversmith's income. While three-fourths of the income is from the trader, the other fourth comes directly from Zuñi, who buy stones and silver from the trader and commission a silversmith to make it into jewelry. The smith is usually paid in cash, but sheep may be the medium of exchange.

A Zuñi may sell his silver and turquoise if he needs cash, but his jewelry is not pawned. The traders at Zuñi gave up the pawn rack as a method of extending credit to the Indians over seven years ago. The pawn rack was never an essential part of the trading economy at Zuñi, or in any of the other pueblos, as it was on the Navajo reservation. Credit was extended to the Zuñi then, as it is today, but the jewelry is not required for collateral. The amount of credit a given Zuñi can obtain from a trader depends on his past trading record and on the size of his flock of sheep and the size of his grain crop. Therefore, the Zuñi may be seen wearing their silver the whole year around, and there is not the periodic shift of the jewelry from the pawn rack to the owner and back to the pawn rack that there is on the Navajo reservation.

A note about the future of the craft at Zuñi might be added. On the whole, I should say that Zuñi silversmithing, as an art form, stands a better chance of surviving than Navajo silversmithing.

Here I am speaking of the silver that the Zuñi and the Navajo make for sale to the white man. Both tribes will continue to make silver of good workmanship and good design for their own use. Zuñi commercial silver stands a better chance of survival because it has not been imitated by the manufacturers of Indian-style silver as Navajo silver has been imitated. There are several reasons for this. Zuñi silver can not be produced as cheaply as Navajo silver because the labor cost of production is higher and because Zuñi jewelry, with its many small sets, can not be turned out with machinery as easily as Navajo die-marked jewelry. Although the turquoise may be ground and polished by machinery, the stones must be set by hand (at least up to this time no machine has been used to do this work). It is this setting of the stones which takes so much time and makes the labor cost of the Zuñi jewelry high. As long as it takes just about twice as long to make a bracelet with multiple sets as it takes to make a Navajo bracelet with no sets at all or with a few large sets, the manufacturers are going to stake their profits on the Navajo-style silver.

Silver of the Other Pueblos

A Survey

TODAY more silver is made at Zuñi than at all the other pueblos together. The Hopi, Acoma, Isleta, and other Pueblo Indians obtain most of their silver from the Navajo and the Zuñi by trading. The smiths that work in these pueblos make up silver in small quantities, and sell or trade the products of their labor to the residents of their own villages. Commercialization of silver is carried on, for the most part, outside of the pueblo.

There are Pueblo boys who work in the bench-shops of Santa Fé, Albuquerque, Phoenix, and other southwestern cities. Here, the smiths are not making silver in the old patterns, which were known to the Pueblo smiths of the past generations, but in Navajo and Zuñi style, light in weight, for tourist trade.

However, in many of the pueblos, silver has a history which goes back fifty years. In one or two of the villages the craft is just as old as it is at Zuñi, a fact that is little realized. One reason that the silver made in these other pueblos has received so little attention is that this silver is usually mistaken for either Navajo or Zuñi work. In many museums which have collections of old silver, the Hopi and Rio Grande pueblo silver, as well as that which was made at Laguna and Acoma, is all lumped together and called Zuñi, if the pieces are rather fancy, with many sets. If the pieces are plain in design, they are labelled Navajo, irrespective of where they were made.

Another factor which has contributed to this confusion is historical in nature. The Pueblo smiths who made silver of æsthetic importance did their finest work during the nineteenth century. Today these smiths are either dead, or so old that they no longer practice the craft. The younger men who make silver in the pueblo carry on their work during the winter months, when there are few visitors in the village. As a result, most of the white people who

have seen old silver being worn at the fiestas of the Rio Grande
pueblos or at the summer dances in the Hopi villages have con-
cluded that all of the old silver seen in these villages was Navajo
made.

In making a survey of the craft in these pueblos, let us begin
with the Hopi towns and work our way eastward to the pueblos
of the Rio Grande.

Hopi Silver

The first Hopi to learn the craft of silversmithing was a man
by the name of Sikyatala, who lived at Sichomovi, on First Mesa.[1]
Sikyatala learned the art from Lanyade, the Zuñi who was the first
of the tribe to take up the craft.

Lanyade tells of his visit to the Hopi country: "Forty years
ago [1898], after Cushing had left the village and before Mrs.
Stevenson bought my tools, I made a trip to the Hopi reservation
to make silver. I stayed at First Mesa for four months, living with
Sikyatala. None of the Hopi men knew how to make silver at that
time, and I didn't let them watch me at my work, because, if they
learned how, they would no longer buy silver from me. I sold
them the silver jewelry I made for money, and sometimes I would
trade it for mantas and sashes. I made many beads, belts, and bow-
guards for them."[2]

Evidently Sikyatala, with whom Lanyade lived, saw him

[1] Sikyatala (Yellow Light) is listed in the census which Stephen made at
First Mesa (Elsie Clews Parsons [ed.], *Hopi Journal of Alexander M. Stephen*,
Vol. II, page 1123). There are also several mentions of him in the body of the
journal. He belonged to Mustard clan and was a member of Snake Society, and
several passages in the journal tell of his participation in the religious activities of
the pueblo. Stephen, who died in 1894, lived on the Mesa prior to the visit of
Lanyade, from whom Sikyatala first learned the craft about 1898.

[2] This information was checked at Sichomovi by Natoh, a resident of the
village who remembers Lanyade's visit to the Mesa, and how Sikyatala learned
silversmithing from him. Natoh is the father-in-law of Roscoe Narvasi, the pa-
ternal nephew of Sikyatala. Natoh is also listed on the census in Stephen's journal
(Vol. II, page 1114). He is Tobacco clan. Mary-Russell F. Colton in her valuable
paper, "Hopi Silversmithing—Its Background and Future" (*Plateau*, Vol. XII,
No. 1, Museum of Northern Arizona, Flagstaff [July, 1939]), has recorded a different version of how Sikyatala learned the art from Lanyade. This paper contains important information regarding the history of Hopi silver, as well as data
on the craft today.

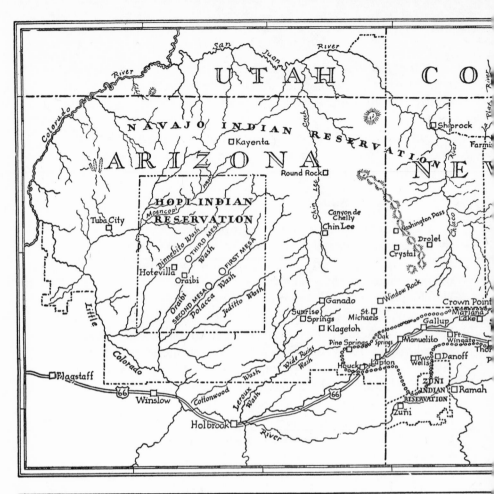

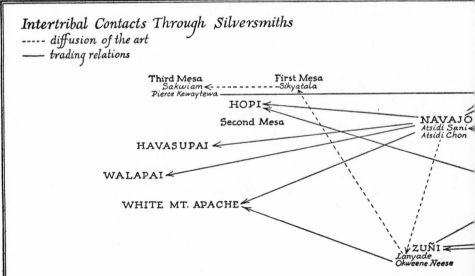

Intertribal Contacts Through Silversmiths

- - - - diffusion of the art
——— trading relations

Third Mesa   First Mesa
    Sakwiam   *Sikyatala*
Pierce Kewaytewa

HOPI

Second Mesa

HAVASUPAI

WALAPAI

WHITE MT. APACHE

NAVAJO
Atsidi Sani
Atsidi Chon

ZUÑI
Lanyade
Okweene Neese

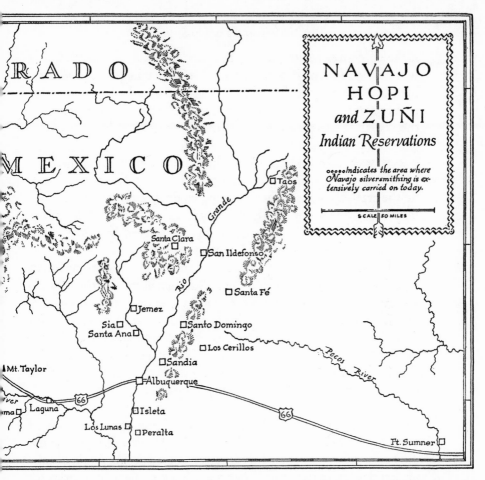

NAVAJO
HOPI
and ZUÑI

Indian Reservations

ooooo*Indicates the area where
Navajo silversmithing is extensively carried on today.*

SCALE 50 MILES

RADO

MEXICO

Taos

Santa Clara

San Ildefonso

Santa Fé

Jemez

Santo Domingo

Sia
Santa Ana

Los Cerillos

Sandia

Mt. Taylor

66

Laguna

oma

Albuquerque

Isleta

Los Lunas

Peralta

66

Pecos River

Ft. Sumner

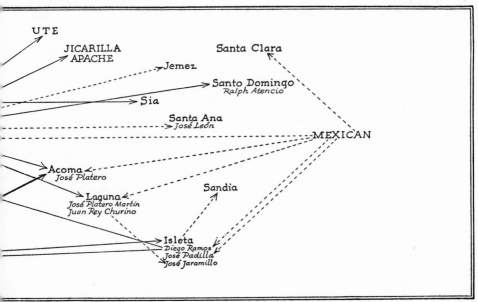

UTE

JICARILLA
APACHE

Jemez

Santa Clara

Santo Domingo
Ralph Atencio

Sia

Santa Ana
José León

MEXICAN

Acoma
José Platero

Laguna
*José Platero Martín
Juan Rey Churino*

Sandia

Isleta
*Diego Ramos
José Padilla
José Jaramillo*

make enough silver to pick up the fundamentals of the art. For it was only a short while after the Zuñi left the village that Sikyatala bought some tools and tried his own hand at making silver. After he became proficient in the craft, he sold some of the jewelry to the trader, Tom Keam, but the greatest part of it he sold to the other Hopi of First Mesa.

It was from Sikyatala that the other Hopi men learned the art. Some of the men who lived on Second and Third Mesa took up the craft. By 1904 silver was being made at Shongopovi. In 1907 Sikyatala made a trip to Oraibi, where he sold some of his silver to the trader. At that time Sakwiam, who lived in Old Oraibi, watched him make silver and learned the craft.

Sakwiam tells of this incident: "I asked Sikyatala to make up a necklace of hollow beads for me. I watched him make those beads and paid him fifteen dollars for them. I saw just how he used his tools and melted the silver. Then I tried it myself. It wasn't long before I could make simple pieces like buttons and rings. A few years later I moved from Oraibi to Hotevilla, where I set up a shop. I still do a little silver work today, when someone asks me to make some jewelry for them, or to repair old pieces."

Today Sakwiam is the oldest smith living at Hotevilla, and one of the oldest of all the Hopi smiths. His teacher, Sikyatala, died over ten years ago. Twenty-five years ago Sikyatala taught his brother's son the craft. This man, Roscoe Narvasi, carries on the tradition of silversmithing at First Mesa, where his uncle learned the art from the Zuñi.

Today there are about twelve Hopi smiths who work on their reservation. There are three smiths at Moenkopi, five at Hotevilla, one at Bakavi, two at Shongopovi, and one at Sichomovi. Unlike many of the Navajo and Zuñi silversmiths, none of these Hopi smiths depend on the art for their living. Their craft is but a part-time occupation, carried on during the winter months, when there is no work to be done in the fields; for the Hopi smith, like the other members of the tribe, measures his wealth in the produce of his land. There is not a smith living on the reservation who makes more than one hundred dollars' worth of silver a year, and the average amount of silver made by one of these smiths is around twenty-five dollars.

The little silver that these Hopi make today is for the most part small pieces—rings, bracelets, and buttons. Once in a great while a concha belt or a bow-guard will be made on special order.[3]

In design Hopi silver follows Navajo and Zuñi patterns. There is only one design element that distinguishes Hopi-made silver from that made by these neighboring tribes. That design is the butterfly, which is frequently seen on rings, bracelets, and bow-guards. The design of the butterfly is usually formed by turquoise and coral, cut to the proper shape to form the wings and body, and set on the silver.

Among the Hopi today the demand for silver is greater than the output of the smiths. Most of the modern silver that one sees them wear has been obtained from the Navajo and from the Zuñi, who come to the villages to trade. The Zuñi frequently trade their turquoise and silver for the mantas woven by the Hopi men, just as they did over forty years ago. The Navajo trade their silver for farm produce; Hopi-grown peaches and apricots ripen earlier than the fruit grown in Canyon de Chelly. During the early summer many Navajo may be seen in the villages, where they trade and watch the Hopi rain- and home-dances.

The art of silversmithing has not developed among the Hopi as it did among the Zuñi and the Navajo. There were many Navajo smiths who were expert at the craft before Sikyatala made his first silver in 1898. At that time the Hopi had been trading with the Navajo smiths for over twenty years. Whenever a Hopi wanted to buy a piece of silver, he could get it readily from a Navajo, as he can today.

This was not so at Zuñi. The residents of that pueblo forty years ago could obtain Navajo silver only by going up to the Navajo reservation, over fifty miles to the north. The Navajo

---

[3] The process of casting silver in a rock mold is known to the Hopi. However, it is not a widely used technique. Harold Jenkins, a smith of Moenkopi, told me: "I taught myself how to do cast work after watching some Navajo smiths make cast pieces. I get my rock up near Red Lake. That is where the Navajo smiths of this region get their rock." Paul Andrews, a smith of Shongopovi, said that the smiths that live on Second Mesa get their stones from the Zuñi.

that live in the region of Zuñi have been making silver for only twenty-five years, but many years before that the Zuñi had become skilled in the art.

An even more important reason for the craft's developing at Zuñi but not on the Hopi reservation is an economic one. At Zuñi the traders have encouraged the silversmiths and have bought their jewelry, but the Hopi smiths have never had this economic backing. The largest post on the reservation, owned by Lorenzo Hubbell, closed down its silver business twenty-seven years ago. Most of the Hopi posts, unlike those at Zuñi, are small stores run by the Indians themselves. These store owners have never been in a position to build up a large silver trade, as it takes considerable financial backing to run a profitable silver business, a backing that the Hopi store owners have never had.

Acoma Silver

Few people realize that the Acoma ever made silver. A photograph of an Acoma silversmith, taken in 1891 by Charles Lummis, proves that this pueblo was acquainted with the art even at that time [Plate 24B]. This smith, Juan Luhan, whose Spanish nickname was Musico, is still remembered at Acoma. Lieutenant Bourke visited Acoma in 1881 and wrote in his diary: "I bought a fine Navajo rug and two silver bangles, the latter made in this pueblo from coin silver. . . . In Acoma and in Laguna, too, there is considerable use of silver upon the dresses themselves, the seams from knee to ankle being held together by rows of silver quarter-dollars fastened to pins; the effect is very pretty. . . . The women wear necklaces of silver beads, with pendants in the form of an archiepiscopal cross, terminating in a heart."[4]

Today the oldest of the Acoma smiths, in fact, the last of the older generation of silver craftsmen, is a man by the name of José Antonio Platero. This Spanish name is in itself indicative of the man's craft. José is now well on in years and no longer makes as much silver as he used to. He tells of how he happened to learn the art.

[4] Bloom, *op. cit.*, Vol. XII, No. 4 (October, 1881), page 365.

"It was over forty years ago [*c*. 1898] that my wife died. One day after her death my father-in-law and I were riding down here to the pueblo from Acomita. This man, who was called Vincente Chavez, knew how to make silver. He said to me, 'Why don't you learn how to make silver? It isn't hard work, and you can earn good money by working at silver in your spare time. If you have something like that to do you will soon forget your sorrow for your wife. I will teach you all that I know about the craft for nothing.' So I learned to make silver from him. A little while after that I went over to the Laguna farming villages. During the next eight years whenever I had any spare time, I used to go over there and make up silver for the Laguna.

"I would sell a string of beads with those blossoms on them for forty dollars' worth of goods. I made a great many of those old silver earrings which were hoop-shaped, and had a hollow bead at the bottom. I charged seventy-five cents apiece for one of these earrings, if the person who wanted them furnished me with the silver. If I furnished the silver I would charge one dollar. I used to do cast as well as pounded silver. My father-in-law taught me how to cast silver with stone, which we got right here on the reservation.

"After I finished a piece of silver jewelry I would wear it myself, so other people could see it. Then they would come up to me and say, 'How much would you charge me to make a bracelet like that?' Then I would say, 'Well, I will sell you this one that I am wearing for ten dollars.' "

At Acoma silversmithing goes back beyond the memory of José Platero, who learned the art from his father-in-law sometime during the 1890's. Vincente Chavez had been taught the craft by his mother's brother many years before. No one at Acoma today knows where this man picked up his knowledge of the art. Since the Navajo first learned how to make silver from Mexican smiths who lived just to the north of Acoma, it is quite probable that the Acoma picked up the art from these same Mexicans. It is possible that they learned the art as early as 1870, which is about the time that the Zuñi first made silver.

There are eight Acoma silversmiths of the younger generation. These men did not learn the craft from the old smiths of the pueblo, but in the shops of Albuquerque.

The silver that the Acoma wear today is largely Navajo or Zuñi made. Many of the women wear Zuñi earrings, with the small sets and bangles which they have obtained at Zuñi during Shalako. A large part of the Navajo silver is traded to them at Laguna, during the fiesta which is held every September; or the Navajo bring silver to Acoma and exchange it for fruit and melons, just as they do at the Hopi villages.

Old Acoma silver is becoming increasingly rare. A few of the old necklaces with the double-barred crosses may still be seen on occasion in the village. There are three men who still wear the old-style silver earrings, which at one time were worn by nearly every man in the pueblo.

From Acoma Lieutenant Bourke went to Laguna, where he made this entry in his journal: "The Laguna women, as we have noticed of those of Acoma, are very fond of looping their skirts together with silver quarters, and also of wearing bracelets of silver and copper which, they told me, were mostly all made in Acoma."[5]

Laguna and Isleta Silver

There are no silversmiths of the older generation at Laguna today. There are twelve young men who work at the craft, and they, like the smiths of Acoma, learned the craft in Albuquerque. But there are a few silversmiths who lived at Laguna during the nineteenth century, and they are remembered by the older members of that pueblo. Marcelino Abeita told me the following story:

"Diego Ramos Abeita, my father's brother, was a silversmith.[6] He was an Isletan. After his wife died, he left Isleta, and he lived outside of the pueblo for many years. He went over to Peralta [c. 1884], which is a Mexican town across the river from Los Lunas, and there he worked on the farm of a Spanish immigrant

[5] *Ibid.*, page 373.
[6] According to Pablo Abeita, of Isleta, this man's name was simply Diego Ramos. He was not an Abeita, but was the son of a Churino mother and an unknown father.

who was born in Valencia. This Spaniard's name was Juan Andres Apodaca, and his nickname was Valencenio.

"This Spaniard knew how to make silver. He also knew how to do leather work, and he used to make saddles when he was not busy working out in the fields. He told my uncle that he had learned these trades in Valencia, when he was a boy. When he was a young man about twenty years of age, he left Spain and went to Mexico City. He said that he didn't like it there, so he moved up to the Rio Grande valley, and settled at Peralta.

"When my uncle went to work there, this Spaniard was about forty-five years old. My uncle and he became great friends. Diego used to watch him make silver. Before he had left Isleta he had worked as a blacksmith, so he knew something about working metal. Valencenio taught him how to make silver. At first he used the Spaniard's tools: a pair of bellows, a blowpipe, clay crucibles, and a pair of fine pliers, with which he bent the wire around the outside of earrings.

"Valencenio made silver jewelry for the Mexican farmers who lived in the valley. My uncle told me that this man used dies on his silver which bore the same designs as those with which he stamped the saddle-leather. The only difference was in the size; the leather stamps were a bit larger and heavier.[7]

"My uncle knew how to work leather. He had learned from the Mexicans who lived near Isleta, where they sold their saddles. One day Diego saw a wooden tool in Valencenio's shop, and he asked him what he used it for. Valencenio told him that it was a leather stamp that he had used as a boy in Spain. He told my uncle that at that time steel and iron were scarce in Valencia, so the only leather stamps that they had were made out of wood. Diego tried to make a stamp out of wood, just like this one. He said that it made a design on the leather, but the impression was not very deep.

[7] This interesting statement lends weight to the theory, first advanced by David L. Neumann ("Navajo Silver Dies," *El Palacio*, Vol. XXXV, Nos. 7–8 [1933]), that the Navajo took over the leather-stamp designs from the Mexicans and applied them to silver. Valencenio's use of dies on silver was a departure from the usual Mexican and Spanish technique of designing silver. All of the Mexican silver that I have seen is etched with an awl, and not stamped with a die. It is quite possible that this Spaniard learned the technique from a Navajo, or hit upon this use of leather stamps after seeing Navajo silver.

"Valencenio earned lots of money at his trade. With his money he bought more land, and hired other men to help him work it. My uncle worked for him for three months during that summer. This must have been about 1885. At that time Diego was thirty years old.

"After that Diego went farther west. He herded sheep out at Silver Creek, Arizona. A Hopi herded these sheep with him. This Hopi was a silversmith. He carried silver and a few tools while he was watching the sheep. He knew how to set turquoise in silver. My uncle had never set stones in silver. This Hopi taught him how to set turquoise, and in exchange he taught the Hopi how to do the fancy bent-wire work which he had learned from Valencenio.

"Diego stayed out in that country for some while. In 1908, after a visit at Zuñi, he came back to this region, and settled down here at Laguna, where he worked at silver. Before he came here, the Laguna knew how to make silver jewelry, but they didn't do much fancy work. When Diego set up his shop, there were about five other smiths in the village. As far as I know he was the first smith at Laguna to set turquoise."

At Isleta I learned that toward the end of his life Diego Ramos Abeita moved back to his native pueblo where he lived until he died. He died, an old man, in 1918.

The fact that there was considerable influence between the pueblos in silver designs is borne out by the fact that Diego Ramos Abeita came in contact with Hopi, Zuñi, Laguna, and Isletan smiths. We have also seen that a Zuñi worked on the Hopi reservation, and an Acoma at the Laguna villages. So the diffusion of silver designs from one pueblo to another was a natural consequence.

Silver which was elaborate in workmanship and baroque in design, such as the silver made by the Mexican smiths, became popular with the Pueblo Indians. Because of the diffusion of design, it is impossible to tell in which pueblo a particular piece of silver was made.[8] And often it is difficult to tell whether a piece

---

[8] In a chapter called "Lo, Who is Not Poor" Lummis writes: "The silver rosaries, bracelets, rings, buttons, earrings, etc. are made by their own silversmiths who achieve remarkable results with a mud forge, a hammer, files, a punch and a little solder, resin, and acid." (Charles F. Lummis, *The Land of Poco*

was made by a Mexican smith who sold it to a Pueblo Indian, or by a Pueblo smith in imitation of the Mexican jewelry [Plate 20D].

I showed a photograph [Plate 24A], taken by Charles Lummis at Isleta in 1900, to Marcelino Abeita. He said: "The smith in that picture wasn't an Isletan. He was a Laguna. I know this because that man happens to be my grandfather. In 1879 there was a religious dispute here at Laguna, and at that time my grandparents moved to Isleta, where they were adopted into the pueblo. That man made silver here at Laguna before he moved to Isleta. Those are his children with him in the picture, my aunt and uncle. My grandfather's name was José Platero. His children's names were Pedro Martin and Marcelina Martin.[9] I remember that house well, and I passed through that gate many times. He owned a few goats, so he built that gate across the door to keep them from coming into the house. He made a pair of those large earrings, with a hollow bead at the bottom, for me. Those big earrings sure hurt your ears when you were riding. We used to turn them up over the top of our ears when we were on horseback."

Marcelina Martin, the little girl who appears in this picture, is still living at Isleta. She was delighted to see a picture of her father, who had been dead for many years. The plain silver beads, which she wears in the photograph I took of her, were made by her father, and the other strand was made by an Acoma smith [Plate 24C].

Marcelino Abeita tells me that his grandfather made silver long before he was born. Therefore the Laguna have known the art since 1870, if not before. They, like the Acoma, probably learned the craft from the Mexicans. If the women of Laguna purchased most of their silver ornaments at Acoma in 1881, it indicates that at that time the craft was practiced by very few Laguna

Tiempo, [New York, 1893], page 54.) Here Lummis is talking about the economic life of the Rio Grande pueblos in general. Most of his knowledge of pueblo life was derived from living at Isleta for a number of years.

[9] Elsie Clews Parsons mentions this man in her paper, "Isleta, New Mexico," *Forty-seventh Annual Report, 1929–30*, Bureau of American Ethnology, (Washington, 1932). José Martin, the father of Pedro Martin, whose Laguna name was Uakwi, is included in the author's lists of the immigrants who came to Isleta from Laguna in 1879 (pages 348–49). His wife's name is given as Josefita Martin, and the native name, Tsiuyaitiwitsa, or Kwaiye.

men. Possibly after José Platero and one other smith moved to Isleta in 1879, the village was left with no smiths at all.

The other smith who moved to Isleta, at the same time as José Platero, was Juan Rey Churino.[10] According to Pablo Abeita, a resident and former governor of Isleta, there was a silversmith who occasionally worked at the craft long before that time. His name was José Padilla. It is said that this man was captured as a child from the Navajo, and was raised by Tomas Padilla. Pablo says that José told him that he learned silversmithing by seeing a Mexican, in El Paso, Texas, do some tinwork, making frames for santos. He told Pablo that it took much more heat to melt silver, but he finally learned how, and made buttons and other pieces. From this evidence it would seem that silversmithing at Isleta and Laguna originated at about the same time.[11]

Before 1879 there was one Isletan who worked in copper and brass. This man, whose name in translation is Spotted Eagle, was

[10] Juan Rey Churino's name is also included on the lists mentioned above. After living at Isleta for many years, Juan Rey moved to Sandia. Dr. Parsons says of this man: "Juan Rey who was headstrong even in old Laguna, used to fight with Pablo Abeita. Because of this hostility in 1923 Rey decided to leave Isleta and go to Sandia to live." (*Ibid.*, page 355.)

His daughter lives at Sandia today. She showed me several pieces of silver made by her father, one of them a necklace, on which there were many small crosses, and a large pendant cross at the bottom. She also showed me a manta clip made of three fifty-cent pieces fastened together, and a pair of earrings, with fancy bent-wire work at the bottom. These she said he made just before his death. She told me that her father made very little silver after he moved to Sandia. There are no smiths in that pueblo today.

Dr. Parsons says that Juan Rey was an important medicine man at Isleta. "Juan Rey was a stick swallower and he maintained that Keresan ritual at Isleta, using the room of the Laguna Fathers for the ceremony which only the Laguna colonists attended and which was thought of as their peculiar medicine ceremony." (*Ibid.*, page 355.)

For further details on the medicine activities of this interesting man, see the report mentioned in note 9 above. Juan Rey's extensive participation in the ritual of curing ceremonies is indicative of his activity as a smith. Silversmithing must have been a minor activity for him, as it was to the other Pueblo smiths.

[11] Pablo gave me another bit of information about a Mexican smith by the name of Anastacio Burgos, of Pajarito, New Mexico, who was a good friend of his father's. This Mexican learned how to make silver from his own father, who had learned the art from some Isleta del Sur Indians. (These Indians are the descendents of Isletans captured by Otermin in 1681, who settled fourteen miles below El Paso). They, in all probability, learned the craft from Mexicans in the region.

nicknamed "Copper." He made buttons, bracelets, and rings of that metal. At Isleta we find that jewelry was made of brass and copper before silver came in, just as it was at Zuñi and on the Navajo reservation.

The oldest smith in the village today is José Jaramillo. He learned the craft from Juan Rey Churino about thirty-five years ago. There are fifteen younger Isletan smiths. Ten of these work for shops in Albuquerque, and the others work in the pueblo.

The most interesting pieces of silver made at Isleta were the necklaces. Necklaces with silver crosses were popular here as they were in the other Rio Grande pueblos. Sometimes the beads were interspersed with coral, or with jet, which gave a most pleasing effect. Many of these crosses were of the double-barred type, such as are found at Zuñi. Frequently there was a larger pendant cross at the bottom of the strand, on which was the sacred heart [Plate 14D]. Pablo Abeita says that these necklaces were made with fifty beads to the strand and represented rosary beads. In the days before the Indians made silver jewelry, when the Isletans were married in the Catholic church, they were given a rosary bead as a symbol of obedience to the marriage pact and as a sign of obedience to the Catholic faith. Later these beads were made of silver, or of coral, and were interspersed with silver crosses. The man gave the woman such a string of beads, and after a period of years it became customary for the woman to give the man a similar string of beads which were smaller in size. In the wedding there was a ceremony, accompanied by prayers, when the beads were exchanged and blessed by the padre. These beads are still used in the marriage ceremonies. However, Pablo said that today almost everyone wears these beads whether married or not.

Isleta is the only one of the pueblos, other than Zuñi, which continues to make jewelry in traditional styles. Diego Abeita, a well-educated Isletan acquainted with American methods of merchandising, runs a silver shop in the pueblo. Here he employs a few young men of the village, who are experienced smiths. Diego encourages them to copy the designs of old Isleta silver. Old-style crosses and beads are made in this shop, as well as traditional bracelets, earrings, and bow-guards. The shop is well equipped with modern tools and the silver produced is not only of good design, but is well constructed.

On the whole, there is more interesting old silver to be seen in the Rio Grande pueblos than anywhere else in the Southwest. Dead pawn in the trading posts on the Navajo reservation has been well picked over, and fine old pieces of silver are becoming increasingly rare. The Pueblo Indians of the Rio Grande never pawned their silver. Many fine old pieces of both Navajo and Pueblo silver remain as heirlooms in the possession of these families, where they will remain for many years to come, for it takes more than mere money to separate these Rio Grande Indians from their old silver.

Santo Domingo, Santa Ana, and Other Pueblos

The history of silversmithing in the other eastern pueblos is a more recent one. Santa Domingo is the only one of these pueblos where the craft is of any importance today.

The oldest smith at Santo Domingo, and one of the first members of that village to learn the craft, is Ralph Atencio. He learned the fundamentals of the craft in 1893, not from a Mexican or a Navajo, but from a white man, a jeweler who had a shop in Santa Fé. Ralph still makes silver, using only a blowpipe, and charcoal to melt his silver. He taught the craft to his son, Ralph, who is now the best craftsman in the village. The father also taught the art to five other men in the village. These five men each paid twenty-five dollars to him for their instruction.

These seven men sell most of their silver to the tourists in Albuquerque, and Santa Fé. That silver which they make for the members of their own pueblo is heavier and set with better turquoise than that which they peddle in the cities.

The Santo Domingo own quantities of Navajo silver. They are the greatest traders of all the southwestern Indians. Every summer they take turquoise beads, which they have worked up from the rough stones, over to the Navajo country. There they trade these beads for Navajo weaving and silver. Wherever there is a large gathering of Navajo, there will be many Santo Domingo with their packs. They go by the carload to the Inter-tribal Ceremonial at Gallup, to the pow-wow at Flagstaff, and to the Navajo fair at Shiprock. Part of the goods which they get from the Navajo they sell to tourists, or to dealers in Santa Fé and Albuquerque; but the best pieces of silver they keep for themselves.

On Christmas Eve the natives of Santo Domingo make small clay objects in the shape of wild and domesticated animals, and in the form of corn, squash, and other crops. These are taken to the church and placed before the altar to receive the blessing of Jesus. They are left there for several days so that the herds and the crops will increase and prosper during the year. It has been reported that at this same time the silversmiths in the pueblo place tools and bits of silver before the altar in order that their craft may be blessed by Jesus during the year to come.[12]

During the 1890's the craft was taken up at Santa Ana.[13] At that time José Rey León, who lives at the farming village, Rancheros, learned the craft from a Navajo in the San Ysidro region. José has taught the craft to several of the younger men of the village.

At the present time there are four men who make silver at Rancheros. As one would expect, the craft is carried on as a minor occupation, most of the work being done during the winter. José Rey León, in Santo Domingo fashion, peddles his silver in the near-by towns.

At Jemez the craft has a similar history. It was learned from the eastern Navajo about the same time. There is only one smith in the village now, the son of the man who learned the art from the Navajo.

Silversmithing goes back to the 1880's at Santa Clara. At that time a Mexican *platero*, who had been living near San Ildefonso, where he made silver for the members of that pueblo, came up to Santa Clara. Three men of that village picked up the art from him, and they made silver jewelry up to the turn of the century,

[12] Dr. Leslie A. White gave me this information in the course of a discussion about the silver of the Keresan pueblos.

[13] Lieutenant Bourke noted at Santa Ana in 1881: "Saw Apache baskets, Navajo bridles, ... drums." (Bloom, *op. cit.*, Vol. XIII, No. 2 [April, 1938], page 217.) Bourke also noted the presence of Navajo silver bridles in the pueblo of Sandia (November 3, 1881).

when the art seems to have died out in the pueblo. There are three younger men, brothers, who work at the art today. They picked up a knowledge of silversmithing from their Navajo brother-in-law.

During the last ten years the craft has spread to San Ildefonso, where there are three men who make jewelry on occasion. One of these men is the well-known painter, Awa Tsireh, who makes some silver for the tourists who visit his shop during the summer.

At Sia there is one smith, a Hopi, who is married to a Sia woman. He makes silver for the members of that village, and he sells the rest of his ware in Albuquerque.

Taos has one silversmith, Candido Romero, who learned the craft recently in Santa Fé.

Generally speaking, the history of silversmithing in each of the eastern pueblos follows the same pattern. During the last two decades of the nineteenth century, there were many men who worked at the art. Then, during the next twenty years, the number of smiths working in the pueblos decreased. Only a few men continued to make silver. About 1920 many young men took up the craft, but they did not learn it from the older smiths in the pueblos. For the next ten years the population of smiths increased.

How may one account for this fluctuation in the population of silversmiths? The answer is found in economics. During the last twenty years of the nineteenth century, silver jewelry was relatively scarce and was in great demand, both among Navajo and Pueblo Indians. Silver jewelry commanded a high price, so that a craftsman could realize a good income from his work. By the turn of the century, Indian-made silver attracted the attention of the white man, who saw its commercial possibilities. This commercialization started on the Navajo reservation. The number of Navajo smiths increased. As the number of Navajo smiths increased, the number of Pueblo smiths decreased. Silver was no longer at a premium among the pueblos. Silver could be obtained easily from the Navajo. The pueblo silversmith no longer found it profitable to make jewelry for the members of his village. As more tourists flocked to the Southwest, the demand for "tourist silver" increased. This steadily growing market created a demand for more and more smiths. The returned students in the pueblos were quick to realize that here was a trade which did not require long years of professional training, and the craft could be carried on in the pueblo, or one could get a job at one of the bench-shops in Santa Fé or Albuquerque. The owners of these bench-shops found that it was difficult to keep Navajo smiths on the job. They would continually run off to the reservation to attend a squaw-dance or a Yeibichai. Therefore, the shop owners began to hire Pueblo boys.

We find a complete break in the tradition of pueblo silver-smithing. The smith of fifty years ago worked in the pueblo and made jewelry of a fine design for the residents of his village. His craft was but a part-time occupation.

The modern pueblo smith, for the most part, makes silver in the bench-shops of the near-by cities. The silver which he makes is sold to the white man and is apt to be light in weight and stereo-typed in design. For him the craft has become a full-time, factory worker's job.

Thus we see that silversmithing, although a comparatively recently acquired craft among the Navajo and Pueblo Indians, is nevertheless of importance in their culture and their economy. The Navajo and the Zuñi have the greatest number of silversmiths, and they make the majority of the silver jewelry which is sold both to members of their own and other Indian tribes and to the traders for white consumption. The bench-shops in cities close to their pueblos furnish other Pueblo Indians with employment in manu-facturing silver jewelry and ornaments and provide the greatest threat to the continuation of silversmithing as an art. However, some traders and the Indian schools are encouraging the smiths on the reservations to fashion a high type of handmade silver, using traditional designs but employing all the aids of modern tools. Fine craftsmanship of this type will always command appreciation and a market.

PLATE 21

A. Lanyade, first Zuñi to make silver

B. Keneshde, Zuñi silversmith
with old bellows

C. Acoma, wearing old-style earrings

D. Leekya, Zuñi turquoise-worker

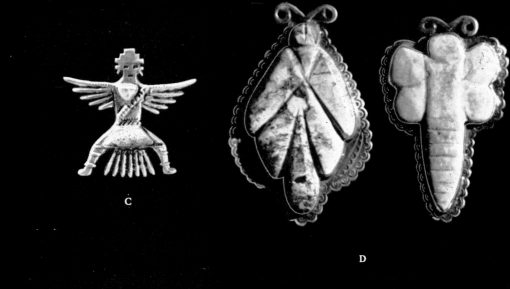

PLATE 22

A. Horace Aiula, Zuñi silversmith
C. Knife-Wing pin
B. Carving Knife-Wing mold
D. Turquoise Dragon-Flies

Appendices

Important Dates in the History
of Southwestern Silver

Navajo

c. 1850   Navajo learned to work iron.

1850–70 Navajo learned to work silver at some time during these two decades (the author favors the year 1868).

c. 1880   Turquoise first set in silver.

c. 1885   Dies bearing designs first made.

c. 1890   United States government forbade use of American silver dollars by silversmiths; Mexican pesos began to be used.

c. 1895   Arrows and swastikas stamped on silver.

1899   Commercialization of silver begun by the Fred Harvey Company.

1938   Indian Arts and Crafts Board inaugurated the stamping of quality silver with the mark *U.S. Navajo.*

Zuñi

c. 1835   Zuñi men made objects of copper and brass wire.

1872   Zuñi learned to work silver: Lanyade learned from the Navajo smith, Atsidi Chon.

c. 1890   Zuñi smiths first set turquoise in silver.

c. 1920   Commercialization of Zuñi silver began.

1938   Indian Arts and Crafts Board inaugurated the stamping of quality silver with the mark *U.S. Zuñi.*

Hopi

1898   Sikyatala of First Mesa learned to make silver from Lanyade.

c. 1904   The art was taken up at Oraibi.

c. 1907   The art was taken up at Hotevilla.

Acoma

1870–90   The Acoma first learned to make silver at some time during this period.

Laguna

c. 1870   Learned to make silver.

Isleta

1879   Silver was made at Isleta by Laguna immigrants.

Santo Domingo

c. 1893   Learned to make silver.

Santa Ana

c. 1890   Learned to make silver.

Santa Clara

c. 1880   Learned to make silver.

San Ildefonso

c. 1930   Learned to make silver.

APPENDIX II

Silversmiths

A. Hopi silversmiths (1938)

At Moenkopi
Harold Jenkins   Earl Numkina   Frank Nutaima

At Hotevilla
Sakwiam   Katchioma   Jean Nivawhioma
      Titus Lamson   Dan Kwiamawioma

At Bakavi
Willie Coin

At Shongopovi
Paul Saufki   Washington Talaiumtewa

At Sichomovi
Roscoe Narvasi

Appendices

Outside the Reservation

Ralph Tawagioma, of Hotevilla, works in Phoenix
Bert Frederick, of Oraibi, works in Flagstaff
Pierce Kewaytewa, of Oraibi, works in the pueblo at Zia
Homer Vance, of Shipaulovi, works at Williams
Randall Honowisioma, of Mishongnovi, works at Williams

B. *Smiths who made silver for the post at Pine Springs during 1938*

Tom Burnsides	Peter Roans	Atsidi Yazzie
John Burnsides	Joe Thomas	Willie Shaw
John Six	Mr. Blacksheep	John Yazzie
Atsidi Nez	Charlie Houck	Earl Vicente
	Tom Joe	Sanla Chi

C. *Navajo silversmiths* (1940[1])

Fred Adaki	Astzan Shorty Becuh	Zuñi Begay
Luna Adaki	Atsidi Yazzie Begay	Charlie Bekis
George Adikai	Brown Begay	Naljeh Yazzie Benulli
Glen Adikai	Cecil Begay	John Berman
Bessie Anderson	Chaki Begay	John Bia's Wife
Frank Anderson	Charlie Begay	Tom Bia
John Anderson	Charlie Shorty Begay	Billie Biggs
Rex Anderson	Dagrai Begay	Tsinajini Bilis No. 2
Rudolf Arlentino	Francisco Begay	John Billie
George Atazick	Frank Begay	John Bernalli
John Billie Atazick	Frank Deschee Begay	Atisidi Yazzie Bitsilli
Luna Atazick	Jake Begay	Toadlena Begay Bitsilli
Fred Atsidi	James Begay	Atsidi Yazzie Bitsui
Harry Atsidi	James Begay	Charlie Bitsui
Leo Atsidi	John Clyde Begay	John Bitsui
Tom Atsidi	Johnny Begay	Otis Bitsui
Victor Atsidi	Keets Begay	Mose Blackgoat
Wart Atsidi	Luke Begay	Charlie Bodie
Frank K. Smith Ba'ad	Naljeh Begay	Henry Bodie
Kee Yazzie Ba'ad	Pinto Begay	Nelson Bodie
Atsidi Yazzie Badani	Roland Begay	Shorty Bodie
Kattas Bah	Sam Begay	Bonaventure
She Bah	Sam Begay	Ahe Lee Mother Boy
Kee Bahi	Silao Nez Begay	Earnest Boy
John Bailie	Tohat Glennie Begay	Johnson Brocitty
George Becente	Tom Atsidi Begay	Cowboy's Brother No. 1
Jack Becente	Wallace Begay	Cowboy's Brother No. 2

[1] A year of peak production. At present some smiths are doing war work; some are in the army.

Fred's Younger Brother
Otis' Brother No. 1
Otis' Brother No. 2
Charlie Brown
Mrs. Charlie Brown
Frank Brown
Fred Brown
Joe Brown
Sam Jim Brown
Dan Burnsides
Husky Burnsides
Isadore Burnsides
John Burnsides
John Burnsides' Son No. 1
John Burnsides' Son No. 2
Tom Burnsides
Mrs. Tom Burnsides
Frank Cadman
Charlie Chai
James Chai
Joe Chai
Margaret Chai
Mrs. Chai
Tom Chai
Lee Chase
Tom Chappo
John Charlie
Julio Charlie
Mabel Charlie
Peacock Charlie
Sam Charlie
Sam Charlie
Tom Charlie
Weston Charlie
Willie Charlie
Wilson Charlie
Charlie Chavez
Marnhelda Chavez
Tony Chavez
Allen Chee
Charlie Chee
Eski Chee
George Chee
Herman Chee
Husky Chee
James Chee
Kee Chee
Tom Chee

Tuli Chee
Toe Chummy
Billie Cornfields
Little Cowboy
Cripple
Frank Curley
Horace Curley
Jim Curley
Buck Dalgarito
Jim Dalgarito
Mrs. Jim Dalgarito
Jim Curley Dalgarito
Philip Dalgarito
Mrs. Philip Dalgarito
Willie Davis
Clara Davis
Jeff Davis
Tom Davis
Chee Dawes
Charlie Day
Hosteen Deel
Kenneth Denet Dele
Dave Dixon
Emerson Dixon
Harvey Dixon
Ben Dubois
Mrs. Ben Dubois
Jim Dubois
Mrs. Jim Dubois
Nellie Dubois
Mrs. Easy
Billie Emerson
Earnest Emerson
Lee Emerson
Tommie Emerson
George Endito
Juan Ray Endito
Willie Jim Endito
Henry Esson
Kee Esson
Nellie Esson
Tom Esson
Alfred Francis
Charlie Francis
Esther Francis
Irene Francis
Joe Francis
John Frank

Frosszy
Bah Ganado
Sam George
Billie Goodluck
Frank Goodluck
Little Hunter's
    Granddaughter
Little Hunter's
    Grandson
Charlie Gray
Agnes Groody
Guy No. 1
Kalth Halwolt
Kee Haswoot
Frank Henio
John Henio
Juan Henio
Tom Henio
Edmund Henry
Charlie Houck
Joe House
Len House
Billie Hoxie
Mrs. Billie Hoxie
John Hoxie
Mrs. John Hoxie
Julio
Tom Jack
Sam Jackson
Mrs. Sam Jackson
John Billie James
John Jim
Tom Jim
Tom Jim, Jr.
Willie Jim
James Joe
Sam Joe
Tom Joe
Mrs. Tom Joe
Richard John Joe
Frank Johnson
John Johnson
Kee Johnson
Sadie Johnson
Charlie Jones
Wilfred Jones
Tom Katon
Robert Kee

Kee's Wife
John Kenneth
John King
Ben Knocki
Mrs. Ben Knocki No. 1
Mrs. Ben Knocki No. 2
Frank Largo
Mrs. Frank Largo
Frank Jim Largo
Fred Largo
Sam Gray Largo
Mrs. Tom Largo
Wayne Largo
Wilson Largo
Agnes Lee
Ben Lee
Frank Lee
John Lee
John Lee
Juan Lee
Robert Lee
Tom Lee
Ambrose Lincoln
Mrs. Joe Lolly
Eski Long
Mrs. Eski Long
Jim Long
Joe Long
John Long
Kenneth Long
Mary Long
Rena Long
Loren
Thomas Lorenzo
Andrew Loy
Myrna Loy
Mr. Little Man
Mrs. Little Man
Philip Manuelito
Frank Marianito
Tillie Marianito
Rose Marie
Big Mary
Charlie Martin
Eski Martin
James Martin
George Martinez
Glen Martinez

Joe Martinez
Prestiano Martinez
Jack McCray
Mercio
Johnson Miller
Stanley Mitchell
Francis Morgan
Herbert Morgan
Jim Morgan
Louise Morgan
Ned Morgan
Willie Morgan
Ben Mose
Ben Navajo
John Navajo
Sam Navajo
Joe Ned
Mrs. Joe Ned
John Nelson
Johnson's Nephew
Joe Nett
Atsidi Nez
Hastin Nez
Jim Nez
Rink Nez
Mrs. Jim Nez
Slim Nez
John Nichols
Two Gun Nick
Tom Yazzie's Niece
Bruce Nlaya
Mrs. Bruce Nlaya
Billie Norton
Mary Norton
Frank Peralto
Fred Peralto
Lee Peralto
Willie Peralto
Francis Parker
Jackson Parker
William Parker
Anderson Peshlakai
Andrew Peshlakai
Bruce Peshlakai
Fred Peshlakai
Mike Peshlakai
William Peshlakai
Robert Pino

Charles Pinto
Mrs. Charles Pinto
Frank Pinto
Allan Platero
Canyon Cito Platero
Charlie Platero
Eva Platero
Jim Charlie Platero
Joe Platero
Juan Platero
Juanito Platero
William Platero
Scott Preston
Joe Price
Tom Rafael
May Ration
Tom Ration
Haskie Tsosie Red Eye
Ambrose Roanhorse
Jim Roanhorse
Nazbah Roanhorse
Peter Roanhorse
Sam Roanhorse
Tom Roanhorse
Rose
Juan Russel
John Sam
Philip Sam
Willie Sam
Marito Sanchez
Jimmie Sanders
Nina Sandoval
Wilson Sandoval
Chee Saunders
Wilson Saunders
Astzan Shorty
John Silver
Sam Silver
Chee Silversmith
Descheny Silversmith
John Silversmith
John Silversmith
Sam Silversmith
Sam Silversmith
Tom Silversmith
John Billie Sister
David Six
Guy Six

197

John Six
Emerson Skeet
Roger Skeet
Slicker
Albert Smith
Atsidi Smith
Charlie Smith
Mrs. Charlie Smith
Frank Kay Smith
John Smith
John K. Smith
Lee Smith
Mabel Smith
Tom Smith
William Smith
Wilson Smith
Frank Snyder
Joe Snyder
Little Hunter's Son
John Spencer
Spigi
Fred Stevens
Hosteen Suey
David Talliman
Low Tarson
Sammy Teba
Joe Thomas
Joe Thomas
Mrs. Joe Thomas
Ray Thomas

George Thompson
Howard Thompson
Kee Thompson
Sam Thompson
Togi
Toho Charles Tom
Earl Tom
Joe Tom
John Tom
John Tom
Little Tom
Howard Tomas
Tsosie
Billie Tsosie
Bitani Tso
James Tsosie
Juan Tsosie
Eskie Tsosie
Todichinni Tsosie
Anderson Watchman
John Watson
Raymond Watson
John White
Frank Whitegoat
Joe Whitehorse
John William
John Willito
Austin Wilson
Katherine Wilson
Red Woman

Sam Wood
Herbert Woody
Yadebah
Andrew Yazzie
Mrs. Andrew Yazzie
Annie Yazzie
Atsidi Yazzie
Mrs. Atsidi Yazzie
Atsidi Yazzie
Beet Yazzie
Ben Yazzie
Bitani Yazzie
Chee Yazzie
Frank Yazzie
Garnet Yazzie
Joe Yazzie
Juan Yazzie
Justin Yazzie
Kee Yazzie
Leuppe Yazzie
Mary Yazzie
Tom Yazzie
Mrs. Tom Yazzie
Todichinni Yazzie
Willie Yazzie
Chester Yellowhair
Husky Yestah
John Billy Young

D. *Zuñi silversmiths* (1940)

Mrs. Achowa
Horace Aiuli
Albert Alipo
Mrs. Alipo
Joseph Bankita
Lowell Bankita
Baubillo
Mrs. Baubillo
Beketewa
Franklin Beketewa
Beku (Pescado)
Betaskuli
Bewonike
Allen Booque
Beka Booque

Bennett Boone
Logan Boone
Clarence Calavaza
Casi
Della Casi
Hazel Casi
Frank Celia
Irene Chavez
Paylem Chyalii
Mrs. Paylem Chyalii
Lou Comasoma
Juan Deleosa
Emerson Dickson
Jerry Dickson
Alec Dieusee

Liki Dieusee
Mrs. Dieusee
Sidney Dieusee
Dishde
Mrs. Pauline Dishde
Virgil Dishde
Tom Eonotie
Eplouis
Moses Eorocho
Mrs. Moses Eorocho
Maxime Eustace
Newman Eustace
Steve Gia
Dena Guam
Luciano Guam

Benny Hamon
Mrs. Benny Hamon
Earnest Hamon
Simon Hamon
Merle Hootchtey
Merle Hotina
Lee Itaike
Merle Itaike
Harry Johnson
Mrs. Harry Johnson
Herman Johnson
Scotty Kaskalla
Mrs. Scotty Kaskalla
Ketseu
Ketsiney
Douglas Ladd
Pincion Lahela
Ray Lahela
Paul Laidti
Noble Lanyade
Clarence Larsoleo
Conrad Larsoleo
Bruce Lasalu
Eli Lateice
Charlie Latima
Leekya
Leopolo
Bennie Lesarley
Dick Likity
Nick Likity
Douglas Lisene

Albert Louis
Bill Loweki
Tom Luhi
Luna
Roy Lunasiee (Nutria)
Eli Lyte
Irene Martinez
Lola Martinez
Ben Malkella (Nutria)
Metsie
Milton
Nashponetewa
Natachu
Denis Natachu
Natchapone (Pescado)
Nat Neese
Okweene Neese
Noskie
Mrs. Noskie
Warren Ondelacy
Mrs. Warren Ondelacy
Daisy Oucho
Leo Pablano
Paque
Edison Paque
Tom Paquin
Fred Paynetsy
Bowman Pewa
Dan Phillips
Robert Saisiwa
Johnson Santiago

Clyde Sheeka
Eddie Sheeka
Francis Sheeka
Oscar Sheeka
Arnold Shebola
Jerry Shebola
Mrs. Shebola
Leslie Shebola
Philomeno Shebola
David Siaekewa
Simone (Pescado)
Dan Simplicio
Henry Sivewa
Mrs. Ray Tekela
Wilbur Tekela
Mrs. Wilbur Tekela
Mike Teslakai
Mrs. Mike Teslakai
Pat Teslakai
Melvin Tseechu
Walter Tspia
Charlie Tucson
Harold Tucson
Mrs. Harold Tucson
Raymond Watson
Willie Wiakwe
Wistika
Barbara Wistika
Nick Yoselo
Casa Zuñi
Willie Zuñi

APPENDIX III

A Note on Standards and Quality of Indian Jewelry

THE TURQUOISE that the Navajo and the Zuñi prefer to all other stones is a clear, deep robin's-egg blue. This turquoise the Navajo call "male" turquoise, and the less rare stone of a greenish hue they call "female" turquoise. The natives value stones of a uniform color with none of the matrix from which they have been removed, showing. The best grade of stones is shipped into Gallup and the surrounding regions largely from Nevada, although a smaller quantity comes from Colorado. Inferior stones are obtained from the vicinity of Kingman, Arizona, and also from mines in the southern part of Arizona. In the past, great quantities of this cheap turquoise have been shipped to Germany, dyed a deeper color, and shipped back to the Southwest to be set in silver by the Indian smiths. Inferior grades of stones are also given a deeper color by soaking them in grease. More than one buyer has been surprised to find that stones left accidentally in the sun have become greasy, because the grease has sweated out of the stones. Stones treated in this way have been used extensively by the manufacturers of Indian silver in the Rio Grande valley. Turquoise may also be produced synthetically in a laboratory, even to the extent of having a simulated veining of matrix.

The best turquoise of deep blue retains its color, while the softer stones of a lighter blue and of a greenish cast eventually become a dull and unattractive green. The buyer learns to distinguish good from poor or imitation turquoise only with experience, after having seen and handled many pieces. The best assurance of quality, for the novice, is in buying from reputable dealers who will guarantee the quality of the stones.

Most of the stones set in silver for sale to the white man have been polished by professional lapidaries who are employed by the miners and the dealers in turquoise. It is difficult for the traders to obtain the best grade of stones in a raw state from the dealers or the mines, since there are larger profits for the dealers in selling turquoise already cut and polished. These stones have a high polish and an evenness that is not characteristic of those that are polished by the Navajo and Zuñi turquoise-workers, who use crude tools. Their stones, with the exception of the ones produced by a few skilled craftsmen are duller and slightly less even of surface than those finished on the more elaborate wheels of the professional lapidary. Some buyers prefer the stones with a high polish, others like those with the rough finish.

At the present time there are two types of Navajo and Pueblo silver being sold to the white man: the silver made as a curio which sells for a low price, and that, made in much smaller quantities, which is heavier, with finer design applied by more careful workmanship. This latter type is more than a souvenir. It has the good qualities that any fine handmade silver possesses, and is bought for its æsthetic merit alone.

A few years ago the Indian Arts and Crafts Board, a government organization set up under the Department of the Interior, began to stamp Indian silver of the second type. These stamps were designed to guarantee the quality of the silver to which they were applied, and they served to encourage the making of the better class of silver following the traditional Navajo and Pueblo silver designs. The finished work is inspected by a representative of the board, and if the prescribed standards of hand craftsmanship are met, the silver is stamped with a small mark on the under side of the piece; U.S. NAVAJO and U.S. ZUNI are the marks that are used, with a number designating the trading post or the Indian school where the piece was made.

In my opinion the best of the silver that is being made today for the white consumer is produced in the shops of the Indian schools which are located at Santa Fé, Albuquerque, Fort Wingate, Shiprock, and Tuba City. Here Navajo master craftsmen instruct the young silversmiths in the methods of the craft, using designs of the best traditional patterns. Many of the oldest types of designs have been revived: filed bracelets, cast bracelets and rings, squash-blossom beads, buttons, and conchas, all of which are simple in pattern and appeal to the modern buyer of fine silver.

APPENDIX IV

Additional Material on the
Economics of Silver

From June through December, 1940, I conducted a survey of the economics of Navajo and Pueblo silversmithing for the Indian Arts and Crafts Board, Department of the Interior, Washington, D.C. That part of the collected data which is pertinent to this volume is summarized below.

The survey was made on the Navajo and Pueblo reservations and in the adjoining centers of white population. The method used was that of personal interview; a schedule of some thirty questions was drawn up as a guide and outline. Eighty Navajo silversmiths were interviewed, and an analysis of their silver production was recorded on the schedules. If the apprentices to the silversmiths are included, it may be said that the survey covered the work of 136 smiths. Twenty-two Zuñi craftsmen were consulted, three at Santo Domingo, and one at Cochiti.

Navajo

I estimated the total number of Navajo silversmiths in 1940 at around six hundred. Appendix II C lists by name 456 smiths. This census is virtually complete for the southwestern reservation and adjacent nonreservation territory where the craft has been commercially exploited. It also includes the names of the silversmiths living on the western and northwestern reservation who spend only a limited amount of their time at the craft, but the actual names of about fifteen smiths who live in the Shiprock–Hogback–Fruitland area were not obtained. The census includes the names of apprentices who are well on their way to becoming master craftsmen, but it does not include students of the craft working in the various government schools, nor does it include the names of silversmiths following assembly-line bench methods in Albuquerque, Santa Fé, Winslow, and other near-by cities.

The eighty smiths questioned averaged thirty-five years of age. Only ten were more than fifty, while forty-seven (58 per cent) were less than forty years old. Sixty-three smiths out of eighty answered the question: "How long have you worked at this craft?" The average was fourteen years. This indicates that the smiths learn the art at around twenty-two years of age. However, one-third of the craftsmen questioned have known the art for five years or less, a fact which indicates that in the last five years there has been an increase in the sales of Navajo reservation-made silver that has prompted the traders to hire more craftsmen. A dealer in Gallup attributed the increase in sales to the government regulations which exclude manufactured Indian silver jewelry from the National Parks. The silversmiths on the northern and western reservation average forty-four years of age. These smiths, who make silver on occasion for their own people and not for the traders, have, in many instances, known the art of making silver since the early days of the craft.

Ninety-five per cent of the silversmiths questioned were male. I believe that, in reality, from 8 per cent to 10 per cent of the Navajo smiths are women, but it is difficult for the field worker to establish a contact with them. There are many women who know how to work silver unbeknownst to the trader, since they are wives of smiths and work on silver issued to their husbands.

Eighty-one per cent of the silversmiths live in hogans, and the remaining 19 per cent live in log houses, which are for the most part in the Smith Lake–Pinedale area. Twenty-three per cent of those questioned have shops separate from their living quarters. Fifty-five per cent of these shops are in the Smith Lake region.

Only a relatively small number of traders have silver made up for them. There are approximately thirty (18 per cent) of the total number (170) of traders that "work" a "string" of silversmiths. Nearly all of the silver that these traders farm out to the Navajo is in slug form and is purchased either directly or indirectly (through the wholesalers in Gallup) from a refining company in Los Angeles, California.

The schedule of questions included the current wages of the craftsmen. Seventy-four smiths answered, and fifty-nine of them said that they worked on an ounce basis. The average pay per ounce is fifty-one cents, and the range is from twenty cents to seventy-five cents. Forty of these fifty-nine work for store credit only, receiving no cash at all; nineteen get some cash from their work, and of these eight are paid half in cash and half in credit. The silversmiths who work on an ounce basis are paid for each turquoise they set, the pay depending on the size of the stones. For setting small stones most smiths are paid ten cents, and for large ones they are paid twenty-five cents. A few traders pay their workers by the piece rather than by the ounce; this is particularly true of the traders in the Smith Lake–Pinedale area, where the craftsmen specialize in bead-making. They are paid one cent for a bead less than a quarter of an inch in diameter, and four cents for a bead twice as large; a bead more than half an inch across brings eight cents. Most of the beads made in this region are extremely light in weight and are sent all over the "silver area." Thousands of them are sold annually at Zuñi, where the traders have their silversmiths assemble them into necklaces.

Out of seventy-three silversmiths 59 per cent work for only one trader and 41 per cent for more than one. Of the latter group 63 per cent work for two traders, 27 per cent for three, and 13 per cent for four. There are several reasons for this: (1) silversmiths seek out traders other than the one they customarily deal with, thinking that they may find higher wages or get a larger percentage of their wages in cash; (2) they may want to establish credit at another trading post, where they think the price of goods is cheaper or where there may be a larger stock; (3) it is also often true that a Navajo owing a large bill at some post will go to another trader and work where his credit is still good, and his wages will not be used up in paying off his account. An interesting correlation to these figures is that 41 per cent of the smiths questioned do not work for the nearest trading post, but for one more distant from their hogan.

Thirty-five per cent of the smiths interviewed on occasion buy their own slugs and turquoise and "peddle" their jewelry, most of them selling it in Gallup for cash.

During the last ten years there has been a growing tendency for the traders to set up living quarters and shops near their trading post for silversmiths. This practice greatly facilitates production and shortens the period between the farming out of the raw materials and the completion of the jewelry. During the winter of 1940 there were more than forty Navajo craftsmen living at Zuñi and working for the trading posts in the pueblo. At Smith Lake the trader has built at the rear of his post a large shop which accommodates over twenty-five silversmiths, who live in near-by hogans and come to work at the shop daily.

Silversmiths work not only for the traders but also for their own people; 64 per cent of those questioned make jewelry for fellow Navajo, who customarily supply the raw materials and usually pay in the form of sheep, other livestock, saddle blankets, peaches, or other products.

The eighty silversmiths interviewed may be divided into three economic groups. First, there are the professionals who work at the craft all the year around. Fourteen per cent fall into this group, and they earn individually from $400 to $800 a year; two or three earn more than $1,000. The second group (50 per cent of those questioned) work intermittently during the entire year and earn from $100 to $400 a year. The third group (30 per cent) work only during the winter months and earn less than $100. From checking with traders I found that the silversmiths were prone to underestimate their earnings, of which they keep no written record, so that these figures are consistently low throughout the three groups.

It was stated at the outset that the eighty schedules covered the production of 136 smiths, because many smiths have assistants. Fifty-seven per cent receive help from someone, usually a relative, and of these, 51 per cent receive help only from their wives.

Seventy-five per cent of the smiths work at night as well as during the day. Seventeen per cent of these work at night only during the winter when the traders have the most orders, and when it gets dark early. Nearly all of these smiths use gasoline lanterns for light.

During recent years the roller has been introduced to the reservation. This tool greatly expedites the work of the craftsmen. It is especially useful in producing from the slug a sheet of silver thin enough for the bezel in from seven to twelve minutes, an operation which would take at least forty-five minutes to perform in hammering by hand. Twenty per cent of the silversmiths questioned used rollers, and of this number less than half (38 per cent) owned their own rollers; the others used those of relatives or friends, or in some cases ones which the traders kept for the use of the smiths who worked for them. Many of the smiths use the roller only for making the bezel, but others use it to reduce the silver to the thickness essential for bracelet-making.

Not more than 50 per cent of the craftsmen interviewed know how to do cast work, and actually only about ten of them make cast silver to any great extent. One reason for this is that most traders do not pay extra for cast work, which takes longer to produce than the wrought silver.

Zuñi

Twenty-two silversmiths were interviewed at Zuñi, out of a total population of 139 craftsmen, thirty-nine (11 per cent) of whom are women. Zuñi women spend more time at the craft than the Navajo women; at least 10 per cent of them have separate accounts at the trading posts. The others, like most Navajo women, work up silver under their husbands' names. As a rule the women grind all the turquoise for their husbands.

Five of the 139 craftsmen live outside of Zuñi proper in the farming villages; three live at Pescado, and two at Nutria.

The average age of the craftsman is thirty-seven—a bit older than the average Navajo, but only one smith interviewed was over fifty, while there were ten in this category among the Navajo. There are also several very old men in the village who used to make silver, but who no longer follow the art.

The average Zuñi silversmith has known his craft for nine years, five years less than the Navajo, a circumstance reflecting the more recent commercialization of his art. He tends to learn the trade at about twenty-eight years of age, and he does his work right in his house, in the main room of which he has a workbench.

Although there are four trading posts in the pueblo, all of which do a business in Zuñi silver, all but one of the smiths questioned sell their work in Gallup on occasion, and 18 per cent of them do not make any jewelry for the traders in the village. It would be conservative to say that one-fourth of all the jewelry made in Zuñi (by Zuñi) is sold directly by them in Gallup or outside the pueblo, some going as far as Albuquerque. These outside markets are sought to bring in more cash than would be allowed by the local traders. Of the seventeen who answered the question concerning cash payments, eleven said that they get only a small amount of cash, and that only when they ask for it; the others get paid in credit only.

At Zuñi the traders pay for most jewelry by the piece. The

PLATE 23

A. Leekya's wife

C. Della Casi, Zuñi silversmith

B. Navajo woman grinding turquoise

D. Leekya's wife wearing manta pins

PLATE 24

A. José Platero, Isleta smith (1900)

B. Juan Luhan (1891), Acoma silversmith   C. Marcelina Martin, Isleta

lowest wage for a single-row bracelet with fourteen small turquoise sets is $1.00, and the top price for such a piece is $1.50.
This is just for the labor, since the trader owns the raw materials.
The usual pay for setting stones in brooches, rings, etc., is from
fifteen cents to twenty-five cents.

Thirty-five per cent of the smiths do inlay work, using white
and pink shell, jet, and turquoise. For work of this kind they are
paid from $3.50 to $4.00; for example, this would be the amount
paid for a Knife-Wing bird two inches high, which takes a full
day to make. Larger pieces bring proportionately more. Jerry
Shebola was paid $10 for an elaborate piece that he made in two
and one-half days.

At Zuñi 60 per cent of the smiths questioned receive help
from a relative. The craftsman's helper is nearly always the spouse,
and together the two can turn out as many as ten cluster rings in a
day, or eight single-row bracelets.

Among the Navajo 78 per cent of the silversmiths work the
year around, but at Zuñi only 50 per cent work during the summer season, when there is much agricultural and ceremonial activity.

Only 23 per cent of the Zuñi smiths earn less than $200 a year
from their trade (Navajo—36 per cent), 57 per cent of those questioned earn more than $200 a year and less than $800, and 20 per
cent of them earn annually $800 or more. There are two reasons
why the per capita income of the Zuñi smiths is higher than that
of the Navajo. The total output of silver is much smaller at Zuñi,
the market is therefore less glutted, and there is little or no machine
competition to force down the market prices.

Thirty-eight per cent of the smiths questioned said that they
make Navajo-style jewelry if the traders ask them to, but that they
prefer their own style. Twenty-eight per cent said that they know
how to do cast work.

Santo Domingo

At Santo Domingo there are seven silversmiths who work in
the pueblo. In addition to these there are about nine who work in
Albuquerque for large commercial houses, and a dozen or more

boys who are learning the craft at the Santa Fé Indian school. Since the average yearly income of the seven smiths in the village is $200 apiece, the craft is distinctly a spare-time pursuit for most of these artisans. Francisco Teyano, the leading silversmith in the village, earns $500 a year. Most of the jewelry he makes is peddled by his father on the streets of Albuquerque and Santa Fé.

In design, Santo Domingo silver is an imitation of the Navajo. At the United States Indian school in Santa Fé, the head of the arts and crafts department, Miss Alfreda Ward, felt that the students from this pueblo should make a type of jewelry that was distinctively their own; therefore, with the help of Mr. Kenneth Chapman, of the Indian Arts and Crafts Board and the Laboratory of Anthropology, designs appearing in his book on Santo Domingo pottery were selected as possible patterns. Wilfred Jones, the Navajo teacher in silversmithing, helped the Santo Domingo boys adapt these designs to the actual steel dies. The outcome of this experiment has been very successful. The delicate curves of the leaf designs are well suited to the medium. The bracelets are made in simple flat bands that effectively set off the die-work. Lapel pins are made after the various bird designs and appeal to the buyers of costume jewelry.

The experiment should prove to be a success financially as well as æsthetically for it gives the Santo Domingo boys at the Indian school a distinctive type of silver which they should be able to make when they return to the pueblo, a type of silver unique in design, which should have a ready market.

Cochiti

At Cochiti there are five smiths who do work for a company in Santa Fé and bring their work into town periodically. Joe Quintana is one of the most successful of these smiths. He reported that he had made $1,000 from working silver during the last year, working at his bench from nine to ten hours a day. In design the silver made in this pueblo is Navajo in type.

The Navajo Arts and Crafts Guild

During the school year of 1939–40 the Educational Division

of Navajo Service set up at Wingate Vocational High School a craft project known as the Wingate Guild. Ambrose Roanhorse, formerly teacher of silversmithing at the Santa Fé Indian School, was the director of the craftsmen, who were graduates of the high school, and men and women on the adjacent reservation. The purpose of the project was to afford employment for the fine craftsmen who had learned their art at the Indian schools. The project also handled vegetable-dyed rugs.

In September, 1941, the Indian Arts and Crafts Board established the Navajo Arts and Crafts Guild. The Wingate Guild was used as a nucleus for this larger craft project. Craftsmen on the reservation were invited to take part. Centers of guild activity grew up in the Window Rock–Fort Defiance area—where Ambrose Roanhorse had formed connections with excellent craftsmen in 1940—and at Toadlena and Shiprock.

The purpose of the guild is to increase the tribal income from the sale of arts and crafts by the promotion of fine handicrafts which will sell in quality stores in the East, Middle West, and Southwest. The tourist market is purposely avoided, as it does not yield as high a return per man hour as the more exclusive stores and shops.

The type of silverware that the guild promotes is similar to that which has been at the Santa Fé, Albuquerque, and Fort Wingate Indian schools; a revival of the old simple types of jewelry, without sets for the most part. Emphasis is placed on cast work. The guild also handles vegetable-dyed rugs and some aniline-dyed rugs of simple patterns and excellent workmanship.

During the first two years of its existence, the guild has never been able to fill all of its orders—proof that there is a good market for large production of the very finest type of Navajo handicraft.

Vocabulary of Navajo Words
Pertaining to Silversmithing

anvil	beḱé·ʔacité
bead, silver	yo·ʔnómaẓá
bead, squash-blossom	yo·ʔnéʔmazeʔdisyá·gi·
beads, loop of turquoise worn at the bottom of the turquoise and shell necklaces (also refers to the turquoise ear-pendants and to any earring tied to ear)	ẓa·ʔx̌ó·ł
bellows	bé·ʔalʔẓołle
belt, of any kind	sis
belt, silver	bé·šlagaiʔsis
belt buckle, silver	bé·šlagaiʔbé·ʔáłʔč̨ʔdéλǫ́ *or* bé·šlagaiʔsisʔbé·ł·daʔnaʔtaʔé·
bezel, or rim, around turquoise	ʔínozʔáʔhiʔ
bezel, notching in	ʔátáʔísčiž
borax	be·ʔáʔdaʔťí·ẓeʔhéʔłagaigí
bow-guard	ḱéʔtoh
bow-guard, cast	ḱéʔtohʔcéʔbí·dolyį́·gi·ʔ
bowl	łe·ċa·ʔ
bracelet	la·coné
bracelet, cast	la·conéʔcéʔbí·dolyį́·gi·ʔ
bracelet, thin, triangular	la·conéʔtose
brass	bé·šʔłe·có
bridle, silver	ʔani·ʔx̌ó·ł
button, silver	yo·ʔnilčiní
button, one, worn by a woman	ʔasẓą́·nʔbiłdanáťáiʔi·
buttons, women's	ʔasẓą́·nʔbí·yo·ʔníłʔčin
canteen, tobacco (also used in describing a modern cigarette box)	náťohʔbizis
charcoal	ťe·š

concha, round, has either round or diamond slot in center, smooth surface, design only around edge — sisʔnázbąsi·gí·

concha, oval in shape, oval or diamond slot in the center, plain surface with design only around edge — sisʔdelʔkǫʔi·gí·

concha, set with turquoise, file-work or cold-chisel work in center, stamped design on outside — do·x̣iži·bi·ʔna·sʔnili·gí·

concha, stamped and embossed (raised center) — sisʔhabídaʔẓisʔneʔi·gí·

concha, stamped designs, no turquoise — sisʔbí·gehʔásčini·gí·

concha, fluted design made with cold chisel or file, stamped around edge — sisʔnoʔẓihi·gí·

copper — bé·šłaʔčí·ʔi·

die, descriptive form, definite — bé·šʔbeʔbíkílčihí

die, nondefinite — béʔaʔkíʔiłčihí

dividers — be·kinaʔacói

drawplate — béʔháʔílzǫʔdé·ʔ

earring, of type which ties to the ear — ža·ʔx̣ó·ł

earring, silver, of the old type with the hoop and ball (also refers to any earring which is hooked directly through the pierced ear, but not tied to the ear) — bé·šłagaiʔža·ʔaɣánáʔáhí

emery cloth — na·lʔcosʔbé·ʔači·si·

file — bé·ʔači·ši·

file, round (rat-tail file) — bé·ʔačiseʔní·yízigí·ʔ

gold — o·la

hammer — be·ʔáʔcidé

hatband, silver — bé·šłagaiʔčahʔbená·sdí·ʔi·ʔ

iron, or any dark-colored metal — bé·šʔdo·x̣iž

jewelry, general word for — yodé *or* ǹx̣iz

knife — bȩ́·š

pawn, word used in speaking of one piece of pawned silver — ʔą̧ʔasla

pawn, word used in speaking of more
  than one object in pawn
    ʔą ʔnasnilígi·

pawn rack
    ʔą ʔnasnilʔgóneʔ

pendant, crescent-shaped, worn on
  necklaces
    nažaʔhéʔ

pendant, attached to bridle
    tɣá·nažaʔhé

pliers
    be·ʔo·cágí·

raindrops, small balls of silver
  mounted on the prongs of a ring
    mą·zoh

ring, finger
    yo·sʔca

rock salt
    cédokǫ́ž

ruler, wooden
    bé·ʔaʔdaʔnilą ʔį́·ʔ

silver
    bé·šłagai

silver slug, or Mexican dollar
    na·ka·iʔbeʔbé·so

silversmith
    bé·šłagaiʔaʔcidí·ʔ

smith
    ʔaʔcidí·ʔ

spoon, silver
    bé·šłagaiʔbé·šiʔté

steel
    bé·šǹX̌izigí·

steel, scrap of, from which dies are
  made
    bé·šʔǹX̌izí·

stone, used for casting silver
    céʔbi·yaʔdaʔí·nilʔígí *or*
    céʔbi·ḱįʔžéʔęʔadílyehę

torch, gasoline
    koʔdo·X̌íge *or*
    koʔdí·ʔcaʔéʔ

turquoise
    do·X̌iži·

turquoise, a set (the turquoise in
  position)
    do·X̌iži·ʔbi·ʔsaʔą́ʔ

turquoise, more than one set in silver
    do·X̌iži·ʔbé·šłagaiʔbi·ʔdasinǹ

tweezers, made of silver or other
  metal, used for plucking facial hair
    dáɣáʔbé·ʔyéʔnižé

wire, pointed, used in welding
    bé·naʔací·

wire, silver
    bé·šłagaiʔáłʔto·sé

Bibliography

Bedinger, Margery. *Navajo Indian Silver-work, Old West* Series of Pamphlets, No. 8. Denver, 1936.

Benedict, Ruth. *Zuñi Mythology,* Columbia University *Contributions to Anthropology,* XXI. New York, 1935. 2 vols.

Bloom, Lansing (ed.). "Bourke on the Southwest," *New Mexico Historical Review,* Vols. XI–XIII (1936–38).

Bunzel, Ruth L. "Introduction to Zuñi Ceremonialism," *Forty-seventh Annual Report, 1929–30,* Bureau of American Ethnology. Washington, 1932.

———. "Zuñi Katcinas: An Analytical Study," *ibid.*

Burge, Moris. "The Silversmithing of the Navajos," *Indians at Work,* United States Bureau of Indian Affairs (December 15, 1934).

Bynner, Witter. *Navaho Silversmithing, The Collector's Viewpoint,* No. 7, Indian Art Series, New Mexico Association on Indian Affairs. Santa Fé, 1936.

Campa, Arthur L., and Cornelius C. Knipers. *Arts and Crafts in New Mexico: A Survey of the Present Status of Handicrafts in New Mexico* (unpublished manuscript), a survey made under the Federal Emergency Relief Fund and completed under the National Youth Administration, University of New Mexico, 1936.

Chapman, Kenneth M. "Zuñi Silversmithing," *Indians at Work,* United States Bureau of Indian Affairs (September 15, 1936).

Colton, Mary-Russell F. "Hopi Silversmithing—Its Background and Future," *Plateau,* Vol. XII, No. 1, Museum of Northern Arizona, Flagstaff (July, 1939).

Coolidge, Dane, and Mary R. Coolidge. *The Navajo Indians.* Boston and New York, 1930.

Cushing, Frank Hamilton. "My Adventures at Zuñi," *The Century Magazine* (February, 1883).

———. *Zuñi Breadstuff, Indian Notes and Monographs*, VIII, Museum of the American Indian, Heye Foundation. New York, 1920.

———. "Zuñi Fetishes," *Second Annual Report, 1880–81*, Bureau of American Ethnology. Washington, 1883.

Douglas, F. H. *Navaho Silversmithing*, Leaflet 15, Denver Art Museum. Denver, 1930.

Espinosa, Carmen. "Fashions in Filigree," *New Mexico Magazine*, Vol. XVII, No. 9 (September, 1939).

Franciscan Fathers. *An Ethnologic Dictionary of the Navaho Language*. Saint Michaels, Arizona, 1910.

Hesselden, Elizabeth C. "Indian Silver of the Southwest," *Design*, XXXII (1930).

Hill, Gertrude. "The Art of the Navajo Silversmith," *The Kiva*, Vol. II, No. 5, Arizona Archeological and Historical Society, Tucson (February, 1937).

Hodge, F. E. "How Old Is Southwestern Indian Silverwork?" *El Palacio*, Vol. XXV, Nos. 14–17 (October 6–27, 1928).

Jones, Wilford H. "How I Make a Silver Ring," *Indians at Work*, United States Bureau of Indian Affairs (April 15, 1936).

Kluckhohn, Clyde. "Some Personal and Social Aspects of Navaho Ceremonial Practice," *The Harvard Theological Review*, Vol. XXXII, No. 1 (1939).

———, and Katherine Spencer. *A Bibliography of the Navaho Indians*. New York, 1940.

———, and Leland C. Wyman. *An Introduction to Navaho Chant Practice, Memoirs* of the American Anthropological Association, No. 53. Menasha, Wisconsin, 1940.

Kroeber, Alfred Louis. *Zuñi Kin and Clan, Anthropological Papers* of the American Museum of Natural History. New York, 1917.

Lummis, Charles F. *The Land of Poco Tiempo*. New York, 1893.

———. *Mesa, Cañon, and Pueblo*. New York and London, 1925.

———. "Our First American Jewelers," *Land of Sunshine*, Los Angeles (July, 1896).

Luomala, Katharine. *Navaho Life of Yesterday and Today*, National Park Service. Berkeley, California, 1938.

Martin, Paul S. *Navajo Silver Jewelry*, Field Museum *News*, No. 8 (1930).

Matthews, Washington. *Navajo Legends, Memoirs* of the American Folklore Society, V. Boston and New York, 1897.

———. "Navajo Silversmiths," *Second Annual Report, 1880–81,* Bureau of American Ethnology. Washington, 1883.

Miller, Wick. "The Navajo and his Silver-work," *New Mexico Magazine*, Vol. VIII, No. 8 (August 8, 1930).

Neumann, David L. "Navajo Silverwork," *El Palacio*, Vol. XXXII, No. 8 (February 24, 1932).

———. "Navajo Silver Dies," *ibid.*, Vol. XXXV, Nos. 7–8 (August 16, 23, 1933).

Nusbaum, J. L. "Swedged Navajo Bracelets," *Masterkey*, VIII, Southwest Museum, Los Angeles (1934).

Oglesby, Catharine. *Modern Primitive Arts of Mexico, Guatemala, and the Southwest.* New York, 1939.

Parsons, Elsie Clews (ed.). *Hopi Journal of Alexander M. Stephen,* Columbia University *Contributions to Anthropology,* XXIII. New York, 1936. 2 vols.

———. "Isleta, New Mexico," *Forty-seventh Annual Report, 1929–30,* Bureau of American Ethnology. Washington, 1932.

Pogue, Joseph E. *The Turquois, Memoirs* of the National Academy of Sciences, XII, Part II, Third Memoir. Washington, 1915.

Stevenson, James. "Illustrated Catalogue of the Collections Obtained from the Pueblos of Zuñi, New Mexico, and Walpi, Arizona, in 1881," *Third Annual Report, 1881–82,* Bureau of American Ethnology. Washington, 1884.

Stevenson, Matilda Coxe. *Pueblo Clothing and Ornament* (unpublished manuscript), in the Bureau of American Ethnology, Washington, D.C.

———. "The Zuñi Indians," *Twenty-third Annual Report, 1901–1902,* Bureau of American Ethnology. Washington, 1904.

Van Valkenburgh, Richard. *A Short History of the Navajo People*, Navajo Service. Window Rock, Arizona, 1938.

West, Louis C. "Standards for Silver Jewelry," *Indians at Work*, United States Bureau of Indian Affairs (November 1, 1936).

Woodward, Arthur. *A Brief History of Navajo Silversmithing*, ·Bulletin No. 14, Museum of Northern Arizona. Flagstaff, 1938.

Wyman, Leland. "Navaho Diagnosticians," *American Anthropologist*, XXXVIII (1936).

Anonymous. "Navajo Silversmithing," *Indians at Work*, United States Bureau of Indian Affairs (October 15, 1936).

Index

Acoma: 178–80; trade with Navajo, 97; trade with Zuñi, 165; diffusion of silver, 174–75; trade with Laguna, 179, 183

Aiuli, Horace (Zuñi silversmith): 137–42, 163 n., 198

Anvil: old Navajo, 18; modern Navajo, 56, 62, 76, 79; modern Zuñi, 138

Apache Indians, Jicarilla: trade with Navajo, 97, 175

Apache Indians, White Mountain: trade with Navajo, 97; Okweene Neese's trip to, 146; trading relations of, 175

Apache Wind-Way Chant: 104, 106

Apprenticeship: of Francis Yazzie, 79 ff.; of Navajo silversmiths, 81, 87 ff.; of Zuñi silversmiths, 142, 163

Beads: shell, 9; silver, 20, 23, 26–27, 203–204; glass, 88; rosary, 185; see also squash-blossom

Bell, mother-in-law: 7, 15, 52

Bellows: early Navajo, 16–17; early Zuñi, 126, 130–31; modern Zuñi, 138

Bezel: old type, 38; technology of Navajo, 66–67, 85; Zuñi, 132

Big Star Way Chant: 100, 106

Bitsui, Charlie (Navajo silversmith): 52, 78–86

Blacksmithing: Mexican, 4–5; Navajo, 4, 6; Zuñi, 121–22; Isleta, 181

Blanching: 19, 60–61, 77, 82, 101, 145

Blessing Way Chant: 100, 106

Blindness: 10–11, 104, 106

Borax: early use of, 18; modern use of, 57, 59–60, 72

Bourke, J. G.: 42, 46 n., 49, 109 n., 127, 178, 180, 187 n.

Bow-guard: see ketoh

Box: 53

Bracelets: 20–22, 24, 26–27, 95, 99, 109–11, 131; design of, 35–40; technology of, 56–61

Brass: jewelry at Fort Sumner, 5; worn by Ute, 11; first bracelets of, 36; canteens, 51; tweezers, 53; alloy in slugs, 56; Zuñi jewelry of, 121

Bridles: 8, 41–43, 123

Buckles: 33–34

Burnsides, Tom (Navajo silversmith): 55–78

Buttons: 20, 22, 24, 95, 109–11; Navajo, 45–49; Zuñi, 125, 133

Canteens: early, 7; history of, 11–13; mentioned by Matthews, 20; design of, 51–52; technology of, 67–72, 80–82

Charcoal: Navajo, 57, 64, 65 n.; Zuñi, 140

Cheyenne Indians: 11, 46

Chon, Atsidi (Navajo silversmith): 9, 13–14; bridle made by, 42

Cochiti: modern silver, 208–209

Coins: used for buttons, 46–47; see also pesos

Comanche Indians: 11, 30

Commercialization: beginning of, 25–28; of bracelet, 36; of ring, 50; effect of, 53; tableware, etc., 53–54; modern centers of, 86, 116; of Zuñi silver, 134–35; of other pueblos, 172; present trend, 201; increase in sales, 209

Conchas: 23, 88, 95, 123; design of, 29–33; Zuñi, 133, 155

Copper: jewelry at Fort Sumner, 5; worn by Ute, 11; canteens, 12, 51;

The Navajo and Pueblo

Silversmiths

has been planned for typographical clarity.
The important and authoritative text has been
set on the Linotype in eleven-point Janson,
with two points of leading, for attractive legi-
bility. The specimens of silver work have
been reproduced in 150-line-screen halftone
for definition of detail

UNIVERSITY OF OKLAHOMA PRESS

NORMAN